The Direct Option

The Direct Option

Richard C. Bartlett

Texas A&M University Press

College Station

All royalties to be paid to the Direct Selling Education Foundation for
use in educating the consumers of America.

Certain material in this book is derived with permission from copy-
righted publications of Mary Kay Cosmetics, Inc., including the *Perfect
Start Workbooks* 1 and 2 and the *Consultants Guide* for which all rights
are reserved by Mary Kay Cosmetics, Inc. 1991, 1993.

The paper used in this book meets the minimum requirements of the
American National Standard for Permanence of Paper for Printed Library
Materials, Z39.48-1984.
Binding materials have been chosen for durability.

^{TM}

Library of Congress Cataloging-in-Publication Data:
Bartlett, Dick, 1935–
    The direct option / Richard C. Bartlett. — 1st ed.
    p.   cm.
    ISBN 0-89096-583-8 (alk. paper). — ISBN 0-89096-584-6
(pbk. : alk. paper)
    1. Direct selling—United States—Case studies. I. Title.
HF5438.25.B37   1994
658.8'4—dc20   93-19819
                                                      CIP

To Mary Kay Ash, who has meant so much to so many in her lifetime in direct selling. It is from her that I have learned the true joy of this profession, the "paycheck of the heart" that comes from sharing with others. Mary Kay, your life is a tribute to your philosophy that "all you send into the lives of others comes back into your own."

Contents

Foreword

The Direct Option is a fascinating book. It is a veritable cornucopia of anecdotes, facts, ideas, and insights about direct sellers and the direct-selling industry. Indeed, to be fully appreciated, *The Direct Option* must be read at least three times to glean the various pearls and nuggets of wisdom it contains.

The first time I read *The Direct Option*, I was left with a happy feeling. Dick Bartlett's exuberance and the many success stories he tells are welcome relief from the trials and tribulations in the world of gigantic, impersonal corporations. The second time through, I was struck by the comprehensive perspective I was getting of the direct-selling industry. By the time I had digested all the chapters, I realized that Dick, in his own way, had subtly educated me about the why's and wherefore's of direct-selling strategies and the distinctive competitive advantages that accrue to direct sellers, advantages that are available through no other mode of marketing or distribution.

My third reading of the book produced yet a different response. On reflection, *The Direct Option* is not so much about direct selling as it is about how to achieve success in business and life, regardless of whether you are interested in a direct-selling career.

What makes *The Direct Option* so special, apart from its content and message, is the fact that all of the royalties it generates will be donated to the Direct Selling Education Foundation. It is clear—from reading the book and knowing Dick Bartlett—that Dick is fervently committed to the ideals and objectives of the Direct Selling Education Foundation. The mission of the foundation, "To serve the public interest with education, information and research, thereby encouraging greater public awareness and acceptance of direct selling in the marketplace," has been whole-heartedly embraced by Dick, his company, and a multitude of like-minded executives and companies.

For three years, I had the privilege of serving on the board of the DSEF as one of two members representing the academic community. I must admit that initially I was a bit unsure of my role on the board. But with every board and committee meeting, I was increasingly impressed by the commitment of the foundation to its mission statement, and, consequently, I became comfortable with my role on the board.

The DSEF has evolved from being an organization whose implicit purpose was to improve the image of direct selling to being an organization that is uniquely proactive in addressing consumer problems and issues that extend far beyond the realm of direct selling. Through conferences, publications, and grants, the foundation has well served the public interest and, in effect, has taken on the aura of a consumer advocate.

Simultaneously, through its academic programs, the foundation has become highly involved in marketing education. For example, in 1990 the DSEF co-sponsored, with the American Marketing Association and the Academy of Marketing Science, a symposium whose purpose was to peer into the future and foresee what retailing would be like in the year 2000. Several dozen retail executives (direct sellers included) and professors interacted intensively for nearly three days. At the conclusion of the symposium, a series of retailing predictions was produced. Not surprisingly, there was virtual consensus that direct selling—broadly defined—will become an increasingly potent form of retailing as the decade progresses. Its inherent benefits—the ability to create and maintain strong customer relationships, the opportunities it provides to achieve financial and personal rewards, the lack of entry barriers, and many other attributes too numerous to name—position direct selling as a force with which all retailers, present and future, must contend. Perhaps this is why so many fixed-location retailers are adopting, adapting, and emulating various forms of direct selling and why manufacturers are purchasing or starting their own direct-selling operations.

In brief, the DSEF is a catalyst in bringing together diverse groups of individuals, companies, organizations, and even educational institutions in a fashion that benefits all parties. I wish other industries had a similar foundation and that Dick Bartlett could be cloned so that more people could benefit from his wit, his genius, and his largess.

Robert A. Peterson
John T. Stuart III Centennial
Chair in Business Administration
University of Texas at Austin

Preface

The Direct Option is not just a catchy book title but a means of achieving economic independence. This is a book that has been written not just by myself but by people currently succeeding in direct selling. You will hear their thoughts expressed through stories, anecdotes, and quotes from hundreds of interviews. It is likely you will find someone very much like yourself in this book, whether you are a college student or a retired grandparent in need of extra income, an out-of-work middle manager seeking a new opportunity or a woman frustrated by juggling work with the demands of raising a family. By virtue of its rich array of examples, exploring why and how people have chosen direct selling, *The Direct Option* offers a commentary on American economic life at the close of the twentieth century.

In interview after interview, I found an exuberance for life, and at the same time an almost tangible release of tension that accompanied the decision to join a direct-selling organization (DSO). Being in business for themselves, but not by themselves, had satisfied something far more important than the desire for money alone—although in the deteriorating job market of the 1990s, money is certainly important: (1) The rewards were as much psychological as financial; and (2) becoming an independent entrepreneur had, in addition to supplying income, enhanced self-esteem, renewed self-confidence, and allowed many to enjoy self-sufficiency, often for the very first time. The optimism of those who have joined DSOs stands in sharp contrast to many millions of Americans whose attitudes and behaviors have been demoralized by economic pressures.

The night I sat down to write this preface, there was a Longaberger basket party scheduled at my home. It was co-hosted by Holley Ramsey, a Discovery Toys Consultant. Looking for an excuse to avoid the task I had at hand, I watched Longaberger Consultant Gina Buck set up her baskets for what was to be her first "real" party (her other parties had been with family members, a common beginning).

Gina was thirty-four years old and had worked her way through school at the University of Tennessee as a Sears salesclerk. Gina had then joined a major corporation where, in her words, she "hit a brick wall—not a glass ceiling." A conflict with a male supervisor had stopped her career cold. A corporate restructuring ended her next job as a sales representative. Gina was frustrated, and she had next come to Longaberger.

Holley had married at seventeen and had divorced at twenty-one. She was trying to rebuild her life and complete her college education. Her Discovery Toys income would allow her the flexibility of attending college part-time when her children started school. "It [direct selling] will allow me to produce an income while I stay home to raise my kids," Holley said. She had been inspired by one of her best friends, who had recently left her corporate job to join Tupperware. Holley knew her friend had already earned the use of a car and was making good money. The morning after the party, which took in over $500 and included a free picnic basket for my wife as her hostess gift, I came down to have breakfast. I made toast with Rawleigh cinnamon marketed by Golden Pride/Rawleigh, from bread stored in a Tupperware container, cooked on a Kitchen Fair griddle. After using my Mary Kay men's skin care products and Amway toothpaste, I brushed up with a twenty-five-year-old Fuller hairbrush, then resumed my place before my PC.

I was struck by the way the timing of the party coincided with my writing of this preface. The room had been full of women and one out-of-work man who were as interested in opportunity as they were in the excellent baskets and decorative items. They were a real-life, real-time example of what direct selling is all about.

Although I have been at an executive level in this most fascinating of industries for over three decades, today I feel a fresh intensity. I believe this intensity comes mainly from the vast changes brought on by the baby boomers who are now trying to cope with widespread income stagnation. The incomes of eight out of ten Americans have not kept pace with gains in the Consumer Price Index—inflation—since the early 1970s. Median household income in 1990, adjusted for inflation, was $29,943, about $1,000 less than in 1973, according to the Census Bureau.

Most of America still doesn't know much about direct selling. A few major brand names—such as Mary Kay, Tupperware, Fuller, Avon, World Book, and Encyclopaedia Britannica—have captured the fancy of many. But little is really known about the breadth and scope of this industry, which I have come to love and respect. Even Encyclopaedia Britannica, its eminence pioneered by direct selling, fails to acknowledge the industry. I know, because I looked it up in my own set, bought from a direct seller. It includes an entry for "Direct Mail Marketing" but not "Direct Selling."

Collectively, the direct sellers I interviewed—particularly the baby boomers, born between 1946 and 1964—seemed to be weary of the reins and halters clapped on by traditional organizations, the steel bits of restraint of traditional institutions, or the callous ways their "careers" were ended. They wanted choices, particularly those which would give them more personal freedoms. The direct option had freed them to be themselves, to express themselves, to know and enjoy their uniqueness and individuality.

Baby boomers tend to be uncomfortable with organizations and institutions that rigidly confine them and restrict their personal and financial growth. At the same time, many business organizations are fighting for their lives, downsizing, becoming "flatter" and much more efficient. The enlightened businesses will come through the lean nineties with, I believe, radically altered organizational forms. They will have to learn to acknowledge, celebrate, and, most of all, empower the individual. But that's for the next century, for most companies. It already exists in direct-selling organizations today.

So many people who have thought about owning their own retail businesses have found direct selling to be the most attractive way to achieve their dreams. I wish Gina and Holley and their friends the best of success. Somehow, I think they will succeed. They have taken the first bold step. What is ahead for them—and you—is spelled out in this book—everything you should know to make a decision to join a DSO and much of what you will need to know to be successful with one.

One of my first direct-selling jobs was at Tupperware Home Parties' public relations department in the late 1950s. In that position, I would often act as the Direct Selling Association's government affairs representative at City Council hearings (defending not only Tupperware, but also Avon, Britannica, and many other association members). Direct selling, thanks to a group of companies I called the "fraudulent fringe" composed of disreputable fly-by-night outfits, had worked its way into the "top ten" of industries on the Council of Better Business Bureaus' worst offenders list. Faced with municipal councils composed mainly of local business persons armed with the BBB data, I usually had an interesting communication challenge. In fairness, most of the local business members of such councils were men and women of integrity, able to set aside their own competitive interests in reaching a judgment on the local licensing issue involved. So our position usually was adopted. But the industry was growing rapidly in the sixties, as was the consumer movement, and the need for a strong ethical code and effective self-regulation grew.

In 1969, the new president of the DSA, Robert Brouse, one of the nation's leading career association leaders, retained another well-respected professional, Gerald Gilbert, a partner at the Washington law firm of Hogan and Hartson, to begin writing a Code of Ethics that would eventually set a new standard for business self-regulation. For his pioneer work on the code, Robert Brouse was honored in 1990 with the Direct Selling Education Foundation's Circle of Honor award. In 1992, Gerry Gilbert was still general counsel of the DSA, hard at work on a new DSA Code of Ethics, and recipient of the DSA's coveted Hall of Fame award.

In a 1991 interview, Gilbert reflected: "One of my greatest rewards in working on the original Code of Ethics came when my son, Bruce, returned home from a CUTCO/Vector training session very excited about what he had learned, especially about the DSA Code. He asked me, 'Dad, are you familiar with the Code of Ethics?'"

A major key to the success of the DSA Code of Ethics is the fact that an independent administrator of the code is named. This is a position always occupied by a person of stature and impeccable credentials for competence and integrity. The administrator operates with complete autonomy and exercises independent judgment on issues brought for consideration.

What, then, of those BBB complaints of the 1960s? Well, in 1991, both DSA President Neil Offen and I were elected to the Board of Directors of the Council of Better Business Bureaus and thus were in a unique position to view the progress of DSA member companies over a thirty-year span. Today, the direct-selling industry can be proud of its record for protecting the interests of consumers and for the strength of its Code of Ethics. The review process has worked well to protect products and services and also serves to protect those who seek opportunities within the direct option, such as, perhaps, you yourself. The first question to ask of an organization you are considering joining is: "Are you a member of the Direct Selling Association?"

My first bicycle was earned in 1947 through the direct sales of magazines in Tampa. Part of my education was financed by direct sales of Kirby vacuum cleaners. My first "real" job after college and the Army was in advertising direct sales, and I went from there to a fourteen-year career with Tupperware. Without a doubt, the last two decades at Mary Kay have been the finest years of my life, rewarding in every way.

One purpose of this book is to "pay back," through the contribution of all royalties received to the Direct Selling Education Foundation (DSEF), for all the good that has come into my life as a result of direct selling.

But it's the good that has come into other lives that gives me the biggest thrill of all. I call it the "paycheck of the heart," and it has brought me riches beyond my wildest imagination.

Dick Bartlett
Dallas

Acknowledgments

A direct "Thank you" goes to many. Direct sellers are taught to *ask* (for an order, for someone to join their organization, etc.). And ask I did, for without the help of scores of wonderful people, this book would not have been possible.

The major stumbling block to the book's creation was time to conduct the lengthy, in-depth interviews that, in my opinion, lent so much to the value of this work. So my first thanks are to those persons from the Mary Kay staff who volunteered their time to call the independent salespeople of more than twenty direct-selling organizations recommended to me by the CEOs of those participating companies.

The interviewers included: Peggy Anderson, Suzy Collins, Elga Desautel, Garret Glaser, Randall Graham, Debby Hennebury, Debby Hooker, Sharon Lasater-Boothe, Kay Levi, Gina Long, Michael Lunceford, Carole Merritt, Sheila O'Connell-Cooper, Elaine Raffel, Charlotte Selaiden, Rhonda Shasteen, Marcelle Trammell, and Ronnie Veals.

Thanks also go to Kathy Boone and Betty Conner, who helped with information about Mary Kay salespeople.

Unlike other, more time-blessed—and I'm sure more organized and talented—writers, I must write on the go, both literally and figuratively. So, copy would flow spastically from my PC to that of a very talented person named Monica Haverkamp, where it magically began to take on the appearance of a civilized document. Monica joined me with the promise that once the book was finished she would go on to much better things in Mary Kay, which she has. Reflecting back, I can see that the motivation to finish—both with the book and with me—drove her to high levels of productivity! There is no way that I can thank her enough, short of wishing her the kind of success she deserves and can achieve in her life, most of which lies ahead.

Other Mary Kay staffers who deserve special mention are Sandra Nottestad, who has served as chairman of the Direct Selling Association's Communications Committee; Susan McNeal, who prepared the questionnaire used in the initial interviews; Liz Barrett, whose behind-the-scenes organization made the interviewing process run smoothly; and Virgil Pulliam, vice-president for Legal Affairs and a member of the Direct Selling Association's Ethics Task Force, who made major contributions to Chapter 3, "Evaluating Direct Selling Organizations."

My longtime friend George "Jay" Hescock, executive vice-president of the Direct Selling Association, volunteered to be our technical editor. His more than twenty years' experience on the DSA staff helped me avoid embarrassing corruptions of fact. Also lending an experienced eye was Joseph Brinker, international project manager of the DSA.

As always, my severest editorial critic, Camille North, deserves much thanks for her ever-humbling help in making the work more readable.

Indirect "Thanks" go to all the marvelously cooperative independent entrepreneurs of the companies profiled and to the executives of these same organizations who contributed their time and knowledge to make this book possible.

Dick Bartlett
Dallas

Introduction

The future of retailing lies in delivering genuine value to customers. More and more, the very survival of retail enterprises will depend on selling the right products at the right prices in the right way. Poorly made products are out. Wasteful distribution methods that needlessly inflate prices are out. Customer-unfriendly stores are out. Value is in; value in retailing is everything.

Well-managed direct-selling organizations are participating in the value revolution in America and beyond. And this is why *The Direct Option* is an important book. Direct selling is one of the best ways to deliver value to customers, and this book tells readers how to jump on this fast-moving train, why, and how to be successful.

The first rule of career management is to join an industry that has a future. Direct selling, with its value connection, clearly has a future. Not all sectors of retailing do.

The second rule of career management is to try to control your own destiny. Direct selling meets this test, too. In direct selling, as Dick Bartlett points out in these pages, you want to find a product line to sell that you believe in and a company that will stand behind you. The rest is up to you—your enthusiasm, your determination, your hard work, and your integrity. Identify the right product to sell and the right company to represent, and you can control your destiny. This book is filled to the brim with the stories of people who built personally and financially rewarding careers from humble beginnings. As Dick Bartlett emphasizes, the key is not where you start, but where you finish.

The third rule of career management is to take great care of your customer. Things have a way of working out for sellers who do this. Direct selling offers you the opportunity to listen to your customers, to explore their preferences and needs and find just the right selections for them. Direct selling provides you an opportunity to surprise your customers with uncommon grace, uncommon courtesy, uncommon commitment to really helping them. Direct selling gives you an opportunity to build ongoing relationships with customers, to build a customer network, to build your own business.

The Direct Option is a wonderful book. It's fun to read. It's inspirational. It's honest. It's practical. It's wise. I hope my youngest son, who is still in college, and my wife, a leading volunteer worker in my community, will both read this book. I am glad I did.

Leonard L. Berry
Director, Center for Retailing Studies
JCPenney Chair of Retailing Studies
Professor of Marketing
Texas A&M University

The Direct Option

Chapter 1

Choosing the Direct Option:
The Benefits and Rewards

It was a sweltering summer in the Bronx in 1954, and I had just started selling Kirby vacuum cleaners. Accompanied by a very patient manager, I had already knocked on dozens of doors without making a single sale. I was a shy teenager, and the repeated rejection was, to say the least, painful. My tendency to blush kept giving away my emotions, which were anything but calm as door after door was shut in my face. I was miserable and just wanted the day to end. Silently, I vowed to quit.

Finally, a woman opened her door to reveal a home without rugs. Nothing in my excellent Kirby training had prepared me for pitching a vacuum cleaner to someone who had no rugs—especially for my first sales presentation! I must have actually bumped into my manager trying to back out the door, but he gently urged me forward into I didn't know what. All I could think was that I was bound to fail. No rugs!

Under the watchful eye of my long-suffering manager, I sweated my way through my carefully rehearsed demonstration, to which the woman paid rapt attention. I dutifully pushed the upright Kirby, one of the world's finest vacuum cleaners, across the bare boards. After a few bold swipes, the sales manual taught that the Dealer—me—was to pause, remove a cloth filter from the machine, and, with a flourish, show the prospect how much dirt had been removed from the carpet. But how much dirt could there be on waxed, hardwood floors?

To my amazement, the filter was clogged with dirt—sucked up from between the tiny cracks in the wood flooring by the Kirby's powerful Black & Decker motor. The woman was a superb homemaker and had fretted about the dirt she knew was there but which had resisted removal until I came along. After fumbling my way through the rest of the demonstration, I fearfully asked for the order. She paid cash on the spot, no financing for her. I left exhilarated, the first fifty dollars of my college funding secured.

Also secured was my future, but I didn't know that yet. I was my own boss. I had made a deliberate choice to control my income. I was in business for myself, but not by myself, for good Kirby people stood ready to help at every turn.

In 1994, some 5 million Americans will choose to join (or rejoin) a direct-selling organization and become independent entrepreneurs—to be in business for themselves but not by themselves. Nine out of ten will be female. *The Direct Option* is about who these people are, why they made the decision to join a member company of the Direct Selling Association, how they learned to be direct sellers, and what success many of them have achieved.

Despite the current economic climate, pessimism simply isn't part of the world of direct selling, where individuals make choices, make commitments, have purpose, and deeply care about other people. Millions of people are doing what they really want to do in direct selling, and many are making excellent livings. Whether they sell Mary Kay cosmetics or Kitchen Fair cookware, World Book encyclopedias or Shaklee cleaning products, they have learned to interact with others, relate to others, grow, and change. And while they are achieving self-sufficiency, they know they are linked to a positive, sustaining culture that cares about them.

Dr. Marvin A. Jolson of the University of Maryland provides a comprehensive description of the direct-sales industry in his teaching manual, *Direct Selling—The Personal Touch*:

> Most of us are so accustomed to thinking that marketing is a complex chess game of intricately related components . . . producers and consumers, advertising specialists and marketing research directors, wholesalers and jobbers, and dozens of other people and factors . . . that we are likely to forget that way back when business got started, it consisted of just two people . . . a buyer and a seller. This was, in essence, DIRECT SELLING, and it still is. There's no mystery about direct selling. In simple terms, it permits a straight line flow of products or services from a manufacturer or national distributor directly to the household end user through an organization of salespeople. If we think about it, we realize that direct selling is a form of retailing . . . in fact, the world's oldest form of retailing. Any time an organization sells products and services to household consumers for personal use, retailing has taken place. And so direct selling is an alternative to in-store retailing. Unlike the store merchant who hopes the prospective buyer will

seek him out, the direct selling firm distributes products by using salespeople who make personal visits to the consumer prospect's home or office for the purpose of product demonstration and an ultimate sale.

In order to fully understand direct selling, however, it's useful to look back at its beginnings in this country and how it has developed over the past forty years.

That Was Then

In the 1940s, 1950s, and 1960s, our country enjoyed a period of unprecedented growth and prosperity. The average annual growth rate for each of these decades was 4.5 percent, 3.3 percent, and 3.8 percent, respectively. In 1980, the growth rate slipped to 2.6 percent and stayed down at this level entering the 1990s. Investment was still anemic, real wages were stagnating, and the economy's debt burden was still heavy.

During the fifties and sixties, unemployment rates fluctuated around 2 to 3 percent, and our national "insurance" system cared adequately for those people out of jobs due to technological change or the small shifts in labor markets that produced what our politicians of those halcyon days called "frictional unemployment."

Unemployment rose steadily in the seventies, reaching double-digit proportions during the energy crisis of the late seventies and early eighties. Although the U.S. economy improved a little, it was virtually stagnant through the latter half of the eighties, and in early 1992 the Labor Department announced that the rate had reached a five-year high of over 7 percent—and the rate stayed at this level as the decade progressed. Millions of manufacturing jobs have disappeared since 1979 as America has attempted to regain its productivity through modernization, robotics, and quality improvement or as companies have downsized to cope with heavy debt incurred in the "Excessive Eighties." The media shook us up in the early nineties with daily reports of layoffs—some mind-boggling, such as General Motors' loss of 74,000 workers; Sears, Roebuck and Co.'s 50,000 layoffs and closures of more than 100 stores, IBM's attrition of 100,000 jobs; and the closings of scores of military bases. Many highly paid jobs created in the 1980s have disappeared, especially in the banking and defense industries. It was Wall Street against Main Street, and Main Street lost as personal savings evaporated, unemployment rose, and poverty soared to 13 percent, with 20 percent of all children living in poverty by the end of the decade.

The American middle class, about 60 percent of the U.S. population, or roughly 150 million people, was mutinous. Americans didn't like to read about F. Ross Johnson's $53 million "golden parachute" at RJR Nabisco when his "true greed" takeover failure cost 2,600 people their jobs. They also didn't want to read about "Call Me Roger" Smith, the GM chairman who led the company into decline in the eighties but received a $1.2 million annual pension when finally ousted.

The choices I and many others had back in 1954, when I began in direct sales, have narrowed substantially forty years later:

♦   College graduates back then just *expected* to get jobs upon graduation. When my son Chris graduated in 1992 with a degree in aerospace engineering, no job awaited him—nor did one for most of his class of highly skilled aeronautical engineers. Even M.B.A. degrees weren't worth what they used to be, with up to one in four 1990s graduates not reporting job placement upon graduation. Law school graduates were in the same boat.

♦   In the 1950s and 1960s, layoffs of middle managers were virtually unheard of. According to a 1992 American Management Association survey of 910 companies, over half of the employees who were laid off in the twelve months ending June 30, 1991, were middle management personnel—that's up 36 percent from the prior period. And although middle managers represented only an estimated 8 percent of the U.S. work force, they accounted for 16 percent of the reductions—twice the statistically expected number of people out of jobs. Professionals, managers, and administrators accounted for over 40 percent of total job losers in 1992, twice the proportion of the two prior recessions (1975 and 1982). Permanent job losers as a percent of the labor force were on a steady rise among thirty-five to fifty-four year olds in the early 1990s. The depressing, demoralizing concept of the "contingent worker" had been spawned by employment agencies by 1993. And worse, labor economists coined phrases such as "disposable" and "throwaway worker" to describe part-time or temporary employment.

♦   I bought my first house in the 1950s, a three-bedroom home that cost about half of what my car did in the 1990s. Like every other young home buyer, I didn't even consider the possibility that the value of my home could go down. For most of us, our homes are our principal asset, and home values in America have not experienced a major decline since the Great Depression. But home values are indeed declining in the 1990s, leaving many homeowners bewildered and uncertain about the future.

♦ In the 1950s, people between the ages of twenty-six and forty-five were at the top of their careers, earning more real income every year, with time to enjoy their families. Today, people in this age group—particularly women—are experiencing a form of "burnout" caused by longer work hours, more work pressures, and incomes that are declining in real terms. In December, 1991, *American Demographics* magazine reported a Gallup Poll finding that 43 percent of employed women between the ages of twenty-six and forty-five, and 33 percent of employed men in the same age group planned to reduce their job commitments by 1995. And 23 percent of employed women in this age group say they will quit their jobs altogether by then.

During the 1990s millions of Americans, and millions more around the world, are finding themselves stepping *down* their life ladders. As they look to the years ahead, many can see that their future quality of life is uncertain. (See Table 1-1.)

Table 1-1

American Households
Average Yearly Median Real Income Changes

Decade	Unrelated Individuals	Families*
1950s	2.1%	4.3%
1960s	5.0%	3.9%
1970s	3.0%	0.5%
1980s	0.3%	0.2%

* households with two or more members of a nuclear family
Source: *Current Population Reports*, P-60 Series, Bureau of the Census, 1990 and 1980. Reprinted courtesy of Dr. Jack Kasulis, University of Oklahoma.

In fact, the ratio of savings to disposable income in the United States and around the world has fairly steadily declined since the 1970s, further proof that Americans are falling behind. (See Table 1-2.) In addition, outstanding consumer credit has steadily increased in the United States since the seventies, rising from 18.3 percent of disposable personal income in 1970 to 20.6 percent of disposable personal income in 1989. (See Table 1-3.)

Table 1-2

Ratio of Savings to Disposable Income

	United States	France	West Germany	United Kingdom	Japan	Canada
1970	8.1	18.7	14.7	9.0	18.2	5.5
1980	7.1	17.6	14.1	13.1	17.9	13.3
1985	4.4	14.0	12.7	9.7	16.0	13.1
1989	4.6	12.3	13.9	6.7	14.8*	10.8

*1988 data
Source: *Statistical Abstract, 1991.* Reprinted courtesy of Dr. Jack Kasulis, University of Oklahoma.

Table 1-3

Consumer Credit Outstanding

	1970	1975	1980	1985	1989
Installment (in $billions)	103.9	167.0	298.2	518.3	716.6
Non Installment (in $billions)	27.2	37.9	52.1	73.8	61.4
Ratio to Disposable Personal Income	18.3%	17.9%	18.3%	20.9%	20.6%

Source: *Statistical Abstract, 1991.* Reprinted courtesy of Dr. Jack Kasulis, University of Oklahoma.

Furthermore, millions of workers in the bottom 75 percent of America's labor force are making less in real dollars than they once did. Over the last three decades, real hourly earnings of manufacturing workers were 2 times greater in Britain, 6 times greater in France and West Germany, and 12 times greater in Japan than in the United States.

U.S. Secretary of Labor Robert B. Reich, while a Harvard Lecturer in Public Policy, stated, "Upward mobility is becoming a vanishing idea." The American dream has become almost unattainable for millions who are in a downward spiral of mobility. In fact, almost all Americans below the top 20 percent are working harder than their parents and yet still falling behind. Hidden in the hoopla of our increasing national productivity is the loss of more than 3 million manufacturing jobs since 1979.

As noted earlier, many middle management jobs have vanished as well. Part of the increasing productivity of American companies has come from "flattening" organizations, shedding many levels of management made unnecessary by the proliferation of modern information systems. In the first two years of the nineties, U.S. companies reduced their middle management staffs by more than 500,000 employees, with more cuts coming faster and faster as the information society erupts.

From my experience as the president of a billion-dollar retail organization employing more than 2,000 people, I can tell you the route from the production room floor or clerical job is no longer easily followed. In fact, production jobs now require high skill levels, and there are very few "secretarial" jobs left in our streamlined company. For us, and many other companies, a major trend is toward self-directed work forces. This empowers workers but also eliminates many supervisory and middle management positions. Looking for a traditional job with us, or almost any employer, has never been tougher—except, of course, as a member of an independent direct-selling organization (DSO), where just the reverse is true.

Switching careers—which requires competing against others with much greater experience and usually means working for less money—has also become more difficult today. Companies are looking for the very best "players" in every position, and experience in an area of specialization counts for much. Those switching as a result of corporate "slimming" also make job hunting more difficult for new college graduates, who have to compete against well-educated and experienced workers also seeking entry-level jobs.

Millions more workers are hitting their heads against the ceiling in traditional jobs. Even long-tenured jobs can disappear in the blink of an eye. Men and women, young and old, are all affected equally. And while the solution is not the same for everyone, there is an answer that can work equally well for young and old, men and women, managers and clerks alike: direct selling.

The Future Is Now: Getting Started in Direct Selling

Let's take a look at some of the starting points of individuals who have gone on to achieve great success within DSOs. Many of these examples have been drawn from one company, Mary Kay Cosmetics, for the simple expedient of being able to follow life stories for a number of years. But as you will find in later chapters, the starting points and the positions of individual life ladders are very typical of people succeeding today in scores of other DSOs. It should be noted that my DSO is primarily composed of businesswomen, and that the study I refer to in this chapter reflects the opinions of more than 250,000 women. Quantitative research was done to substantiate the validity of the results indicated here. The final quantitative research confirms these findings with a high degree of statistical accuracy and precision. (We will meet many other "voices" from this chapter later on.)

Age

Let's start with age. One of the most frequent myths believed by unemployed workers, according to James Challenger, president of an international outplacement firm, is that entrepreneurship is a young person's game. Many believe, "Don't try it if you're over forty." Challenger says just the opposite is true, "About one in five discharged managers are starting their own businesses. More than 70 percent of them are over forty." But, in fact, age need not be a barrier to starting a business.

Evelyn Flippo from Hamilton, Mississippi, notes: "I'm a great-grandmother with seven children, thirteen grandchildren, and three great-grandchildren. I was working in nursing and had never sold anything in my life. But I was *very, very* tired of my job. My first goal was to just make an extra $20 a week, not to really change my life. But my first week I sold $600, and from that time on, that was it."

In fact, there are many people in their seventies and eighties who have made very successful careers of direct selling. They have literally started their lives over.

By the year 2020, one in three Americans will be age fifty or over and eligible for membership in the American Association of Retired Persons (AARP). The number of men in their sixties will increase by 75 percent to 17 million, and the number of women in their sixties will increase by 68 percent to 19 million by the year 2020. The entire concept and definition of aging will continue to undergo radical redefinition.

Direct selling will appeal to many of these men and women. Many older Americans will have the motivation, resources, and energy to join DSOs, to become entrepreneurs, and to run their own businesses. DSOs offer a safe haven where older Americans can learn new skills, earn the extra money their fixed incomes often demand, make new friends, and provide welcome services to their peers.

Age sometimes teams up with disability to make it more difficult to find employment in the traditional workplace. Trudy Jackson from Livermore, California, had been in the grocery business for almost thirty years when she hurt her back in an automobile accident. "I enjoyed the physical side of my work as a grocery checker and 'throwing stock' at night, but I could no longer do it. I was never a salesperson, but if you find a product you're comfortable with, you really don't have to be a great salesperson to be successful in direct selling. You just tell others what you know and like about your product."

The Physically Challenged

The physically challenged are welcome in this industry, and a direct-selling career allows the individual to function in his or her own choice of location, in a manner and means that accommodates almost any disability. For instance, much excellent sales work can be done via telephone, even from a bed. In my DSO, we have highly successful saleswomen who are legally blind—family members drive them to homes where they teach customers "skin care basics." Scores of top saleswomen confined to wheelchairs are recognized at our special events each year—we've installed special elevators to facilitate their on-stage appearances, always to enthusiastic applause. The physically able are quick to recognize the extra effort required for those with disabilities to excel, and I believe the added recognition is often emotionally beneficial. Member companies in the Direct Selling Association (DSA) show great diversity within their ranks, as the "Welcome to All" chart shows.

Welcome to All

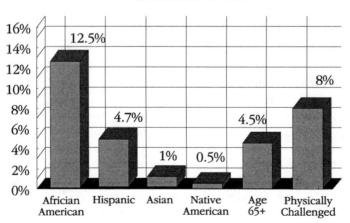

College Students

College students also often encounter barriers in finding employment because of their age and lack of experience. But there are several DSOs that offer great opportunities for students. Joel Broadbent of Brentwood, Tennessee, says, "Direct selling appealed to me as a career, because as a college student I had a chance to get my income at a level higher than anything I could get coming out of college."

In addition to having more money, Joel also has much more besides. "In my direct selling career, I have developed more resilience. I have learned the ability to be tough enough to bounce back from failure. I understand what it is like to have temporary setbacks, but I don't let them overcome me."

And Perry Bigelow of Nashua, New Hampshire, comments: "My attitude when I first went in was, 'Even if I don't make a dime, I'm going to walk away with some experience.' I overcame the negative image that some people have of direct selling by turning it into motivation. At first, people laughed at me and gave me a hard time, but I just threw it back into their faces. I have become much more assertive. I am no longer afraid of people and have a lot more self-confidence."

In fact, thousands of college students elect the direct-selling option annually. "I joined my DSO when I was eighteen, just out of high school," reports Pam Tull of Bridgeville, Delaware. "My motivation was to make enough money to pay for my tuition, books, and all the expenses that go with college." Pam is a good representative of the flexibility of direct selling at various steps on the life ladder. She explains: "I've been in direct selling as a young single, as a married woman, and while working another full-time job. Now, I have a four-year-old daughter, and direct selling is my full-time career. It fits all of those stages!"

Ethnicity

Furthermore, despite America's progress with respect to racial equality and decades of affirmative action, ethnicity is also often a barrier. Blacks, Hispanics, Asians, and other ethnic groups may face special challenges making their dreams come true in the nineties. In fact, as recently as 1988, when nearly 5.6 million women were employed as executives, administrators, and managers in the United States, black women represented just 2.9 percent of all workers at these levels.

Ruell Cone, an African American from Atlanta, Georgia, started out in life as the daughter of a sharecropper, harvesting Georgia cotton. When she attended her first direct-selling event, she watched guests make their purchases and thought to herself, "If I could just make $50 a month doing this, we could buy some furniture for our house and some curtains, too." Reminiscing, Ruell says, "At the time, we had only two trundle beds—the entire family was sleeping on them—plus a refrigerator and a piano."

Ruell's story is truly inspirational: all three of her children are now practicing medicine, graduates of the nation's finest medical schools— thanks to Ruell and her direct-selling option.

The direct option also helped Hispanic Florence Rivera of Miami, Florida. "I was working in import/export, a mother of nine kids. I decided I needed more time to dedicate to my children, and I liked the independence that direct selling gave me. You work the hours you feel like working; you program your time; you set your own goals; and you make the amount of money you want to make. There's no limit. I like to share with others and tell them if I could do it and reach this high, then I think anyone can do it as long as they set their goals."

In addition, direct selling was also a perfect choice for Yong Lee from Glendale, California, a naturalized U.S. citizen from Korea who simply wanted to "work at some American place to speak or learn English." Yong first tried work as a cashier and then at a home implement warehouse before choosing direct selling.

At first it wasn't easy for Yong. "I couldn't even think about selling," she says. "But then I discovered that it was more than selling . . . it was about becoming a better person, achieving personal growth, and gaining self-confidence. But many Asian Americans run away when I tell them about direct selling. They don't like the idea (as I didn't) at first. They don't like to sell, but I tell them about how I changed after I was involved with direct selling.

"People coming to the United States from Asia, Taiwan, China, and Korea who have difficulty with English can get a good start with direct selling."

As the song "It's Not Where You Start" from the musical *Seesaw* by Cy Coleman says, "It's not where you start. It's where you finish." You can even start from a completely foreign culture with a completely different language and succeed.

Maria Elena Alvarez arrived in America as an escapee from Castro's Cuba via Puerto Rico. Now a single mother with two children, Maria has been joined by her parents, and the family lives together.

Maria says, "I divorced by the time I joined Mary Kay, and because I had a nine-year-old boy and a one-year-old girl, I needed the income but wanted to raise my children. At the same time, I wanted to be successful by achieving big goals. I was searching for the 'American Opportunity' and thought that through Mary Kay, not only could I achieve all my desires, but I could also give my family a sense of *pride*."

Maria is especially excited about the opportunities direct selling offers to the Hispanic community. In *Vista*, a magazine for Hispanics, Maria
wrote, "I want to help break the barriers for Hispanic women by teaching
them to believe in themselves and realize that they, too, can gain success."
She has proven it by achieving a position of high leadership in one of the
world's largest DSOs.

Education and Status

Another barrier in many occupations is education. Thomas Wotruba,
a professor of marketing at San Diego State University and one of the
nation's leading academic authorities on direct selling, points out that
direct selling also provides "an entry into the business world for people
without the formal work experience required for employment in other
organizations." Our own studies show that direct sellers come from every
market segment—different education levels, ethnic groups, income levels,
household sizes, and occupational groups.

Sometimes, a high degree of formal education can work against the
decision to join a sales organization. Many people with an advanced degree or multiple degrees simply can't see themselves in a role that involves
"salesmanship" and interpersonal skill development. Others, however,
have seen through this artificial barrier to become highly successful in
direct selling.

Carol Anton of Fairfield, California, remembers when she was just
completing her college education with a degree in psychology. "I wanted
to plan my life in a way that I could raise my children, but I knew that I
would have to wait for a teaching job for three years, and then raise
children after that. It looked like I would be getting old quickly and going
nowhere fast. So I looked at direct selling but said to myself, 'No, I'm too
good for that. I want to have a *real* job.' But the opportunity looked so
good, I decided I would be a fool if I didn't try. . . . I planned to give it
a year." Carol is now one of the top fifty in commission earnings in an
organization of more than 250,000 women. Similarly, having achieved a
certain "status" in the community may have been reason for Anne New-
bury of Detriot not to consider a direct-selling career. "Back in 1969, as a
mother of two little girls who filled her leisure hours doing community
volunteer work raising money for the arts, I felt my life as a homemaker
was complete.

"On a visit to Dallas, my cousin and her husband invited me to
dinner. During the course of the evening I tried to make intelligent conversation talking about my fund-raising projects and how many community dollars we had generated. My cousin's husband, a very successful real

estate developer, leaned over the table and said, 'Anne, for all the time you spend raising money for everybody else, have you ever thought of doing something for yourself?'

"I said, 'I don't know what in the world you think I could do!' And with that he asked me if I had ever heard of Mary Kay Cosmetics. Of course I had not, but I had an instant idea of what I thought it was, and I assure you I was not interested!" But it became a seed planted that was destined to blossom into a career that would take Anne to the very top of Mary Kay.

"After high school," recalls Alma Gaines of Little Rock, Arkansas, "my parents could not afford to send me to college, so I began working in a small county courthouse. The pay was not very good, and the hours were long. But because I didn't have a college degree, it was difficult to find a job that paid well."

Alma took an office job that paid 50 percent of the salary paid to the men in her office. In 1964, she heard of a new DSO in Dallas, and with her husband, Bill, made the 350-mile trip to find out more. To start, she needed to purchase a $25 kit, and on the long drive home, Bill would ask her every so often, "Do you think we lost that $25?" Alma is still with the same company today, retired on an income equal to 60 percent of the best three of her last five years' commissions, earning six figures annually.

Cathy Bill from Westmont, Illinois, was labeled a "slow learner" in grade school. "I had a learning disability, and I was with children who had behavioral problems—children who would get suspended all the time. I could never comprehend anything I read. I walked around thinking I was dumb, so college never entered my mind. But I was searching for something. I chopped onions at a hot dog stand for $1.85 an hour, pumped gas at a gas station for $3.85 an hour, did clerical work for $4.00 an hour—and got fired from all jobs!"

Electing the direct option changed Cathy's life. "Only my mother and my husband believed in me until I joined my DSO. People believe in you every step of the way, until one day you wake up and believe in yourself."

Direct selling does not present the same barriers to entry that are found in traditional employment, where job opportunities favor people with experience in a closely related area of activity.

Training

The well-established direct-selling companies offer excellent training materials and educational programs to aid the new entrant in getting started in the business. Most important, the best companies provide a "take-you-by-the-hand-and-show-you-how" type of educational opportunity designed to guide salespeople to ever-higher levels of achievement. Most companies offer free, weekly education sessions (usually through highly motivated independent businessmen and women) and periodic major educational events, which may bear a modest fee or cost travel expenses, but are usually well worth the investment of time and money. However, beware those companies which charge large sums for their basic training programs. These expensive programs, since they obviously benefit the company as well as the trainee, usually signal that something is not right with the company. (Some legitimate DSOs do offer more advanced education programs, which can be an excellent investment in the future—but learn the difference before committing.)

Each direct-selling company has its own marketing style, techniques, products, and service characteristics, as well as its own philosophy of business, so a new learning experience awaits those who move from one to another. But the programs are geared so that virtually everyone can learn and advance.

Experience in other fields may be of some limited help, but the individual's ability to assimilate and build on the knowledge base of the DSO's optional training and educational programs will usually be far more important than prior experience. We have found that a background in some teaching or training-oriented profession is helpful—for example, nursing, education, corporate training, or human resources. The most important qualities of all are human relation skills and perseverance. Those who enjoy being with people and can relate to many kinds of people can find extraordinary success in the direct option.

Even those who think they have little or no human relations skills may want to inquire further. The direct-selling option is one where tens of thousands have improved such skills, almost always to their overall betterment, even if they do not stay in direct selling. There is no better way to improve these valuable skills than in direct selling.

Rubye Lee of Alpharetta, Georgia, was a homemaker with no job experience, who had a strong fear of speaking to more than two people at the same time. She joined her DSO to see if she could learn to be more comfortable around people. For a while, Rubye sold her company's products strictly as a hobby, something she did in her leisure time. After committing herself to more of a full-time effort, Rubye began to succeed and, naturally, her success threw her into the spotlight.

Even high tech, high-education-required jobs can be dead ends. And it doesn't matter where individuals from these upscale career areas start. They may be facing the acrylic ceiling or job discrimination or career burnout. The direct option can therefore be a solution for these highly qualified or highly educated persons who feel themselves at a dead end in life.

"I was in a salaried position stuck in a structure that wouldn't allow me to advance any further without a promotion," says Larry Banks of Atlanta, Georgia. "I worked for the Federal Reserve Bank in Atlanta, and I wanted unlimited earnings and control of my own destiny." Larry scrutinized his life ladder, saw the S&L and subsequent banking crises coming, and realized that "unlimited earnings" and a career in banking in the nineties were not at all a likely match.

Larry made his choice quickly. "I walked out of the bank and said, 'I'm going to sell encyclopedias!'" Larry has since gone on to make a full-time career in his DSO, earning the kind of income he desires to support his wife and three children while also having the freedom he desires.

Diane Hartung of Slidell, Louisiana, obtained a master's degree in computer science and still felt unfulfilled. "I designed databases for mainframe IBM computers and went to school for many, many years to get that job," Diane remembers. "I thought I had really arrived, but I wasn't happy. There was just something missing. Direct selling was the only thing I could see that would fit my life. I am still amazed at the impact I am having on the lives of other people as a leader in direct selling."

Benefits and Rewards of the Direct Option

In a major research project at my company, probing at decisions to join DSOs, we found that the majority said they joined with the intention of pursuing the position part-time, and many said they regarded the "job" as a hobby, social outlet, or a way to make extra money—but that money was not their major motivation.

Nonmonetary rewards were mentioned more than monetary ones, and many participants said the nonmonetary rewards meant the most. Study participants mentioned that the person who led their unit was the primary source of support, particularly in helping a newcomer survive the rough times during his or her first year with the DSO. Peers were given high ratings for support in areas of encouragement, recognition, friendship, and sharing of successful sales techniques. This is very typical of the quality DSOs in the DSA.

Overall, the social support system received high marks and was cited as one of the primary advantages the direct option has over more traditional business structures or corporations.

In addition, study participants rated their training as excellent, including major company meetings, regional workshops, the marketing plan, and audio cassettes and videotapes.

Our research found that some women joined our DSO with the intention of making it a career or as a second career, and for these women, money was an important factor. Aspects of the career that appealed to the majority included flexibility, independence, low risk, growth opportunity, and the ability to transfer the career if they moved.

Why Choose a DSO?

Most of the women who participated in the study said that the decision to join was not influenced by a family member or a friend; in fact, many said they joined without discussing it with others. Of those who discussed the decision with a spouse, most said their spouses were supportive of the decision to join. Although some considered other self-employment, they chose a DSO because it was lower risk, did not require a large investment, and offered support and training.

The initial expectation for many of the study participants was low. Many said they didn't know what to expect. Others said that after they got started they found it totally unlike what they expected, mostly in positive ways. Generally, reality exceeded expectations in areas of financial potential, advancement opportunities, training, social support, and emotional rewards. Negative reactions, where they existed, were most often related to difficulty of sales and recruiting—especially handling rejection.

The study participants were almost unanimous in agreement that potential for advancement and growth in a DSO was unlimited. Many participants who did not aspire to higher levels at the time of joining, now are (or plan to be) at higher levels. Others said they were "taking it one step at a time" or were happy at their present level.

Few of our study participants mentioned any undesirable consequences of progression. Those few undesirable consequences which were mentioned included conflicts with other responsibilities and frustrations with lower producers in their units of salespeople.

Most participants said they have made more money as they progressed, enabling them to enhance their standard of living and increase their financial security. Although participants generally appreciated the material value of cars and prizes, these awards (especially the cars) were mainly viewed as symbols of achievement and success.

In addition to material benefits, study participants cited many nonmaterial benefits as a result of progression with the DSO. They said progression has meant a change in status, an increase in self-esteem and self-confidence, rewarding experiences in helping others, and improved leadership and professional skills.

The majority of participants said they spend thirty hours or less per week on their DSO activities. Some at lower levels said that although compensation may be currently lower than they would like, "it will pay off in the long run." This, as you will see later, is a very typical reaction for people building their own retail business—one good customer at a time.

Finally, few of the study participants could identify other jobs that would be comparable to their direct-selling businesses. If they were to leave, participants were almost unanimous that it would be for a position in which they owned their own business.

Former professional viola player Deborah Dudas of Niles, Michigan, speaks for many in the study: "I was running a hospital laboratory working days, nights, and often past midnight and had maxed out on salary. I had two little girls, ages one and four, and my husband Dan worked swing shifts. It's no wonder I elected direct selling!"

"I was a corporate accountant," says Maggie Rader from Westlake, Ohio. "Sounds real glamorous, but it was a real low-stroke, no-recognition job; and although I was paid very well, it just wasn't worth the hassle. I elected to stay home with my children for a few years, until I was ready for something new. That something new was direct selling, although I had no sales background. But when I went to a function and saw for the first time in my life successful women who hadn't given up anything morally or ethically to get where they were—they had self-confidence, they liked themselves and they were open—I really just wanted that with all my heart.

"My husband and I had wanted to start our own business. We had looked at a lot of opportunities, and all of them required great amounts of time and capital investment, but not the DSO we were investigating. You could start for as little as $95! Now my husband has joined me full-time, giving up a job of thirteen years, and we have our own successful company!"

DSOs have known for years that the net gain in family income of having both spouses hold two full-time salaried jobs is frequently much less than anticipated. Some of the key factors involved are taxes, child care, and job-related costs (including the necessity for expensive clothing for work). Therefore, the economies often do not add up for many two-paycheck families. The direct option, however, often offers a superior earnings opportunity both full-time and part-time, especially when computed on a real earnings-per-hour basis. In addition, the direct option offers many legitimate opportunities for tax-deferred savings as well as for tax deductions that are not typically available to persons earning a paycheck as an employee.

Incomes tied to a paycheck also have other potential liabilities. First, the paycheck can be easily terminated, leaving the worker high and dry. Experts agree that it is risky for families to rely on one partner (usually the husband) as the sole wage earner because of the harshness of today's business climate, the increased incidence of divorce, and the possibility of losing a spouse to death. DSOs offer the opportunity to learn a valuable job skill, regardless of future circumstances. The ability to market yourself as well as a product or service is one that retains its value for a lifetime.

Olivia Theriot of San Antonio, Texas, had reached the rank of colonel in the Air Force. When she retired after twenty years, she looked around for a new career and chose direct selling. "The very first meeting I went to I couldn't believe what was happening," Olivia says. "There I was, and they were singing, and someone came and hugged me. I'm a very private person, and I thought I would die. I thought I'd come to a wrong decision—that these people must be crazy. But I tried again, and now my own business is eleven years old, and I've been very successful."

Workplace equity issues for women, especially those to do with equal pay, continue to be a major problem with traditional forms of employment. For instance, although middle-aged and older women make up an increasing portion of the work force, they are paid substantially less than men their age. Women tend to reach their peak earnings a decade earlier than men and are still largely segregated in traditional "women's jobs." Most women remain confined to lower paying "women's work"—employed as secretaries, retail salesclerks, waitresses, nurses, teachers, and librarians. This job segregation gets more pronounced with age.

While men's median earnings climb steadily until the age of fifty-five and then begin to drop, women's earnings peak at the age of forty-four, then start to decline. Even in the years when women's wages are rising, they do not increase nearly as fast as men's. One estimate places women's wages at 80 percent of men's by the year 2000. While that estimate is an improvement from 65 percent in 1990, it's still an insult to women—one that contributes to the burnout noted earlier.

According to Wendy Reid Crisp, national director of the National Association for Female Executives, women still have a long way to go to catch up monetarily. She explains: "As women get into a field, salaries go down, because women are willing to work for less. Women are desperate for opportunity, so they undersell themselves."

Judy Baker of Orlando, Florida, one of the first women in pharmaceutical sales in the southeastern United States, worked for companies such as Warner-Lambert Company, the Parke Davis Group, and Lederle Laboratories. "I was very unhappy," says Judy. "I found myself playing games that I didn't like to play. I learned corporate gamesmanship, and I found that the corporate world really reinforced mediocrity—every year I was penalized because I was really a super achiever. Then the next year I had a higher goal to achieve with no incentive other than the fact that I was glad to have my job . . . I got to keep my job if I did well.

"Even though I had the college degrees needed for promotion, because I was female, because I was a wife, and because I really did not want to move to New Jersey or wherever they wanted us, I was absolutely not considered as a prospect for upper management." Judy adds, "In fact, being top in sales didn't even give me job security! I lost my job when a new manager decided to 'sweep with a heavy broom' and replace everyone with new salespeople of his choosing. Job security only comes when *you're* the boss."

Former executive recruiter Ginny Granke from Bridgeville, Pennsylvania, found herself pulled in many directions at once as a single mother of three. She obtained a nursing degree from the University of Pittsburgh and a master's degree in psychology. But despite her education, Ginny found that she had hit the glass ceiling—there were no advancement opportunities and tremendous office politics.

Ginny was skeptical and at first rejected the direct option. "I said I needed another job like I needed a hole in my head. The person who recruited me said, 'Intelligent women listen.' And that was enough to make me give her the time to explain her DSO. I signed up as a lukewarm part-timer, then went to a major meeting in Dallas. I sat on the edge of my chair with my mouth open watching all those wonderful women having fun and making money. I went home and walked away from a $40,000-a-year job to go full time in my own DSO. It's been my sanity, my fun, and my comradeship."

Family

College instructor Bett Vernon from Winter Haven, Florida, had been teaching for fifteen years. "Because of stress, lack of money, and lack of time to be with my two and three year olds, I was really looking for something that would allow me to be more positive," Bett says. "Back then, I didn't know how to dream, I didn't know what was out there. Growing up on a farm in South Dakota, my future seemed very limited. My DSO has provided me with badly needed self-confidence, people skills, financial independence, and a positive outlook on life that I can pass on to my children."

DSOs offer a great opportunity for people to pursue careers while putting their families first. Our DSO's founder, Mary Kay Ash, has for decades espoused the philosophy of "God first, family second, career third," showing a deep recognition of the crisis facing millions of American families.

Families in which both spouses are employed have major challenges in balancing the competing demands of work and home; this is especially true among younger families. DSOs often have incentive programs that offer opportunities to win fabulous prizes and vacation trips that are not the routine items most budgets allow. Women especially want a more liberal social agenda and the enhanced affiliation and acceptance offered in the direct option. They rate security and safety higher than men and are less materialistic.

Take the case of Nancy Tietjen, formerly of Madison, Minnesota: "Before I joined my DSO, I was working the graveyard shift packing shotgun shells on an assembly line. I was the sole support of my two daughters, Susie and Kristi, who were then thirteen and eleven years old. I can tell you, I didn't get a bang out of that work!" After discovering the DSO that met her personal needs, Nancy invested in an "old, rusty Mercury for $250. It didn't even have a heater, which is not good in wintertime Minnesota. I can remember having to sell a toll bridge operator an item of my merchandise to get across, because I didn't even have change for the toll."

Nancy found little that was emotionally and psychologically rewarding in her shotgun shell plant. She found her life hard and very confining. She sought her own identity—her key demands were for respect, self-worth, and individuality. But she was at an impasse in her life.

Through DSOs, excellent earnings can be obtained on schedules that place family time above work time. In addition, the family (especially children) can be involved in DSO activities and begin to find out how the world really does work. Thus, a career in a DSO can help reduce the disequilibrium that is created between the need to work and the need for the traditional values of marriage and parenthood.

Kristin McNally of St. Petersburg, Florida, says: "Before joining a DSO, I had two choices: stay home with my two children and be under financial stress, or work full time and let someone else care for them. Thanks to direct selling I can stay home with my children *and* earn an income."

Barbara Peasel of Silex, Missouri, sums up the position of many women: "I took up direct selling on a part-time basis because I had three little ones. I first got into my DSO as an outlet and to make extra money. I liked it and liked being with people. I have grown with the business.

And as I've had time and as my family has grown, I grew into a full-time position."

Almost two-thirds of all mothers with children under eighteen years of age are now in the work force, a 300 percent increase since 1960. By the year 2000, 75 percent of working mothers will be in this category. The most frequently heard praise of DSOs, mainly from women (whether married or single heads of household) and a few men as well, has to do with the availability and flexibility of time direct selling allows to spend with their children.

"I really was not successful by any measure," states Susan Ehrnstrom of Forked River, New Jersey. "I wanted to do something, but didn't want to leave my four children, ages two, four, nine, and eleven. Direct selling allowed me to stay home and be a full-time mother and make a lot of money in just a few hours . . . and still give my family the consideration I thought they deserved."

The number of births in the 1980s and 1990s has been much higher than the demographic experts predicted. In 1990, 4.2 million babies were born in the United States, according to the National Center for Health Statistics. Between 1980 and 1990, birthrates among women in their thirties were up more than 33 percent, according to the Census Bureau. (The baby boomlet, which started in the late 1970s, slowed a little in 1991.) Much of the boomlet's vigor seems to come from the fact that many younger women are deciding to have children. (See Table 1-4.)

Table 1-4

Fertility Rates of U.S. Women

Year	Rate	Year	Rate
1945-50	3.0	1965-69	2.6
1950-54	3.3	1970-74	2.1
1955-59	3.7	1975-79	1.8
1960-64	3.4	1980-84	1.8
		1985-89	1.9

Source: *Statistical Abstract, 1991, 1988*. Reprinted courtesy of Dr. Jack Kasulis, University of Oklahoma.

The 1990s are bringing other changes. Sociologist Marc Miringoff reports in his "Social Health Index" that social health sank to its lowest point in twenty years in 1991, with a 51 percent drop since 1970. The five worst problems were child abuse, teen suicide, income polarization, great numbers of people without health insurance, and people over the age of sixty-five spending a high percentage of income on health care. Divorce rates are up more than 50 percent since 1970.

Stanford University research for the years 1980 through 1986 showed a ten-hour decrease per week of potential parental time—in just five or six years. The reason for this sharp decline goes back to the influx of great numbers of women into the work force starting in 1960, jumping from 30 percent in 1960 to almost 70 percent in 1990. (See Table 1-5.) Some demographic and sociological research would indicate that the total amount of time parents spend with their children has dropped anywhere from 40 to 50 percent during the past twenty-five years.

Sylvia Ann Hewlett, in her book *When the Bough Breaks: The Cost of Neglecting Our Children,* points out, "A body of new evidence shows extremely high levels of stress among women who hold both demanding jobs and deal with home and family in their 'spare' time." She continues, "Contrary to conventional wisdom, the most stress-filled occupations are not in the executive ranks; rather, they are the less glamorous jobs in the pink-collar ghetto, held mostly by mothers."

Hewlett cites recent studies, with which our research agrees, that male managers "may actually stress-out less than 'support' workers," such as secretaries, data entry clerks, word processors, assembly line workers, waitresses, and retail sales clerks.

Hewlett concludes that dangerously high levels of stress can be experienced by working mothers, who often deal with children and housework after a full day's job. She adds, "Despite the fact that wives and mothers have entered the paid labor force at a very rapid rate in recent years, men have picked up relatively little on the home front." More than 70 percent of the almost 60 million women permanently employed in the United States at the beginning of the 1990s are suffering from stress in the workplace, according to a survey by the New York Business Group on Health, a nonprofit organization which monitors employee health care protection.

Married women spend twice as many hours each week on family tasks as their husbands, when both hold full-time jobs. According to a *Dallas Morning News* survey, the average working mother spends forty-four hours at work and thirty-one hours on family tasks weekly. Her husband spends a little more time on the job but only fifteen hours pitching in at home. The multiple roles that many working women play add much potential for stress.

Sally Wendkos Olds, writing in *Working Parents Survival Guide,* claims that the two-paycheck families that run the smoothest "often tend to be those in which at least one parent has a flexible or part-time job." She adds, "When flexibility is possible, situations often stop being problems and turn instead into challenging puzzles that, with ingenuity and perseverance, can be neatly solved." This is especially true when the flexibility comes from involvement in a DSO on the part of one or both partners, as the family unit itself is often involved in the "solution."

Table 1-5

Adult Female Participation in the Labor Force

	Children Ages 6-17			(Preschool) Children Ages under 6		
Year	Married	Separated	Divorced	Married	Separated	Divorced
1960	39.0%	N/A	N/A	18.6%	N/A	N/A
1970	49.2%	60.6%	82.4%	30.3%	45.4%	63.3%
1980	61.7%	66.3%	82.3%	45.1%	52.2%	68.3%
1989	73.2%	73.5%	85.0%	58.4%	57.4%	70.5%

Source: *Statistical Abstract, 1991*. Reprinted courtesy of Dr. Jack Kasulis, University of Oklahoma.

Judie McCoy from Waukesha, Wisconsin, started her direct-selling career as a wife and mother of two small children who didn't work outside the home. McCoy says, "I had a lot inside that I just needed to get out, and I wanted something where I could work around my family. For eight years, I chose to be a full-time wife and mother. When I felt it was time for me to pursue a career, I was frustrated with the lack of opportunity. I was full of ambition, enthusiasm, and determination. I felt I would be a great asset to *any* business simply because I *wanted* to succeed! However, the reality was that I did not have a college degree, much less any experience. Direct selling provided a track to run on. And run I have! I often wonder where American businesses would be today if they looked at enthusiasm and desire as much as credentials and a resume when they recruit."

"If you had met me in 1973," says Holly Zick of Bloomington, Minnesota, "you would have voted me least likely to succeed at anything. I was a single parent and the sole support of two children, one who needed braces, the other who needed glasses—neither of which I could afford. I can remember crying late at night while doing dishes—asking God to help get me and my children out of this situation so that I could provide them with the life they deserved. My children and I were eating eggs or peanut butter every night, and I was working fifty hours a week in a dead-end job. I was behind on my house payments; the bank was going to foreclose on my mortgage; my father had just died; plus, I had no hospitalization insurance and no car."

Holly joined a DSO after saving for three weeks to get the $50 she needed for a demonstration case. "I had one suit and one pair of shoes," she recalls. "I either had to have my babysitter's mother take me to a customer demonstration and pay for her gas or take the bus."

Although many advanced corporations are making progress in developing cultures that maximize the opportunities for women and provide the flexibility women often need in corporate careers, the vast majority are still mired in the rigid hierarchical structures of the fifties and sixties.

Flexibility

"I wanted to go into business for myself because I'm an extremely independent person," says Barbara Armstrong-Allen of Indianapolis, Indiana. "I got tired of the bureaucracy! I like working my own set hours. I can work as hard as I want for myself, instead of for someone else, with less stress."

Over one-third of all U.S. employees are reported to have considered quitting their jobs in 1990, and the problem is growing. Almost half of all workers find their jobs stressful, a figure which has doubled since 1985. Seven out of ten workers say job stress is causing frequent health problems and has made them less productive.

DSOs offer an alternative to stress caused by factors in the workplace that are relatively inflexible, such as pressure to work harder and longer for an organization that is in far too much debt because of recessionary trends or bad management. Independent members of DSOs can minimize these and other stresses—even those created by serious health problems—by setting their own hours, by simply not working any "overtime," and by setting their own financial goals.

"I married immediately after high school and began my lifelong dream of being a good Christian wife and soon found myself with three small children," recollects Rena Tarbet of Fort Worth, Texas. "My husband was completing his formal education while I took our monthly income of $300 and tried to make ends meet. I had no car, no money, and was going completely crazy until I decided on direct selling." Rena says today, "To me, a successful person is one who lives well, laughs often, and loves much; who fills his niche and accomplishes his task; who realizes that true happiness is from within and does not depend on outward circumstances."

Those who know Rena know that she is, by her own standards, a very successful person. They also know that she is a special person under constant threat of cancer that would a few years ago have been terminal.

The examples could continue by the thousands. That so many have achieved so much in the organizations with which I've served is all I need to sustain me in any adverse circumstance. I just think of the many women who have done so much with their lives and the lives of others. No, it's not where you start that matters at all. It's where you finish.

As stated earlier, each year, some 5 million Americans elect the direct option as a means of not only earning a living, but earning a living in the style they want as people in business for themselves. To many, the prospect of working in their own way, at their own speed, on hours they select for themselves is very appealing.

The direct option has become a career of choice, accessible to almost everyone in America, and indeed, the world.

The next chapter will demonstrate how direct selling is becoming a dynamic retailing force for the 1990s when contrasted with more traditional forms. It demonstrates clearly that the direct option has many advantages.

Chapter 2

Is the Direct Option for You?

There has never been a better time to re-evaluate where and how you wish to earn a living. If you have the urge to be independent and live a life-style of your own choice—not the choice of an employer or "boss"—now is the right time.

Those who have chosen the direct option have found unlimited opportunities without the stereotyping or discrimination often found in other positions. Women and minorities who make direct selling a full-time career consistently earn above the median income for all categories, including white males.

- 90 percent of all direct sellers are women
- 19 percent are minority group members—Hispanic Americans, African Americans, Asian Americans, and Native Americans
- 8 percent have a physical disability
- almost 5 percent are over the age of sixty-five.

Direct selling provides income opportunities for all Americans—regardless of age, sex, ethnic background, physical condition, or financial status. DSA industry statistics prove that this channel of distribution taps into markets not well served by other retailing channels—direct selling represents a special opportunity to many individuals. Many companies offer virtually all of their training and sales aids in languages other than English, including Kitchen Fair, Mary Kay Cosmetics, and Tupperware.

According to a 1992 survey by Nathan Associates of sixteen hundred independent contractors from DSA-member companies, the top five reasons for selling direct include factors such as liking and believing in the products, being one's "own boss" and having flexible hours issues, the need to earn extra money for self or to supplement a family income, the link between effort and reward, and the enjoyment derived from selling. These results closely resemble those found in the survey work done for my DSO.

Top Five Reasons People Sell Direct

Like and believe in the product	90.7%
Being their own boss, working their own hours	73.1%
Supplement family income or make a little extra money for myself	63.7%
The harder I work, the more money I can make	54.3%
Enjoy selling	48.5%

Age Distribution

Before focusing on the direct option, I will review the many other options available, starting with the fundamental choice of whether you wish to start a home-based business or one that requires a fixed location.

Home-based versus Fixed-location Employment

The U.S. Department of Commerce places 95 percent of all business in the country in the "small business" category. There is a *lot* of competition. There is also a lot of risk. For example, in 1990, more than 12,000 fixed-location boutique retailers went out of business. This is a tip-of-the-iceberg example, representing just one narrow segment of the businesses that fail in the United States each year. The Department of Commerce estimates more than 500,000 businesses are started each year, but that by the end of just one year in business, 40 percent (or 200,000) will fail. By year five, 80 percent will have failed—that's 400,000 dreams and lots of money down the tube.

If you are selecting a business requiring a location away from your home, you will need to do some serious work in advance and have a substantial source of capital.

Commercial banks and life insurance companies continue to experience rising delinquencies and foreclosures, and bank failures will continue throughout the nineties. In short, commercial banks aren't too interested in loaning money to small business start-ups, outside of well-collateralized personal loans. And the Small Business Administration (SBA), once a user-friendly lending source, is becoming harder to get money from.

Even assuming you can get the capital, where to locate is a decision fraught with much uncertainty due to today's highly mobile customers. Then you need to decide whether to lease, buy, or even build. If you choose to build, beware the common mistake of underestimating both the time of construction and the cost.

The retailer's success slogan of "Location, Location, Location" is critical. What will your customers expect of you in the way of access? Do you need a lot of traffic? Check out the competition within a several-block radius. Is a major local corporation going to be in business five or ten years from now?

Some of the fixed-location businesses that should do well in the nineties would include: the automotive after-market, such as auto detailing, tune-ups, oil changes, and repairs; beauty salons; bed-and-breakfast establishments; craft shops; day-care centers; dry cleaners/alterations; educational toys and games; fitness-related items, such as athletic wear, athletic equipment, diet clinics, health food, aerobics, health and exercise centers, and, if you're qualified, health care itself; garden supplies and landscaping; gourmet food stores, products, and restaurants; home decorating centers; laundromats, combined with another retail idea such as entertainment; party rental stores and party planner services; quick printers; retirement facilities; sandwich shops, pizza "joints," and take-out restaurants; self-storage facilities; shoe repairs; specialized clothing, such as children's, professional women's, and large-size apparel; and vocational schools.

This partial list is included to stimulate your creativity with respect to the possibilities in fixed-location businesses. You *must* select well. Few fixed-location businesses that start with limited capital can be built without a large capacity for hard work, determination, courage, discipline, efficiency, resourcefulness, organizational ability, and lots of "street smarts"—to name but a few characteristics of success. But, most important, you must absolutely *love* your business, for you will be with it sixty to seventy to eighty or more hours per week. The fact is, with your own in-store business, you'll usually have less free time than if you are employed. But if you enjoy it and are having fun, it will all be worthwhile.

Although direct selling is mostly a home-based business, many other businesses can also be run from the home which are not characterized as direct selling. For example, you could consider becoming an accountant, an advertising/graphic designer, an auditor, a building contractor, a caterer, a dating service business, a desktop publisher, a financial planner, a home interior decorator, an insurance salesperson, a maid service, a management consultant, a meeting planner, a messenger service, a photography/video producer, a public relations professional, a real estate agent/appraiser, a writer/agent/editor, and so forth.

Perhaps the most important trend in home-based businesses—one that is growing tremendously—is based on the "information age" that will increasingly shift the balance of global economic power. Information is very portable, and modern computers, modems, and networking devices make it possible to work anywhere.

In fact, at Mary Kay we have noted that many husbands, who need not have a time-demanding role in their wife's business, have developed home-based computer-oriented businesses on their own. This is often beneficial to both spouses, in that the wife's business and customer records can usually be managed on the same computer system.

In the baby boomer group alone, almost 5 million say they want their own businesses—their own "world" that they can master and enjoy. And if you can be one of the relatively few who succeed, that dream can be yours. The trouble is, the risks are often staggering.

The direct option is about a way to own your own business without those risks. It allows entrepreneurship with minimal risk. As the 1990s began, the wellspring of direct selling was becoming a river of opportunity for millions of independent entrepreneurs. Many other business options have big price tags, high risks, or perhaps require technical knowledge or other expertise which many would-be entrepreneurs do not possess and cannot easily acquire. The direct option can be exercised by almost everyone, regardless of level of education or net worth.

Franchises

A very appealing option is franchising, a business form that is well established throughout the world. One of the world's largest franchise operations is McDonald's. Each year, about 20,000 people contact McDonald's about obtaining a franchise. Only about 2,000, however, reach the interview stage, and fewer than 200 ever obtain a restaurant.

First, not everyone has the money to obtain a franchise. McDonald's franchisees must invest over $600,000, including an initial franchise fee of over $20,000, and only a portion of that can be borrowed.

Before being awarded a restaurant, applicants must work two years, usually about fifteen hours a week, as unpaid apprentices. Then the applicants are off to Hamburger University for a two-week training session. After all that, most are awarded franchises hundreds of miles from their homes and must relocate at their own expense.

The Retail Industry

In choosing the direct option, you are electing to become a retailer, so it is important that you understand the major changes sweeping the retail industry in the 1990s—all trends that favor your becoming a direct retailer.

The Richmont Corporation, a mortgage banking and marketing counseling service that has done considerable work in the direct selling field, has clearly defined the differences between in-store retailing and direct selling.

"In a retailing organization," says Richmont's John Rochon, "resources are organized primarily to support the selling of products in a store where people come to buy them. The key to success is being able to attract—or 'pull'—customers into the retail establishment to buy the product. Advertising and promotion 'pull' the customer to a specific product once he or she is in the store. Once the customer is inside a retail establishment, the retailer can begin to 'push' additional products to the consumer."

Direct sales, by contrast, "bypasses the 'pull' phase and goes straight to the 'push' phase. Unlike a department store that 'pulls' customers into the store, a direct selling company has sales representatives who, in effect, act as mobile mini-stores who initiate the selling occasion by taking the product to the consumer," concludes Rochon.

In the 1980s, many conventional retail outlets were consolidated and downscaled. The downscaling continued into the 1990s as the industry as a whole was saddled with astronomical debt and bargain basement margins. Of the top twenty discount department stores in 1980, only half were in existence at the end of the decade. By the year 2000, as many as 20 percent of the regional shopping centers are forecast to be closed, and some product categories may be controlled by as few as five organizations. Consumers will be left with fewer retail choices, both in stores and perhaps even in merchandise selection.

The eighties brought new forces and an increased competitive turbulence to store retailing that will continue into the next century. There is a surplus of retail store space beyond that required for population growth and consumer spending. The United States has become "overstored and overmalled" with far too much retail space.

By the year 2000, more than 50 percent of established fixed-location retailers will be out of business. There will be a concentration into fewer marketing-driven "power" retailers. As few as thirty or forty retailers may be setting the competitive agenda—and small retailers had better not be in the line of fire. According to the U.S. Commerce Department, the annual percent change in retail sales in 1991 was the lowest in thirty years. For the entire year, retail sales rose only seven-tenths of one percent.

Retail business failures continued to surge in 1992, with about 230,000 retail workers laid off in 1991. Professor Douglas Tigert of Babson College, a retail expert, has said, "Retailers of today have to be market-driven and use the customer to tell them what to sell." (Tigert has accurately described how the direct option works.)

The Direct-Selling Industry

One of the most appealing reasons to consider a career as a DSO retailer is the sharp decline in customer service among in-store retailers. Far too many in-store salesclerks give the impression they do not care whether they make a sale or not. (There are exceptions, of course, such as mail order giant L. L. Bean, Stew Leonard's famous Connecticut market, or Nordstrom's and Wal-Mart retail chains.)

The poor performance and gloomy economic forecasts associated with in-store retailing don't affect the direct option, for this industry has a tremendous resilience anchored in its ability to provide a source of income when needed, in amounts large enough to sustain individuals, families, and companies.

In a "research note" that appeared in the *Journal of Retailing* in 1989, professors Robert A. Peterson, University of Texas, Gerald Albaum, University of Oregon, and Nancy M. Ridgway, University of Colorado, reported that their nationwide survey revealed that 57 percent of respondents had purchased a product or service from a direct-sales company in the year preceding the survey. Purchasers tended to be younger, more educated, and more affluent than non-purchasers. Convenience was perceived to be the major advantage of buying from a direct-sales company, while the major disadvantage was perceived to be pressure tactics or pushy salespeople.

The direct form of retailing, which provides for a high degree of relationship marketing, has a major advantage over all other forms of retailing, particularly if the sales tactics used are *not* "pushy," but rather service oriented, honest, and conducted with integrity. Direct selling and other forms of non-store marketing are on a growth curve. In 1989 and 1990, DSA member companies reported an increase of over 700,000 in the number of independent entrepreneurs in the United States. In the same period, traditional forms of retailing fell upon hard times because many major retailers had forgotten their consumers as well as their salespeople in a mad scramble for cash flow and short-term earnings.

As the in-store retail industry shakes itself out, and as store closings and consolidations continue, the opportunity for direct selling increases. Direct-option retailers need no store to be effective and can offer proven goods and services to American consumers.

Direct sellers can even choose the customers they want to serve, as Margarita Garcia of Kitchen Fair notes. "You choose the customers you're going to work with," she says. "In a retail store, you have to deal with the people who come in. Here, you choose the people you're going to work with. And that's what I like."

Retail competition for market share has become tougher and tougher. Consequently, consumers have come to distrust many retailers and their so-called "sales." The financial dilemmas facing most consumers have created a preoccupation with price and an emphasis on value and value-added concepts.

Value

Today, the upscale consumer is perceptive, inquiring, tasteful, demanding, sophisticated, and streetwise on price. A new consumer paradigm has emerged for the nineties. Within this paradigm, consumers will pay more for acceptable quality, but they will also demand a fair price and convenience of purchase.

Sue Kirkpatrick of Mary Kay Cosmetics says, "I think you have to have a good product that is in demand. The product has to be related to a service, too. It has to be a product and a service at the same time, because people want service. They'll buy when they feel helped."

Many direct-selling organizations have an advantage in this price war. To begin with, a DSO bypasses the traditional wholesale chain and thus effects significant distribution cost advantages. These savings are passed along to the consumer and to the sales force in the form of compensation and incentives. In addition, because direct sellers go to their consumers, little or no advertising is required. These savings are also passed along to the consumer and the sales force.

Today's consumers also like value and value-added concepts. The teaching-oriented methods of many DSA member companies is the finest possible, so the consumer learns how to use the product most effectively. To most consumers, this is a very important dimension of value, according to John Andrews of Fuller Brush. "People are not going to buy something if they don't think they're going to get a good value," said John. "So therefore, the product line, in reality, was the determining factor in my going into direct sales. Fuller Brush has always had quality products."

At the point of sale, direct sellers are usually not faced with price competition, at least not blatant wars. While price is of vital interest to the consumer, very few direct-buying decisions are made solely on the basis of price. This is particularly true as strong relationships build between the direct seller and the consumer.

Time Savings

Time impoverishment among upscale and middle-scale consumers will continue to be a major problem as the year 2000 approaches. The time people will have to shop will continue to decrease. Work demands just to keep even with basic material needs will increase. Most consumers will face ever-expanding domestic obligations, including parenting and the desire for leisure activities. Although retirees will have more time, they too will be caught up in other activities and have medical and other financial pressures that will make them demand convenience.

Time poverty means that those who have selected the direct option will have another great advantage in the 1990s. In addition to offering excellent products and services, direct sellers are really providing time. The time it takes to make the personal demonstration and delivery services that are typically provided is a luxury in today's hurry-up world. Most DSOs also provide a strong telemarketing opportunity, further positioning the direct service individual as a consumer "timesaver."

Quality of Service

Poor service quality, including unreturned phone calls, missed messages, and processing errors, is responsible for the loss of millions of in-store customers annually. Analysis shows that reducing defection by dissatisfied customers by just 5 percent can increase profitability by 25 percent or more. Nine out of ten customers who have a bad experience with a retail store will not tell the store, thus keeping the problem hidden. Some of these dissatisfied customers (13 percent) will spread the word to at least twenty people. Many of these customers are now being served by the independent salespeople of DSOs, few of whom were affected by the mania for debt in the 1980s.

Retail training consultant Richard Imprescia spoke out in *Cosmetic World*: "The real tragedy is that NO ONE provides the live salesperson (in stores) with the proper tools for successful retail selling. . . . Even when we do train, we get it backwards." And *Training* magazine reports that while 69 percent of organizations with more than fifty employees provide training to managers, only 30 percent train salespeople. On the other hand, DSOs provide training to 100 percent of the sales force.

DSOs greatly emphasize sales force education. Most DSOs stress a program that teaches customers how to best use the product. Hyacinth Brown of Dudley Products, a direct-selling company that manufactures ethnic hair care items, describes the training her DSO provides: "I already had some selling skills from my former position, but the product knowledge training was very important to me. For two weeks, I was trained on how to successfully demonstrate and sell the product. I was then assigned to a successful Dudley salesperson, who took me on her own sales calls to 'show me the ropes.' Only after I knew everything I had to know did I go out on my own. The training was excellent."

Dr. Joseph Hair, chair of the Department of Marketing at Louisiana State University, describes personal selling as "the communication of a company's products, services or ideas to its customers in either a one-on-one meeting or a small group arrangement. The approaches, methods and responsibilities of personal selling are changing rapidly in response to new technologies and a changing business environment."

Dr. Hair points out that in the 1980s, "the sales profession struggled to overcome the negative image that has been ingrained in the minds of customers by overzealous salespeople of past decades. Selling today is not made up of jokes, backslapping, smiles, drinks, gifts, shady deals, expense accounts, high pressure and high living . . . salespeople do not have to resign themselves to lives that are less full, less satisfying or less happy than those other individuals enjoy."

"Today's salespeople," continues Dr. Hair, "seek a more professional image by putting their customers' needs ahead of what they are selling, by providing excellent service after the sale and by not overstating the quality or performance capabilities of their products. The new sales attitude of business focuses on the marketing concept, which is based solely on finding out what customers want and need and providing that product or service to that customer at a reasonable price." DSOs (especially those used as examples in this book and which are members of the DSA) are committed to these modern marketing concepts and often go beyond this definition to offer the finest products at the best value in a sincere attempt to achieve total customer satisfaction.

Quality of Product

James Julian, a distributor for Amway, which is a direct-selling company specializing in household care items, sums up: "The product line was very important when I chose my direct-selling company because if I used it and it didn't work, I would have no faith in it. The quality of the products, the return policies, the guarantees . . . if you didn't like it, they'd take it back. Period."

Personal selling itself is not optional in our economy. It's absolutely essential to a vibrant economy, to achievement of high levels of employment, and to the strength of our nation.

Non-store buying is the major consumer trend of the 1990s. Both direct selling ($12 billion) and direct marketing ($190 billion) will continue to capture larger shares of the consumer's dollar, principally because of convenience. For all of these reasons, millions of men and women will be selecting the direct option in the 1990s. For those who wish to build lifetime businesses and for those who wish to earn substantial incomes, the opportunities in DSOs have never been better. This is especially true of established DSOs (member companies of the DSA), because most of these firms have founded a strong base from which to build by adding thousands of new people to their independent sales organizations.

Targeted Marketing

Modern DSOs make wide use of the most advanced marketing techniques, especially databased marketing. From the beginning, new DSO independent contractors are taught to create detailed files or databases on their customers that allow for a high level of personalized service. Advanced DSOs often give the independent contractor an opportunity to enter customer demographics into a central database, and are then able to provide a great number of computer-assisted services to the independent contractor. In addition, at the request of independent contractors, some DSOs even regularly create and mail elaborate literature to customers in support of individual sales efforts. The economies of scale that are possible when millions of direct mail inserts are prepared and mailed at the same time allow even the smallest independent contractor to impress customers by the first-class appearance of such jointly produced mailings. Other services include computerized customer lists, mailing labels, and tracking that enable the smallest independent contractor to function like the largest in-store retailer—in fact, more efficiently and more personally than most.

Furthermore, databased marketing helps the DSO reach specialized markets. This is often accomplished through lead generation and referral to the independent sales force. Database techniques allow a high degree of personalization, especially at the sales force level. These techniques can be used to help identify, classify, and profile individual customers. In fact, many DSOs have customer profile systems available to their independent sales force for application in the field. This allows for highly personalized communications, finely targeted offers, and, most important, the building of a two-way flow of communication—an ongoing relationship between salespeople and their customers.

Direct selling will benefit from the aging of the baby boomers, because marketing to them will not be very easy for traditional in-store retailers. *Business Week* magazine noted in late 1991 that "an old way of life is ending—the days when a great merchant saw his store as a theater and stocked it with sumptuously presented goods. For these merchant princes, selection of merchandise for their emporiums was paramount." Baby boomers are emerging as self-confident and self-controlled consumers, whose priorities are quite distinct.

The Yankelovich Monitor Management Survey for 1991 calls the values system consumers have adopted as a foundation for life "Neotraditionalism," which is based in "control" and "emotional enhancement." Consumers are achieving more control in their lives by managing risks better and by demanding responsibility from our basic institutions, especially business. Emotional enhancement begins with a "preference for that which is genuine, sincere and of fundamental importance to happiness."

Quality of Life

The baby boomers will thus be spending more discretely, shopping less frequently, and saving more. These trends are very important to DSOs, with which the primary benefit offered is enhancement of life-style.

Furthermore, the baby boomers want to age attractively and comfortably. They believe it is important to look better longer; good health is also important to them. DSOs offer the baby boomer a wide range of choices, including advanced skin care and glamour techniques, health aids and services, and overall life-style enhancements.

Along with baby boomers, working women—as the main shoppers—are demanding the culture of convenience. Increases in women in the work force obviously reduce the time available for purchasing and shopping. Working women are seeking services and products that give them more time for themselves. Businesses that provide home delivery services, such as DSOs, will be sought out by many working women.

Ethnicity and Education

America has always been known as a pluralistic "world nation," a great "melting pot." In fact, the already well-established ethnic diversity of the United States—no other nation comes close—has important implications for in-store retailing, especially with regard to further market fragmentation. Although this can be negative for in-store operations, it can have great positive implications for DSOs.

Stronger ethnic identification and the desire to maintain cultural heritages will lead to market fragmentation. This will change the fabric of American society in many ways—no longer will America be a great "melting pot." I think it is more accurate to describe the United States as a great "chef's salad bowl" mixture of all the world's races, with each "ingredient" and "spice" standing out distinctly in a wonderful entree of diversity. DSOs, by their pluralistic nature, welcome such changes and provide the opportunity for peers to reinforce one another in a positive, supportive environment.

Many immigrants and ethnic groups use retailing as an economic building block. DSOs especially welcome ethnic diversity. Many DSOs offer special programs (complete with translated literature) to enable their independent sales forces to market to these groups.

A tremendous income polarization is taking place in the United States—most dramatically illustrated by the nation's reaction to the Rodney King verdict, especially the violent reaction in Los Angeles, in May, 1992. The Census Bureau revealed that the top 20 percent of the population earned 44.3 percent of reported income, and the bottom 20 percent only 4.6 percent of reported income in 1991. In fact, in the early 1990s, an estimated 25 million people were on food stamps. America now has an "underclass" of more than 3 million welfare-dependent people. The behavior and motivation problems within this group are extremely complex, but DSOs (almost alone among business structures) offer a way up and out of a below the-poverty-line situation. A special task force composed of DSA member companies and chaired by Joe Dudley, CEO of Dudley Products, was formed in May, 1992, to offer specific solutions to independent entrepreneurship questions in the inner cities.

There is also a decline in education. Although more people are graduating from high school, more of these graduates are functionally illiterate. And unfortunately, lower income groups—white, black, or Hispanic—receive a lower quality of education. Again, DSOs offer a way to start up the ladder of success by offering training in fundamental skills and, most important, by instilling the self-confidence and self-esteem needed for the motivation to continue to learn.

The fact is, America's public school system doesn't work anymore, and this disaster offers an opportunity for real service to our nation for those offering educational products and services—DSOs in these categories should prosper in the 1990s. During the decade of the 1980s, real spending on education in the United States increased about 25 percent, to right at $5,000 per student, as our world rank in math and science plummeted to 15th.

"My direct-selling company offered tons of encouragement and motivation," says Steve Smith of CUTCO/Vector, a direct-selling company specializing in cookware and cutlery. "They showed you how to get there—you just had to be willing to pay the price. By that I mean you had to work; you had to learn your fundamentals; and you had to put the hours and the time in."

Once given an opportunity, many thousands of DSO independent contractors go on not only to achieve unanticipated success, but also to become better educated. These independent contractors in turn contribute to meeting others' needs for advancement and to serving their communities as well.

Personal selling, a subject now stressed in many university curriculums, has emerged as one of the most sought-after careers of the 1990s. But more important, personal selling is a profession that can lead not only to significant financial rewards, but to important psychological rewards as well.

Making Your Choice

It's up to you to thoroughly examine the array of options open to you in light of your own needs—psychological, emotional, family, professional, and financial. Then make the choice that best meets your needs—now and for the future.

Perhaps you are now wondering if you are at all suited for a career, even a part-time effort, in direct selling. First, let me say that in my experience I have simply not found an individual—regardless of "social style"—who hasn't been able to achieve success in this industry. It appears that if you want to succeed badly enough, you will. For this reason, I have always found "personality quizzes" to be suspect, especially if they show that a given individual cannot possibly succeed in sales.

However, it may be useful to know a little about your own "social style" and how you may relate to others, especially to those of a completely different style. In test after test, for example, I'm identified as a person with a "driver" social style, and my friends, acquaintances, and co-workers uniformly agree with this assessment. When I'm at full "driver" peak, it is almost a certainty that I will not be building a relationship with, say, a person who is far more "amiable." I don't make many sales when my social style is predominantly "driver"—and I don't make many friends, either.

We should be alert to the effect we may be having on others and modify our approach to allow us to build long-lasting and fulfilling relationships with our customers.

Several studies of direct-selling companies have been done by Wellington Resources Group, a business consulting firm in Green Brook, New Jersey, examining the behaviors of their most successful salespeople. Terry Kurzawa, managing director of Wellington, has used her Social Styles Model to conduct research into DSOs and has developed a "Social Style Profile" exclusively for *The Direct Option*. Kurzawa points out that the single most common factor found in these studies is that successful salespeople have a communication style or social style that encourages the building of relationships with their customers.

One such survey was conducted on a DSO comprised almost entirely of female entrepreneurs. Answer the following questions to find out what your social style is and to compare with the results of the national study.

Social Style Profile

Circle only one answer in each group:

1. When I'm at a party . . .
    a. I can't wait to leave because it's a waste of my time.
    b. I'm the life of the party.
    c. I spend the time catching up with my old friends.
    d. I plan on whom I will talk with and for what reason.
2. When I'm running any type of meeting . . .
    a. I try to keep it short and to the point.
    b. I try to keep it entertaining and lively.
    c. I try to avoid conflicts in the group.
    d. I try to present as much information as possible.
3. When I get stuck in traffic . . .
    a. I go over a list of things I have to do.
    b. I dream about being on a Caribbean vacation.

    c. I get concerned about keeping my appointment waiting.

    d. I think about traffic patterns and how I can avoid this in the future.

4. I believe that clothes . . .

    a. should be neat, clean, and traditional.

    b. should be an expression of a person's personality.

    c. should be quiet and inoffensive to others.

    d. should be good quality and utilitarian.

5. If what I say is challenged by others . . .

    a. I remind them why I know what I am talking about.

    b. I try to persuade them to see my point of view.

    c. I ask them why they feel that way.

    d. I recite the research behind my statements.

6. When I am assigned a project to do . . .

    a. I need only the outline of what has to be done, and then . . . leave it to me.

    b. I need to know what the outcome should look like and what's in it for me.

    c. I need to know where this fits in with what everyone else is doing.

    d. I need to know as much information as possible before I can begin.

7. In making decisions, other people accuse me of being too . . .

    a. objective and detached.

    b. impulsive and emotional.

    c. indecisive and ambiguous.

    d. slow and perfectionist.

8. When I work with others on a project . . .

    a. I like to run the show.

    b. I like to have fun.

    c. I like to help wherever I can.

    d. I like to have rules on who does what.

9. I know I've done a good job when . . .

    a. I see the results.

    b. I get a promotion or testimonial.

    c. I get a pat on the back from my boss.

    d. I do what was expected of me.

10. When I talk, others tell me that . . .

    a. I talk fast and to the point.

    b. I am enthusiastic and loud.

    c. I speak quietly and calmly.

    d. I am careful in choosing my words.

11. In giving others information . . .
    a. I forget the details and give them the big picture.
    b. I forget the facts and go on gut feel.
    c. I tell them how it relates to them.
    d. I give them accurate details.

12. My friends would describe me as . . .
    a. pragmatic, independent, and blunt.
    b. outgoing, fun to be with, and spontaneous.
    c. loyal, cooperative, and patient.
    d. logical, prudent, and serious.

13. To motivate me, others need to . . .
    a. let me do it my way.
    b. persuade and inspire me to greatness.
    c. support and care about me.
    d. give me a detailed plan to follow.

14. If there is one area in which I need improvement, it's . . .
    a. learning to listen better.
    b. learning to check for facts before taking action.
    c. learning to overcome my procrastination.
    d. learning to be less detail oriented.

15. I get others to agree with me by . . .
    a. being forceful and determined.
    b. being charming and enthusiastic.
    c. being sensitive and a friend.
    d. being factual and logical.

16. I prefer to spend my leisure time . . .
    a. in competitive activities.
    b. in social events.
    c. in family activities.
    d. in solitary activities.

17. I get my best results when . . .
    a. I take quick action.
    b. I work with others.
    c. I am patient and unpressured.
    d. I have all the facts.

18. I can't stand it when someone . . .
    a. wastes my time.
    b. double checks my work and questions me.
    c. betrays my trust.
    d. makes a decision without all the facts.

**TO DETERMINE YOUR DOMINANT SOCIAL STYLE,
LIST YOUR ANSWERS IN THE FOUR CATEGORIES BELOW:**

a. _____b. _____c. _____ d. _____

a. = DRIVER   b. = EXPRESSIVE

c. = AMIABLE   d. = ANALYTICAL

The category in which you have the most answers (the highest number) is most likely your dominant social style. If you have a tied score (the same number in two or more social styles), read the accompanying description in the text that follows and you should be able to recognize your dominant social style.

Now that you have taken the profile above and scored your results, let's discuss what the four social styles may mean in relation to your career in direct sales.

Please find your own dominant social style in the figure of "The Four Social Styles" and note the key words at each edge of the four quadrants and under each social style:

The Four Social Styles

TASK-ORIENTED

ANALYTICAL	DRIVER
Facts are important	Time is important
Poker face	Controlled
Speaks slowly	Speaks quickly
Little or no gestures	Sits/stands erect
Likes to work alone	Likes to direct others
Slow to decide	Quick to decide

**ASK-   TELL-
ASSERTIVE   ASSERTIVE**

AMIABLE	EXPRESSIVE
Friends/family are	Novelty/fun is
important	important
Smiles easily	Emotional
Asks for opinions	Speaks with excitement
Small gestures	Lots of gestures
Likes to work with others	Likes applause
Slow to decide	Quick to decide

RELATIONSHIP-ORIENTED

What this illustration shows are the key characteristics of each of the four social styles:

- ♦ If your dominant social style is ANALYTICAL—you are task-oriented and ask-assertive—that means you communicate by concentrating on the task or goal at hand and you ask questions; you tend to be less risk-oriented, you do it *right* or not at all, you appear logical, serious, conservative, and orderly.
- ♦ If your dominant social style is AMIABLE—you are relationship-oriented and ask-assertive—that means you communicate by concentrating on relationship building and you ask questions; you are people-oriented, compromise easily to avoid confrontations, are team spirited and supportive, and appear relaxed and flexible, friendly and informal.
- ♦ If your dominant social style is DRIVER—you are task oriented and tell-assertive—that means you communicate by concentrating on the task or goal at hand and you tell more than you ask; you tend to be action-and goal-oriented; you take calculated risks and tend to appear impatient at times, directive, stoic, disciplined, and blunt.
- ♦ If your dominant social style is EXPRESSIVE—you are relationship-oriented and tell-assertive—that means you communicate by concentrating on relationship building and you tell more than you ask; you are open and down-to-earth, theatrical and bigger-than-life at times; you tend to be impulsive, can be reckless, and appear to be a "social butterfly" who knows everyone.

Now that you know your social style better, let's talk about the social styles that are the best match for direct selling. As you have probably guessed by now, the number-one most successful social style for direct selling is . . . amiable . . . followed not too far behind by expressive.

That's right, these two styles, primarily the amiable social style, have been found to be the social styles of over 70 percent of the biggest moneymakers in direct sales in those direct sales companies surveyed by Wellington Resources Group.

Does that mean that if you did not score as an amiable in the profile, you should give up thinking about going into sales? Absolutely not!

What it does mean is that you need to learn to flex your own social style to match more closely to that of an amiable. How do you do that, you ask? Well, you can begin by studying the verbal and nonverbal characteristics of an amiable and learn to speak, move, and relate like one.

Here's how many amiables make sales: first, they ask a lot of questions about their prospect (not just business, but family and personal needs); then, they express their care and concern for this prospect's well-being, happiness, and success; next they share a little about themselves as appropriate; finally, they mention the product or service they're selling. It seems like a long process, doesn't it? But their sales hold, and they often have long-term customers who buy from them for a lifetime. Some amiables we surveyed have sold to three generations of families and businesses. Since direct sales success is based on repeat business, it is useful to learn to sell like an amiable.

Now let's look a little closer at the results of the national study.

Table 2-1

Social Styles of Top Producers
(Earnings of $50,000 per year or more)

Style	Dominant
Amiable	36%
Expressive	36%
Driver	23%
Analytical	5%

For this top-producing group, amiables and expressives each accounted for 36 percent of the total. Taken together, they constitute 72 percent of the top producers profiled. This shows the strength of relationship building in the top producers of the DSO.

Table 2-2

Middle Producers
(Earnings between $35,000 and $49,900 per year)

Style	Dominant
Amiable	32%
Expressive	32%
Driver	32%
Analytical	4%

Table 2-2 shows the results of the middle producers profiled. For this group, amiables, expressives, and drivers were each at 32 percent of the total. This shows that 64 percent were either amiables or expressives and would be expected to rely on relationship building in the sales process.

Table 2-3 shows the results from the average producers profiled. In this group, 51 percent were amiables and 35 percent were expressives. Taken together, this shows that 86 percent of average producers rely on relationship building in the sales process.

Table 2-3

Average Producers
(Earnings below $35,000 per year)

Style	Dominant
Amiable	51%
Expressive	35%
Driver	7%
Analytical	7%

Tables 2-4, 2-5, and 2-6 look at the data in a different way. They separate each group by style components: Task, Relationship, or both. This was done to show some differences between top, middle, and average producers. Each table will be discussed separately.

Table 2-4 shows the style components for the top producers. As can be seen from the table, 64 percent of the top producers rely on both relationship and task orientations. Only 32 percent rely on only relationship, and a mere 4 percent use task only.

Table 2-5 shows the results for the middle producers. In this group, a smaller percentage uses both task and relationship—55 percent. Of the middle producers, 39 percent use relationship only, and a mere 6 percent use task only. Compared with Table 2-4, this shows a smaller percentage using both task and relationship and a larger percentage using only relationship.

Table 2-6 shows the results for the average producers. In this group, a still smaller percentage uses both task and relationship—43 percent. The majority of the average producers, 51 percent, use only relationship building. A mere 6 percent use only task.

Table 2-4

Top Producers
(Earnings of $50,000 per year or more)

Style Component	Percentage
Both Relationship and Task	64%
All Relationship	3%
All Task	4%

Table 2-5

Middle Producers
(Earnings between $35,000 and $49,900 per year)

Style Component	Percentage
Both Relationship and Task	55%
All Relationship	39%
All Task	6%

Table 2-6

Average Producers
(Earnings below $35,000 per year)

Style Component	Percentage
Both Relationship and Task	43%
All Relationship	51%
All Task	6%

Table 2-6 shows the results for the average producers. In this group, a still smaller percentage uses both task and relationship—43 percent. The majority of the average producers, 51 percent, use only relationship building. A mere 6 percent use only task.

If we take the results in Tables 2-4, 2-5, and 2-6 together, we see a drop in the percentage of producers using both task and relationship (64 percent to 55 percent to 43 percent) as we go from top to middle to average producers. At the same time, we see an increase in the percentage of producers using all relationship (32 percent to 39 percent to 51 percent) as we go from top to middle to average producers.

The most successful sales leaders have a combination of relationship and task orientations in either their dominant or backup styles. The average sales leaders have mostly an all-relationship approach in their social style. They lose a sale or a recruit because they lose sight of their task (closing the "sale") in exchange for keeping the relationship (customer is their friend and still likes them). Even in relationship selling, there must be a task component for the sales leader to be truly successful.

Note that the social styles of the very top income levels—those over $50,000 a year—varied somewhat from the next level. Although the above profile should not be your sole determinant in whether you should pursue a career in direct sales, it can give you an idea as to what social style you should work to develop if you want to match the proven success of the top salespeople in direct selling.

There are many self-help books, seminars, and companies available to help you learn direct-selling skills. The one key ingredient every social style must have to succeed is determination. If you want it badly enough, you'll learn how to get it.

Chapter 3

Evaluating Direct-Selling Organizations

Once you have decided to pursue the direct option, an important early step in determining a course of action is to write or visit the local Better Business Bureau. The BBB publishes a long list of businesses by type, and the list itself will provide a range of choices for you. Once you have zeroed in on a specific business, checking with the BBB is always a good idea, as they will report on whether that particular business has received complaints.

Shortcut to Success— Or Highway to Nowhere?

In a later chapter, you will be introduced to some possible business associates, DSA member companies that have stood the test of time. Many other companies are listed in Appendix A, and they, too, have provided excellent career options to hundreds of thousands of independent sales-people, not to mention great opportunities for advancement.

But we're going to assume in this chapter that you have not yet made a choice, even as to the type of business opportunity that might be appropriate for you and your family. You may be more vulnerable than you imagine to the seductive pitches of business opportunity scam artists or the misleading siren calls of recruiters who will stop at nothing to promise you a "ground floor" opportunity to "get rich quick" and a "short-cut to success."

Beware. That "ground floor" may be a basement from which you never emerge. The only person who gets rich may already be at the top of a multilevel pyramid structure, and the "shortcut to success" may well be a "highway to nowhere." This chapter will help you sort out fact from fiction among the claims sometimes made by unethical DSOs.

Many DSOs are engaged in different forms of marketing through which their products and services are sold to consumers by methods they refer to as "direct sales." Therefore, the term *direct selling* can have various interpretations in today's business environment. Today, however, it is distinguished from *direct marketing,* a term which is used to refer to mail order solicitation by numerous catalog companies which market their goods on a nationwide basis. One of the best known of such companies is L. L. Bean, whose telephone service operators are superb at service over the phone. And our neighbor in Dallas is the Horchow Collection, another outstanding example of a direct-marketing company. It should be noted that direct-marketing operations can be started on a small basis and run from your home. But to achieve major sales, the start-up costs and ongoing investment requirements are substantial.

In direct marketing, the company's sales presentation is accomplished through mailing literature and order forms. The sale is closed when the customer either mails or phones an order to the company. The personal salesperson/customer contact is generally missing in this method of selling, except for some customer interaction that may occur over the telephone.

Other alternatives to in-store, fixed-location retailing include direct-response print and broadcast advertising (such as HBO), computerized shopping services (for example, Videotext), automated merchandising (vending machines), and telemarketing, which, as we'll see later, can also be used as an effective partner in direct selling.

The most generally accepted concept of direct selling seems to involve personal sales—individual-to-individual, point-of-sale contact—as contrasted with typical over-the-counter retail sales at fixed business locations. The process developed by DSOs that enables the salesperson to go to the customer is an integral part of the power of direct sales. These are truly "personal sales" and, in their best forms as described in *The Direct Option,* truly fulfill the mission of providing "Total Customer Satisfaction."

Lauren Debonis of Discovery Toys, a direct-sales toy company, amplifies this important point: "I know that I am a real service-oriented person, and the people who get my business—the stores, the individuals—are the ones that give me good service. And the thing about direct sales that really appealed to me was the service associated with doing direct sales. I knew that if I really loved it and appreciated it, a lot of other people would appreciate it as well. And it would be an asset to my business knowing that we live in a service-oriented society."

Direct selling in today's marketplace is further characterized as "in-home" selling—serving the customer in the place most convenient to the customer, so the customer never even has to leave home. In an age when approximately 70 percent of working-age women are employed outside the home, a new dimension has been added to the concept of direct sales and personal service when the direct seller is able to go to the place of work or enter the work environment itself to provide selling and service functions. This occurs in many offices and plants throughout the United States where employees may attend direct sales presentations during lunch hours or breaks in the workday, sometimes through programs specifically arranged by the host employer. Avon Products now estimates that fully 30 percent of its U.S. sales are made in the workplace. Tupperware U.S. has designed a special party format geared specifically to the workplace.

Less formally, offices throughout the country have employees who function in dual roles, as full-or part-time employees in salaried or hourly occupations and as direct sellers providing a wide range of products and services. Almost every office with a significant employee population, including Mary Kay's own corporate offices and manufacturing facilities, has individual employees who are engaged part-time in direct sales of other products. For many years, Avon's product catalogs circulated in Mary Kay's executive offices. Mary Kay employees, including myself, regularly buy from a host of other DSOs either from catalogs available in the office or from independent contractors of other DSOs who happen to be our own employees. As the vice-chairman of a major company, I prefer that sales to our employees be outside normal working hours, and we don't encourage demonstrations on the premises. But we do encourage free enterprise and the circulation of sales materials within reason, from which after-hours demonstrations, purchases, and deliveries can be arranged.

Telemarketing is a variation on conventional direct selling, which utilizes telephone contacts rather than face-to-face personal contacts between the salesperson and the consumer. The personal involvement of the salesperson may vary considerably from very personalized contacts by direct salespeople who also customarily deal with their customers on a personal, face-to-face basis all the way to automatic-dialing, computer-generated sales pitches—one of the most impersonal methods of direct marketing imaginable. Overuse of such techniques, combined with a proliferation of consumer scams, has generated widespread pressure for legislative reform of telemarketing. Most direct sellers utilize telephone contact only when desired by existing customers, and not as a scheme to generate new business.

The most successful direct-selling companies in today's marketplace are those which have developed sales organizations that specialize in marketing specific product lines. As independent contractors, some individuals involved in direct sales may handle the products or services of more than one direct sales company, but the companies that achieve the greatest sales success—for themselves and for their independent sales organizations—generally have salespeople who concentrate exclusively, either full-or part-time, in marketing branded line(s) of that company's products. A sales organization specializing in a particular product line under the trademark of one DSO tends to be more successful because of the superior product knowledge and superior concentrations of sales effort to achieve a strong market position.

Barbara Peasel of Stanhome, a direct-selling company specializing in home cleaning and maintenance items, summarizes her reasons for commitment to a single product: "The product line was very important in choosing my DSO. It was something that we have always used. It was a quality-plus product. I knew that it was guaranteed, and I knew that the company would stand behind me. . . . In a small, rural community, I wanted to be able to sell something I was proud of."

Distribution Methods

Single-level

A direct sales company may operate through several different methods of distribution. For example, the company's products may be sold to independent contractors at wholesale and they may then re-sell the products at their own retail prices to individual customers. In this distribution system (which could be called a single-level distribution system), the company is represented by different "dealers" who re-sell directly to consumers. This is the distribution structure of companies such as Mary Kay Cosmetics, which has only one wholesale sale from the company to the independent contractor, called a "consultant" or a "representative." The consultant then follows with a retail sale to her individual customer.

As a DSO with a distribution system organized in a way similar to Mary Kay develops and matures, it must provide greater educational electives and offer more sales promotion assistance to increasingly large numbers of salespeople. This often results in the evolution of an independent leadership structure developed from the best and most successful salespeople in the organization. If the company continues to maintain its single-level distribution system, it must develop commission structures to reward individuals from its independent organization who assume new responsibilities for leadership, education, and motivation of groups of individual dealers or consultants. In this process, a more complex commission structure may evolve.

Such a structure may be seen in the evolution of the Mary Kay organization, which began in 1963 with Mary Kay Ash herself as the only leader of a small band of nine consultants. As the years passed, other levels of independent contractor leadership were added to cope with the sheer size of the leadership function. Today, more than 6,000 independent "sales directors" provide leadership to more than 300,000 independent consultants. This organization remains a single-level distribution system but has evolved a hierarchical structure of independent leaders who not only sell at retail themselves, but also receive commissions directly from the company for services that relate to increasingly greater numbers of other entrepreneurs in their organization.

Multilevel

Other DSOs may be formed with a different, multilevel distribution concept, which involves multiple levels of "distributors." Multilevel marketing (MLM) is often called network marketing, and the terms seem to be interchangeable in most MLM companies.

While a given MLM may have a legitimate marketing structure, some of its promoters have wildly misstated its role in American marketing. For example, you may hear the following claims:

- ♦ "*The Wall Street Journal* and *SRI International* have predicted that by the end of the 1990s, 50 to 60 percent of all retail sales will be made by MLM." This is false.
- ♦ "MLM is taught at Harvard Business School." This, too, is false. There are Mary Kay Cosmetics case studies being taught at Harvard Business School, one by Professor John Quelch, another by Professor Bob Simon. Mary Kay is *not* an MLM company, and the courses are teaching use of alternative promotional channels and incentives, *not* MLM.
- ♦ It is claimed that the *New York Times* is considering selling newspaper subscriptions by MLM. This statement is also false. The *Times* has no such plans.
- ♦ "In the United States, 20 percent of all millionaires made their money through MLM." Another blatant falsehood, although many millionaires have been created in direct selling.

Unfortunately, many consumers seem to equate legitimate MLM companies with the illegal "pyramid" schemes that were so prevalent in the late fifties and sixties, culminating in the fall of Holiday Magic and its look-alike, Koscot, when their chain-letter recruiting schemes were declared illegal. Holiday Magic was fined $55 million by the U.S. Justice Department, and Koscot and its sister company, Dare To Be Great, had a $1 billion class-action lawsuit brought by 6,000 dissatisfied investors. Glenn Turner, founder of Koscot and Dare To Be Great, was sent to prison in 1987, but not before much public misconception was created by these and other illegal pyramids. His probation ended in April, 1993, a year after his release.

Some observers speculate that the original pyramids were inspired by the scams of Charles Ponzi, who sold investors on an idea that relied on buying and selling foreign postal reply coupons. What Ponzi was actually doing was paying off initial investors with money obtained from new ones until the well went dry, because he did not actually have a legitimate investment opportunity. In other words, his "product" had no value.

Lawmakers in many different jurisdictions have attempted to prohibit promotional schemes that were designed or operated to take advantage of investors, while preserving opportunities for legitimate direct-selling companies. Currently there are laws throughout the United States which declare "pyramid marketing" programs illegal. These laws provide different statutory definitions of the term, but customarily include a description of objectionable characteristics of pyramid plans, such as charging substantial fees for distributorships or sales kits, substantial investment requirements to enter the business, the sale of the business opportunity, endless chain recruiting schemes, referral sales schemes, payment of commissions solely on distributor purchases rather than retail sales, payment of commissions on investments as opposed to the sale of products, and membership sales rather than product sales.

In 1979, Amway, which had been created by two former Nutralite distributors, Rich Devos and Jay Van Andel, proved to the Federal Trade Commission that its plan was not a pyramid and therefore was legal. What is illegal is any payment for which no product or service of value is anticipated. As long as MLMs pay commissions only on the actual sales of recruits, not for just lassoing the recruit into an organization, they are legal.

The tip-off to an illegal scheme is compensation solely for the act of recruiting and the promise of incredible earnings as a consequence of a chain of recruiting. Mathematically, such schemes would quickly exhaust the 5.5-billion population of the world to achieve the promised wealth for all players.

I had to contend with these pyramid schemes when the legal counsel for Mary Kay Cosmetics called me in Florida in 1968 to inquire why they were having such a difficult time getting started in the Southeastern states. Unknown to Mary Kay, Koscot was reaching a crescendo in the Carolinas, and illegal pyramid charges were everywhere. Certainly, it was not the best time and place for a legitimate cosmetic direct-selling company to begin developing its independent sales force.

It was about then that I accidentally met Glenn Turner in an Orlando restaurant. He claimed to have achieved millions of dollars in sales in just a couple of years. It was obvious to me that a plan founded on the premise of "get rich quick" would fail—but incredibly, this was not at all obvious to his potential investors, whose ranks included lawyers, doctors, and other intelligent, educated, professional people. The appeal was to greed, to "get rich quick without effort."

Keith Laggos, president and publisher of *Money Maker's Monthly*, is quoted as saying, "Exaggerations will be the death of us [MLMs] yet." This statement in mid-1991 headed a column that talked about the exposé of a company called Sunrider by ABC's program *Insider*. "Such exposés of exaggerated product claims hurt the image of the network marketing and direct sales industries," Laggos noted. "This makes it hard to recruit new distributors into the industry and makes it harder to sell the products of network marketing companies."

Bob Paton of Watkins, a direct-sales company founded in 1868 which offers spices, food-related products, liniments, and salves, speaks for many when he says: "It was very important to me that I was able to go to a customer and say, 'Here's an American-made product with a money-back guarantee. If you don't like it, I'll give you your money back.' I didn't have to 'beat around the bush' and make up stories. I could look them right in the eye and tell them that." In evaluating your direct option, one of the key warning flags is greatly exaggerated product claims.

Some MLM systems of distribution are similar to conventional distribution systems for many goods sold through levels of distributors who may be referred to as "jobbers," "wholesalers," "distributors," or "dealers" who sell to end users. In direct selling, many companies have organized distribution systems in this fashion and now account for more than 50 percent of the industry salespeople. For economic success, MLM marketing depends on the ability of each member of the distribution chain to sell the goods at a higher price to the next level, until final sale at retail occurs between the dealer and the dealer's retail customer. It goes without saying that for this system of distribution to be economically viable over the long-term, every level of the distribution chain must be able to sell the products with a sufficient mark-up to adequately compensate that level for its involvement in the transaction. The ultimate end-user price must bear the original manufacturer's price and the accumulated mark-ups. Also, retail sales volume must be sufficient to utilize the quantities of goods flowing into the distribution system on a relatively consistent and steady basis. If the retail market does not absorb these goods at a consistent pace, products will stack up at some point in the system, and distributors who are buying more goods than they are re-selling will experience negative cash flow, loss of income on their investments, and excessive credit costs if they are operating on borrowed money.

The importance of the value that customers see in the end retail price is frequently overlooked by MLM promoters, as is the percentage of profit to the person who is supposed to demonstrate and sell that product at retail. Both oversights can be serious flaws, often given too little thought by the person considering the MLM "opportunity." The simple fact is that in order to sustain a retail business, particularly in the 1990s, you must offer a real value to your customers. Without retail sales, all MLM or network plans come crashing down. This has happened hundreds of times over the past two decades. Table 3-1 is a partial list of former MLM companies that have gone out of business in their original form in just the past few years.

Table 3-1

Defunct MLM Companies

ABI	Coppersmith Company
Jerome Alexander Home Workshop	Daisey
Aloia Joy	Dallas Diet
All American Toy	Dare To Be Great
Allied Marketing Inc.	Dawn Skin Care & Cosmetics
Aloe Charm Inc.	Decora
Aloe Gold	Deco Plants
Aloe Magic	Destiny Products
American Family Marketing	Dianna Berelli Distributors
American Professional Marketing	Diversified Marketing
Amerimex Industries Inc.	Edith Rehnberg Cosmetics
John Amico Cosmetics	Enhance Corporation
APO International	Espree Cosmetics
Aubrey McDonald Creations	Fashcot
Barely There	Filter Pure Products
Bestline Products	First Rate Enterprises
Better Living	Fortunate Corp.
Bon Del Corporation	Furst Cosmetics
Brocco	Genesis InternationalGolden Industries
Bryna Cosmetics	Golden Wunder
Cara Cosmetics	Gold Plate International
Care Free International	Hair Beautiful
Carianna International	Health Glo
Cato Corporation	Heart Cosmetics
Chambre Cosmetic Corporation	Heart of America Corp.
Charmay	Heritage Corp. of America
CIC Inc.	Holiday Magic
Command Performance	HomCare
Community World	Idea Way
CompuClub Marketing Group	Impressions

Table 3-1

Defunct MLM Companies (continued)

Kash is Best Inc.	Sterling Health Services
Kick'n Around	Success Five
Koscot	Sullivan Company
Legacy International	Sunasu
Life Products	Sunsets Unlimited
Lilac Time	Swipe
Living Homes	TCC
Lynell's Skin Care	Thermal-Chem
Manda's World	TNT (Today not Tomorrow)
Marjo	Tomorrow's Heritage
Meditrend	Tomorrow's Woman
McHoven Products	Torza Co.
MFI	Total Fitness
Multiway Associates	Total Success
Nutri-Bio	Total Support Marketing of America
Nutrient Cosmetics	Trinity Computing
Olde Worlde	Tronics
OMA Products	Ultra-Life
Ovation	Universe Foods
People Builders	United Professional Services
Perfume Originals	United Sciences of America ("USA")
Positive Living	Vega Cosmetics
Prestige Products	Venus International
Richline Cosmetics	Vis-A-Vis Inc.
Samantha Jewels	W.I.N.G.S.
Scientia Corporation	WCA
Sev-Co Products	Wellington Laboratories Inc.
Seyforth Laboratories	Wesware Company
("Slender Now")	Windfall Products
Sheer Delight	World Adventures Unlimited
SSI	World of Elegance
STA	World Wide Cosmetics
Star-Com	World Wide Products
Star Laboratories	Yurika

In a later chapter, we will review several MLM companies that have stood the test of time by offering value to their end customers. There are many others in the DSA, and undoubtedly there are legitimate MLM companies that are not a part of the DSA. But many MLMs are formed each year and promoted to "investors" mainly on the premise that they will be able to geometrically increase their earnings by obtaining multiple distributors who each obtain more distributors until an extremely large distributor organization theoretically exists with, of course, profits on all sales flowing to the top-level distributor.

The promotional programs utilizing these plans may attempt to augment their revenue by requiring individuals who participate to purchase distributorships for substantial sums or pay distributor fees that do not directly relate to the sale of products. Or they may require distributors to purchase substantial minimum quantities of inventory to occupy a particular position in the distributorship chain and receive the higher commissions payable to that level. A legitimate company will not need to rely on excessive start-up fees.

"I had to make a very small investment when I got into direct selling," says Norine Rodriguez of Cameo Coutures, a direct-sales lingerie company. She continues, "I think that's what got me into the company. I was ready to turn my Director down right off the bat, but I asked her how much it was going to cost me to get into the company. And when she told me, I was shocked. And I thought, 'Well, I can't lose. I'm not going to lose anything.' And that's what really made me sign the agreement."

Distributors are also often required to purchase additional quantities of inventory on a regular basis, perhaps monthly, simply to maintain their position and commission rights. Because each level of this distribution chain receives profit on the sale of stocks of products purchased by the next level, income can be earned as the goods move through the distribution chain to the lower levels—as long as there are lower levels of distributors who continue to buy. This, of course, is where many such plans unravel—they run out of lower levels willing to buy, primarily because the potential profit at the next sale is far too low, the retail value nonexistent.

An organization formed with an MLM structure will usually continue to grow horizontally at its various levels and may continue to attract multiple levels of distributors through aggressive recruiting premised on the concept that everyone has the opportunity to build huge "downline" organizations below them. Such an organization can grow with great rapidity simply through the dynamics of distributors recruiting and selling to other levels of distributors. However, the result is that product inventories accumulate in the distribution system as it grows and may vastly exceed the volume of actual retail sales to consumers.

An inherent problem in multilevel promotional schemes that rely heavily on "get-rich-quick" claims to promote aggressive recruiting lies in the rapid and undisciplined growth of sales organizations which have no real consumer market for the company's products and lack the training and financial incentives to develop one. Such an organization is literally one with no place to go. This organization does not build sales leadership.

The only talent it really promotes is recruiting—and that tends to focus on earnings claims that bear no resemblance to reality for the average participant. People selling such schemes are essentially promoters who migrate from one organization to another and are often referred to as "multilevel junkies."

Even when their intentions were legitimate, some of the original MLM founders have discovered that they have an organization that is out of control. Recruiters who have no link with corporate personnel, training, or legal discipline make increasingly extravagant claims in so-called "opportunity meetings." These same promoters also often publish outlandish and misleading earnings claims and almost always exaggerate the virtues of their products and disparage legitimate competitors. This erroneous information is then freely distributed throughout the rank-and-file organization to those who lack the knowledge to recognize the misstatements.

By contrast, organizations such as Tupperware, Stanhome, World Book, and Mary Kay, which have been built from the ground up over many years, have established cadres of independent leaders who have proven themselves through experience and performance. Wide dissemination of carefully developed literature and training aids has provided a core of discipline for these organizations, and that has helped them avoid the kinds of activities which can generate major regulatory problems and private legal claims. Ongoing training programs offered to the independent-contractor sales force cover every aspect of product marketing as well as recruiting, so salespeople know how to market products to consumers and how to recruit new salespeople responsibly. An example of responsible recruiting is cited by Bob Paton of Watkins: "When considering which direct selling company to affiliate with, I looked for one that had its feet on the ground. I looked for a company in which there was not a lot of hype and no one was going to tell me, 'Hey, when you come back here next year, you're going to come back here a millionaire.' In other words, I looked for a DSO that was realistic. One that didn't change things every time the moon changed. I wanted a company whose marketing program had been the same for a long time."

Within the DSA, there is a strong Code of Ethics to help maintain such integrity (see Appendix A). This code calls for outside legal investigation of unresolved consumer complaints. At the 1992 DSA Annual Meeting, as chair of the Board of Directors, I presented the recommendations of an Ethics Task Force headed by Alan Luce, then vice-president Administration of Tupperware. This task force had been formed to study ways in which potential exaggerated recruiting claims of member companies could be subjected to review and possible censure. The concept was to replicate the success of the DSA's original code, which protected the consumer of our industry's products, with a new code that protected the *consumers of our opportunity.*

The key amendments to the DSA Code of Ethics as adopted by the membership in June, 1992, are as follows:

- **Recruiting**—No member company shall engage in any deceptive, unlawful, or unethical consumer or recruiting practice.
- **Earnings Claims**—No member company shall misrepresent the actual or potential sales or earnings of its independent salespeople. Any earnings or sales representations that are made by member companies shall be based on documented facts.
- **Buy-back Obligation**—Repurchase by the member company of all marketable inventory purchased by a departing salesperson during the 12 months prior to termination. Repurchase must be for at least 90 percent of the salesperson's original net cost, less appropriate set-offs and legal claims.
- **Expulsion**—Code Administrator is empowered to recommend suspension or termination from Association membership for violations of state or federal law, or the DSA Code.

Wherever exaggerated earnings and product claims have caused a "ballooning" of product inventory in the distribution system, the result will be an implosion. Frustrated "investors" who have placed large amounts of money in distributorships and inventories on the assumption that they could find other distributors to buy from them may become so discouraged with the result that they file complaints with regulatory agencies and the Better Business Bureaus or file private lawsuits against the company and its promoters.

When the media spotlights such developments, it frequently signals the impending demise of the MLM organization, because unfavorable publicity destroys the confidence of both the people already in the organization and the general public. Further, news reports concerning litigation often trigger the attention of other regulatory agencies and prompt more investors to join in legal action, as happened with the $55 million Holiday Magic class action. This is usually sufficient to cause the company to descend in a downward spiral into dissolution or bankruptcy.

As noted earlier, not all MLM organizations are inherently bad—far from it. But it is important for those considering the direct option to know that an MLM or "network" marketing program by itself does not guarantee the success of individual participants. Without great product value and excellent profits for the person who sells the product to the consumer, the risks to an "investor" are considerably increased, and the downfall of such organizations can be greatly accelerated. The same mechanisms which caused rapid growth cause rapid decline.

Legitimate DSOs are always researching new product trends and improving existing products so that their independent sales organizations are not offering obsolete or unwanted merchandise and services. A "Johnny one-note" product line, never-changing, is often the sign of a weak company, or even a scam. The sales charts of such companies often resemble a hockey stick—sharply rising at first through aggressive MLM recruiting, then sharply declining, often to bankruptcy. The abrupt decline usually starts within two to three years for such companies, leaving latecomers to the plan high and dry.

Some newer companies have adopted the MLM label with a twist. These companies may, in fact, utilize what appears to be a commission structure with different levels of commissioned salespeople deriving commissions and overrides from the sales of other salespeople below them. If the emphasis of these organizations is on multilevel recruiting at the sacrifice of adequate attention to building a strong consumer base for their products, they may be subject to the same problems as more traditional MLMs. What should be self-evident, but obviously isn't, to unknowing "investors," is that for any organization to be economically healthy, the consumer base should be many times the size of the sales organization.

Some organizations may encourage large initial inventory purchases by new distributors to generate commissions and may allow sales credit to each of the different levels—not only the products sold by the levels below them but also on personal purchases. These schemes can be designed in such a way that a salesperson is able to maintain a position at a higher level of the organization through personal purchases and encouraging others to purchase substantial inventories from them.

Such a marketing plan may be, in reality, a disguised multilevel distribution that promotes inventory loading by its salespeople to achieve and sustain their positions in the organization and commission structure. These plans will fail if there is not an adequate—and genuine—retail consumer market. The organization will not have the morale and the momentum to continue. *The development of the consumer market must be paced with the growth of the sales organization. To accomplish this always requires expertise and expenditures of marketing funds.*

Many companies in direct selling start with a big recruiting promotion based on unsubstantiated claims, quickly reach a peak, and then end up bankrupt, battered by regulatory investigations or some investigative reporter's exposé. They can't generate sufficient retail sales to support their commission structures. When that happens, most often many members of the sales organization are left out in the cold.

If It Sounds Too Good to Be True, It Probably Is!

Is opportunity really knocking or has someone rung your doorbell and run away? That is the question you may face if unscrupulous members of multilevel or network marketing companies attempt to recruit you. Here are some of the claims you might hear, along with questions you might consider when evaluating their legitimacy.

Beware of the infamous "ground floor" or "window of opportunity." The implied message is that the first people to sign up will "make a killing" while the later recruits won't have a chance. In fact, the literature for one company with huge recruiting success in the early 1990s actually stated, "The first man gets the oyster, the second man gets the shell." A legitimate business should be getting better as each year passes, and achieving success should not be contingent upon beating someone else to the punch or leaving someone else high and dry with no opportunity for success. The great DSOs have one thing in common—caring and sharing people sincerely interested in your success, not in leaving you just the shell.

Constancy is definitely a virtue with a DSO. Dawn Rehbock of Encyclopaedia Britannica states, "My DSO offered me a system that I could rely on and depend on. If I put my orders in, I knew exactly how they were going to be handled. . . . I knew exactly what to expect from the company. They were very consistent, and that consistency was very important to me because my customers were changing—each moment, every two hours, each day. But the company was very reliable."

Ask yourself:

- ♦ Do honest people really want to be responsible for recruiting friends, relatives and neighbors into a "shell game"?
- ♦ If a company expects only a short "growth" period or to be "saturated" in a few years, how can its salespeople expect financial security?

"Earn $5,000 a month in your spare time!" Whether on a matchbook cover or in the "Help Wanted" section of the newspaper, this sort of offer generally commands attention—and skepticism. A variation of this lure is the promise of fantastic commission percentages. Very few activities—with the exception of buying a winning lottery ticket—can bring in the really big bucks with just minimal effort. It is true, as you will learn later, that it is possible to earn six-figure incomes—even high six-figure incomes—in DSOs, but rarely at the beginning level and almost always as the result of a lot of hard work—not with just a few short hours invested weekly or monthly. Barbara Armstrong-Allen of Art Finds International, a direct-sales art company, recalls: "When I first began direct selling, I expected to make a lot of money really quickly. That was a 'pie-in-the-sky' idea—very unrealistic. Not that it's not possible, but it's not terribly probable for everyone. It's like anything else in life—you have to work hard and long at it to achieve what you want."

Ask yourself,

+ How many people are really making that kind of money?
+ How many recruits would one need to earn that amount?
+ What can a beginner expect to earn during the first year or two?

Another come-on strategy is the suggestion that you don't have to sell anything—simply get other people to sign up. Legitimate companies base their businesses on actual product sales to consumers. Pyramid or chain schemes, on the other hand, do not concentrate on selling products, but solely on recruiting. Eventually the pool of new recruits dries up if no one is selling to the ultimate consumer. Unless, as one business writer put it, "they begin recruiting in another solar system."

Ask yourself,

+ If consumers are not buying the products, how can the company support its payment of commissions and incentives?

Beware, too, of exaggerated claims about products.
Ask yourself,

+ Can the company substantiate all of its product claims?
+ Does the company have a 100 percent satisfaction guarantee?
+ Would you feel comfortable selling a product that you weren't totally sure of?

The decision to join a DSO is so important to your future happiness and well-being, I urge you to ask the following questions when someone tries to recruit you or sell you a franchise or so-called business opportunity:

♦ Is the company well known? True, some wonderful companies exist, some even mentioned in this book, that have not achieved major levels of consumer awareness. But if the company is unknown to you and your acquaintances, the burden of investigation becomes greater.

♦ How long has it been in business in its present form? Don't be fooled by length of business under different management or with different plans.

♦ Where has it been in business?

♦ What is its reputation?

♦ Is it sufficiently capitalized to provide reasonable assurance that it can meet its financial obligations to its dealers? (This can be almost impossible to determine, particularly with a multilevel company on a tremendous growth track because of aggressive recruitment. One day, there can be millions in its bank account, the next day, bankruptcy looms.)

♦ Who are the principals of the company, and what is their reputation? Can they be identified with other failed schemes? There are many repeats at the top of chain recruitment schemes, because for them "getting the pearl" is the objective.

♦ Is the company involved in major investigations or major litigation? Are there any federal or state regulatory actions pending against the company? If so, what implications might these actions have for the future of the company? Is the company involved in a bankruptcy proceeding, or has it recently emerged from bankruptcy?

♦ Have you taken a close look at the products or services you would represent? Are they high-quality products or services? Are they consumable? What is the profit margin on sales of products? Often, large profits at the top are skimmed from the lowest level. If there is not a good earnings potential for the person selling the product, the plan will fail.

♦ Can you determine who actually manufactures the product and where it is made?

♦ Is the product or service guaranteed in writing by the manufacturer or supplier? Can you obtain a copy? Is complete, written product information readily available from the manufacturer?

♦   Is the marketing plan sound?

♦   Does the plan provide dealers the right to return their unsold
    inventories for repurchase by the company? Is this agree-
    ment in writing? Does the repurchase agreement allow a
    reasonable time for return? (The DSA Code demands a 90
    percent buy-back policy, minus overrides and bonuses that
    have already been paid, for up to one year. Five states—
    Georgia, Louisiana, Maryland, Massachusetts, and Wyo-
    ming—require a buy-back policy.)

Where to Go for Help

Take the time to answer these questions by consulting some or all
of the following:

♦   Your local Chamber of Commerce, Better Business Bureau,
    public library, or consumer affairs office.
♦   A nearby university, testing laboratory, a local business deal-
    ing in similar products, or an attorney.
♦   Your attorney general's office, a regional Fair Trade Com-
    mission (FTC) office, or the Clearinghouse for Business Op-
    portunity Complaints, 625 South Broadway, Denver,
    Colorado 80209.
♦   The Direct Selling Association, 1776 K Street, N.W., Suite
    600, Washington, D.C. 20006.

You must thoroughly understand the nature of your business relationship. We suggest you contact people who know the product you
would be selling and review with them the claims as to its marketability,
pricing, and projected profits. You should read your organization's contract carefully and perhaps review it with a lawyer.

The Direct Selling Education Foundation (DSEF) has published a
widely circulated booklet entitled *Promises—Check 'Em Out! Business Opportunity Fraud* in cooperation with the Economic Crime Project, National
District Attorney's Association, and a grant awarded by the Law Enforcement Assistance Administration, U.S. Department of Justice.

This booklet lists the "warning signs of fraud":

1. Pressure to sign a contract quickly and to agree to pay
a large sum of money before all claims can be investigated or
legal advice obtained. It should be noted that modern-day

scam operators often disguise the financial "hook" by requiring less investment, in the hopes that you will recruit many participants and that the chain of recruitment will result in huge profits at the top. And this does work, to the chagrin of those left holding the bag and the delight of those who started the scam.

2. Promises of extraordinarily high or guaranteed profits. This is almost a sure tip-off—exaggerated earnings claims.

3. Claims that profits can be achieved easily. A circular distributed in late 1991 openly promoted a multilevel scheme by asserting, "The last thing you want to do is sell anything."

4. A required initial fee greatly exceeding the fair market value of any products, kits, or training. In fact, exaggerated product claims are another hallmark of a business fraud since a claim of some fabulous product superiority is the easiest way to justify the exaggerated earnings claim. One necessitates the other-both together are a sure tip-off. And as for educational options, most of the "get-rich-quick" presentations never mention opportunities to learn the business. It seems "learning to sell" is a dirty expression on the "fast track."

5. A large fee payable before you receive anything in return.

6. Evasive answers by the salesperson or unwillingness to give disclosure documents required by law.

The DSEF booklet points out that these are only "warning signs of the most obvious frauds." The writers add: "An independent investigation is necessary in any case. A fraudulent salesperson may be prepared with glib assurances and authentic-looking documents." You can be assured that the recruiter will indeed be "glib" and will be armed with claims of high checks earned in the scheme and a lot of "instant riches" stories. Remember, "If it's worth your money, it's worth your time . . . to investigate."

The DSEF *Promises* booklet suggests, "If you have reason to believe that a company is defrauding business opportunity investors (whether or not you have invested), notify your local district attorney or other law enforcement agency."

Legitimate DSOs will go to extraordinary lengths to provide answers to your plan and product questions. For just the price of a few stamps, or with a simple phone call, you can obtain a wealth of information on DSA member companies. You should be able to reach a friendly, cooperative person who will send full disclosure information to you by return mail.

Check the service systems on which your DSO relies. *Really* test them. One test is to call the company's 1-800 number to determine its response to product or service questions. If the company doesn't have a 1-800 customer line, it has failed its first systems test.

Remember, this is your business, your career, your life. Take a few days more to check out several companies. Get to know their people in the field; actually buy and use their products if practical. *Get comfortable!* If the opportunity is right for you, you'll be spending a lot of time with these same people.

Chapter 4

Examining Your Motivation

As exciting as the prospects for success in a DSO are, it's helpful to examine your motivations before you sign up. If you join a DSO for the wrong reasons, you may find yourself in trouble later on. Don't join just because you are angry and fed up working for a boss who doesn't appreciate you, or because you think you can get rich quick, or because you imagine you'll be able to make money without too much effort. Working in direct sales takes a positive, not a negative, attitude. If you enter the field with a chip on your shoulder you may find it difficult to get along with others and pass on your pride in your product. Although DSOs offer a wonderful work alternative for many, they're not magical. You won't get rich quick or make money without trying—although you may get rich through hard work and dedication.

If, however, you are driven by the thought that you'll never know how well you can do until you try, and you recognize direct selling as a challenge that can be rewarding at many levels—plunge in! With that attitude, you can expect success in a DSO.

Six Typical Direct-Selling Career Categories

One way to take a careful look at yourself and your reasons for joining a DSO is to review an analysis of the six types of typical salespeople, identified by DSA president Neil Offen. Which one are you?

- ♦ The first type is the individual who signs up as a salesperson and never sells a product. Such individuals sign up to receive a wholesale or discount price that is available only to independent contractors. They are ultimate users of the product and feel strongly enough about it that they sign an independent contractor agreement so they can save money on personal purchases.

♦ The second type of salesperson has a short-term, specific objective in mind. For example, a woman may join a company to sell in the month of November and the early part of December so she can earn enough money to buy Christmas presents for her family. Or someone else may wish to buy a color television or replace a worn-out appliance. That person will sell until he or she has earned enough to purchase the product and then stop. They may do this occasionally throughout the year, and they may do it for many years in a row. These people are interested only in short-term, specific objectives.

♦ The third type needs the income our industry offers on a year-round basis, but has a limited amount of time to give to sales activities. For example, someone might wish to supplement an inadequate family income. These people work five or ten hours a week. Even if they are offered a substantial increase in compensation for a minimal increase in their investment of time, they cannot do so. Often, they use direct selling as a second or third income source.

♦ The fourth type of salesperson is the career entrepreneur. Direct selling is the prime source of income for such people, and they work anywhere from forty to eighty hours a week, generally six or seven days a week. As in most sales industries, 80 percent of the money is earned by 20 percent of the individuals involved. In addition, direct selling probably has more women earning in excess of $30,000, $40,000, or $50,000 a year than any other industry. In direct selling, women earn the same amount that men do for the same work, whereas in the United States generally, women earn only seventy cents to each dollar earned by a man in the same type of activity.

♦ The fifth type of salesperson is attracted to the industry not for its income earning activities, but for the recognition given to people for their efforts. These people, generally speaking, are women who are not receiving such recognition at home and who also seek social contacts outside the home, where they perhaps are raising young children and feel isolated. Traditionally, direct-sales companies run weekly sales meetings and annual conventions where star performers are recognized and everyone is made to feel good about themselves and their accomplishments. (Of course, recognition is a motivation shared by *all* types.)

♦ The sixth type of salesperson joins because he or she believes so strongly in the product's value to society that he or she wants to share it with friends, neighbors, or fellow citizens.

You need to recognize that your success depends not only on the quality of the product, but also on the quality and ability of the salesperson. Just as all the DSOs we profiled guarantee their *products*, you've got to guarantee you will "give it your all" from the very beginning if you want to be successful.

Time Spent Direct Selling & Recruiting

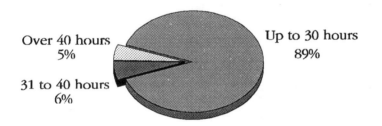

Over 40 hours
5%

31 to 40 hours
6%

Up to 30 hours
89%

Few do. Analysis of the comprehensive Nathan Associates Survey done of member companies by the Direct Selling Association in 1992 shows that only 11 percent of salespeople spend more than thirty hours a week selling products or building sales units. Other information indicates that a substantial number of participants claim less than ten hours a week, and the productivity of those hours is suspect. Part-time commitment and effort will lead to part-time income. Those individuals electing only part-time effort thus join the 50 percent of American workers who fall in this category, but often with an important difference: the per-hour earnings of direct salespeople are typically much higher.

Under the DSA Recruiting Code of Ethics, any DSO presenting its opportunity on an "hourly earnings" basis must substantiate the claims based on actual field experience. You should therefore request this information of any DSO you select for consideration.

My survey of the leading companies finds a remarkable similarity in claims at the "lowest," or part-time entry levels, averaging in the range of $12.00 to $15.00 per hour after all selling expenses. Admittedly, this rate will not make you wealthy—but it is competitive with wages offered across the nation for comparable effort and substantially better than the federal minimum of $4.25 in 1993. With fierce global business competition, hourly wages are likely to stay low, and according to the Bureau of Labor Statistics (BLS), replacement jobs typically average 25 percent to 35 percent less in pay. Earning $12.00 to $15.00 an hour would place you in the BLS's "very good" job category, along with jobs that normally require high skills and years of experience. And you may enter the typical DSO *without* "high skills" or "years of experience" and begin earning almost immediately as you learn the skills you need for rapid advancement.

When you consider that there are virtually no barriers to entry, and that skills can be learned "on the job," the achievements of top direct sellers are truly remarkable. Within the DSA membership, more than 150,000 individuals earn over $35,000, and almost 5,000 earn over $150,000. These are people who have examined their motivation, and who *do* have a positive attitude.

Table 4-1

Estimated Annual Direct Sales Earnings

Amount	Total Number of Salespeople
Over $35,000	152,000
Over $50,000	87,000
Over $100,000	23,000
Over $150,000	4,600

Overcoming Fears and Rejection

When reviewing the original draft of this copy, my editor, a woman, exhorted me to not bring up the specter of "rejection" in this early chapter. At first I agreed. In my years of personal recruiting, I would never have stirred the fear of rejection in a prospect at the outset, for it is the dislike of rejection that stymies many a career in sales. But I have since learned that to face the thing you fear is to master it, and this is especially true of the unfounded "fear of rejection" or "call reluctance." And since we are asking you in this chapter to examine your reasons for joining a DSO, you should be aware that your motivation must be strong enough to handle some discomfort when hearing the inevitable no's.

The best DSOs are aware of this discomfort. Most go to great effort to ensure that your early efforts meet with some success and that you find yourself in a supportive environment. In her powerful work, *Women Who Run with the Wolves,* Dr. Clarissa Pinkola Estes recites the tale of "The Little Match Girl" to remind us of what happens when we are in an environment where people don't care. Dr. Estes states, "Being with real people who warm us, who endorse and exalt our creativity, is essential to the flow of creative life. Otherwise we freeze. Nurture is a chorus of voices both from within and without that notices the state of a woman's being, takes care to encourage it, and, if necessary, gives comfort as well. . . . Every woman is entitled to an Alleluia Chorus."

"Alleluia Choruses" are a trademark of the most successful sales organizations, which have learned that recognition and "praising people to success" are critical components of survival and growth.

Bernard Rapoport, chairman and CEO of American Income Life Insurance Company, writing in Baylor University's newsletter "Professional Selling," gives insights that I believe enable us to put aside any "call reluctance" we may have.

- ◆ **The Perspective**. Successful sales professionals recognize and are committed to the premise that prospective customers need the products more than the sellers need their commissions. Salespeople should believe that the sale is not as important as fulfilling the need of the person to whom they seek to sell.
- ◆ **The Opportunity.** Successful sales professionals believe in the opportunity that selling can afford them. They view the profession of selling as an opportunity to help customers, which can in turn bring success to their firms and themselves.
- ◆ **The Presentation.** Successful sales professionals make sales presentations, not "pitches." Since sales professionals are not baseball players, they do not throw balls. Instead, they make presentations that will inform customers about filling their particular needs.
- ◆ **The Approach.** Successful sales professionals approach selling according to the tenets of professionalism, not amateurism. Amateurs, typified as "blue suede shoe, arm-twisting hawkers," pollute and foul up the opportunity found in selling. Professionalism, on the other hand, calls for integrity,

exemplary conduct, discipline, and dedication to preserving the highest standards for selling.

Mary Rose Schoinost of Watkins says, "I wanted to go into business for myself because I wanted to find something in life that I could stand firm on. And I knew . . . if I worked hard at it, I could achieve a goal or a dream that I wanted to. I have found that through life all things are possible, but you must try."

This is a career that will bring satisfaction and happiness as well as allow you the opportunity to earn what you really deserve. To succeed in a DSO, you will soon recognize, you must be in the business of selling yourself and believing in yourself. Your attitude will be the life-sustaining key to your career. This doesn't mean you won't ever have a negative thought or know fear or become discouraged.

Barbara Armstrong-Allen of Art Finds International explains: "The philosophy I have is every time something negative happens I just have to work harder to overcome it. . . . I just have to believe in myself and say, 'Oh, can I really do this? Yes, I can!' I think Abraham Lincoln said it best: 'A person is as happy as he sets out to be.' I want to be positive, I want to overcome any objection that I have in my life, in my business. That's important to me. . . . You have to work at being positive, at being disciplined."

A good and optimistic attitude will constantly buoy you through the early stages of becoming a competent direct seller; this attitude is crucial because direct selling is challenging. Most often, your number-one hurdle will be dealing with rejection. Bob Paton of Watkins copes with the effects of rejection this way: "You have to put rejection in the back of your mind. Watkins has a good saying, 'Some will, some won't, so what?'"

Shirley Hutton, the top National Sales Director in Mary Kay Cosmetics, earns over $700,000 a year. In her book, *Pay Yourself What You're Worth*, she recalls how early rejections affected her. "My strong suits were energy and enthusiasm. My weak suit was worrying about what others thought about me. I suddenly realized that by giving in to this feeling, I was ignoring what sales really meant. I was letting those worries accompany me to skin care classes and influence me negatively more than I'd suspected. The fact was that I had nothing to be ashamed of! I represented a company that was founded on fine principles and that produced a superior product and offered excellent career opportunities."

I experienced similar feelings when I started out in direct selling as a Kirby Dealer in the early 1950s. My motivation was strictly financial. Unlike those of you reading this book, I had no basis for analysis of the direct-selling industry. I absolutely had to earn money during the summer to afford the tuition, board, and books for my college education that fall. But I also partially mastered my fear of rejection during that long, hot summer. The important point is that, in addition to whatever income I earned, I learned to face problems, focus on problem-solving, and anticipate problems in future demonstrations.

In their excellent book *Earning What You're Worth?* George Dudley and Shannon Goodson address the psychology of sales call reluctance. They point out, "In direct sales, results are critically linked to the number of contacts initiated with prospective buyers. . . . Our studies show that as many as 80 percent of all salespeople who fail within their first year do so because of insufficient prospecting activity." "Call reluctance is a career-threatening condition which limits what salespeople achieve by emotionally limiting the number of sales calls they make," Dudley and Goodson continue. "Some have trouble using the phone as a prospecting tool. Others have trouble initiating face-to-face contact with prospective buyers. Many have trouble doing both."

Rejections are a fact of life. Michelle Buschini of World Book says: "The minus of a direct selling position is that there is a stigma that direct sellers are slick, door-to-door salespeople that get their foot in the door, and you can't shut the door. It takes a while even for you to build your own confidence in the company and the product. But once you start finding out more about the company and about how excellent the products are and how much of a difference they make in people's lives, then that sort of changes. Now I feel proud to tell people what I do."

"During my direct-selling career, my self-esteem has definitely improved," says Kari Brendtro of Discovery Toys. "I feel much more in control of my life. Instead of being so dependent upon someone else, I have the ability to depend upon myself. I never thought you could love doing something as much as I love doing this. I've been in jobs before, but I've never loved something. It isn't like a job, it's a way of life. Everything that we stand for, we live that way, too!"

And John Andrews of Fuller Brush has the solution to rejections. "You are going to get a high percentage of rejections, but the idea is to keep going." With each rejection, you are one step closer to a sale.

A major shift at the university level has taken place regarding career perceptions of various sales and sales management options. I have witnessed this glacial shift over the past forty years since my experience with Kirby.

When I studied marketing at the University of Florida in 1955, my textbook had only a one-line reference to direct selling—and that was negative. Until just the past few years, a career in sales carried with it some sort of stigma, despite the fact that it's one of the best-compensated careers in the world. Some of the stigma stems from "hard sell" practices, dishonest product and service claims, and exaggerated earnings claims. Sadly, there always seems to be a new huckster-type company that comes along and manages to tarnish the image of a fine, rewarding career in sales. Scam artists have added to consumer mistrust but can no longer dim the appeal of the direct-selling option.

Lyndon E. Dawson, Jr., of Louisiana Tech University and Donald P. Robin of the University of Southern Mississippi have done a study entitled *How People in Direct Sales View Unethical Practices.* Dawson and Robin state, "The idea that direct selling is unethical is a hindrance to the productivity and performance of the direct selling industry. . . . Because of the personalized nature of the direct selling activity with its call for immediate action, a belief is held by some that 'door-to-door' salespeople tend to be unethical and characterized as full of hucksterism and out-right deception. In direct selling, trust is even more important than in other marketing efforts because of its fragile nature."

What is striking about the direct option is the constancy of service provided by the *successful* companies. Most are several decades old, some are over a century old. While many in-store retailers are moving away from service, DSOs are maintaining and even enhancing their ability to solve consumer problems, present consumers with multiple options, and provide total satisfaction.

"The most rewarding thing about my position with my direct-selling company is that I'm serving people who want to be served," says John Andrews of Fuller Brush. "They like the product, and they look forward to having you serve them. You make people happy, and you're also making money. What could be better than that?"

Appreciation and Self-Esteem

The DSO salespeople of today see themselves as people whose fundamental purpose is to help others solve their problems. A person concentrating on solving another's problems has taken the first major step toward creating the positive, optimistic attitude that helps assure not only sales success but a highly rewarding life, as self-confidence and self-esteem grow.

Dawn Rehbock has been in direct sales for ten years and sums up her position with her DSO: "The most rewarding thing to me today in my position with Encyclopaedia Britannica is the people—the customers, their satisfaction, how they feel about what I've done for them in terms of serving them by helping them get their books." She adds: "It's addictive to be appreciated. It's addictive for people to be pleased and happy when they get something."

The best part is that the DSO with which you associate yourself will be providing you support and specific educational opportunities every step of the way, an advantage not found in any other form of business endeavor. Most employers are far too busy (they think) to provide the hands on, day-in-and-day-out training and support you will find in any of the DSOs I've identified.

Susan Estes, a Tupperware Dealer, puts it this way: "I joined Tupperware because no one believed in me. I was going to prove to the people who did not believe in me that they were wrong. I was going to show them exactly what I could be and do. Even my husband was against my getting into direct sales, until he saw my first earnings. Then he was pushing me out the door."

In her book, *Revolution from Within*, Gloria Steinem reflects on the lack of self-esteem she experienced in her own life, although she accomplished so much. "The idea for this book began a decade ago when even I, who had spent the previous dozen years working on external barriers to women's equality, had to admit there were internal ones, too," Steinem says. "Wherever I traveled, I saw women who were smart, courageous and valuable, who didn't *think* they were smart, courageous or valuable— and this was true not only for women who were poor or otherwise doubly discriminated against, but for supposedly privileged and powerful women, too."

Steinem observes, "It's a feeling of 'clicking in' when that self is recognized, valued, discovered, *esteemed*—as if we literally plug into an inner energy that is ours alone, yet connects us to everything else. To put it another way, I began to understand that self-esteem isn't everything; it's just that there's nothing without it."

The direct option has to do with determining what you really want out of your life and your work, making a conscious choice of how to invest yourself—for that is what you are about to do. Although there are no guarantees in life, the direct-selling option comes as close as possible to guaranteeing that time well invested will be well spent.

After a year with Cameo Coutures, Deborah Balka says: "Most people complain about their jobs, their bosses, their husbands— something in their lives. I see life differently. This is the first time in my life I feel I've been overpaid instead of underpaid, because I actually have fun in Cameo. And I'm making good money at the same time."

It is certain you will learn a great deal more about yourself in the process of being a direct seller, even if you do not continue in the field as a career. To the extent you persevere in your chosen DSO, you are almost guaranteed gains in vital areas of your life, including self-esteem, self-confidence, self-sufficiency, and the invaluable skill of being able to sell yourself.

Often, a new direct seller will subconsciously "give up" on herself. The early warning signs are usually clear. The demonstration kit or show-case stays hidden away in a closet, and day by day fewer customers are contacted or serviced, until the business has atrophied. This is most often not by intent; it "just happens," even to well-intentioned people. But not to well-motivated ones.

Brian Bradley of Kirby learned this first-hand. "I had a lot of fears when I first began in direct selling," he says. "You wonder if selling is for you and if you can really go as far as they say. Are all the people that can be sold already sold in this area? The doubts seem to increase when you go a week or two without a lot of sales."

"It's natural to have doubts," Brian continues. "I got through it by relying on my wife, because when I was down she helped. You need someone who is supportive of your abilities and who won't kick you in the teeth when you're down. I just didn't give up."

"During my direct-selling career," says Jeanne Moseman of Cameo Coutures, "I think I've become a more sharing person. I share personal bits of me, whereas I didn't before. I've become a warmer person."

You, after all, are the ultimate product, and becoming a warmer, more sharing person plus acquiring the ability to sell yourself will forever reward you—no matter what your ultimate career choice may be. You will also learn to truly reward yourself.

Geri Cray of Watkins sums up this aspect: "I guess because I've always had to struggle, I just wanted to be able to get to the place where I was comfortable and was able to maybe go out and not always have to look for something on sale, like I had for the many years that I raised my children by myself. I wanted to go into business for myself because I just felt that it was time in my life to accomplish something. When I started with Watkins, I didn't feel like I had much ability . . . to build up a business. But now I feel as if I'm gaining it. I've never been a leader, but I feel as if I'm developing into a place where I can become a leader. I really had just planned on being a Dealer, but my aim now is that I'll become a Distributor."

Leadership

Learning to become a leader, as remote as that may sound to you now, is one of the great benefits of a career in direct selling. The late Chief Justice Harry Phillips of the U.S. Circuit Court of Appeals in Cincinnati sold in the Southwestern program in the 1920s. "Southwestern's program is an effective cure for the kind of inferiority complex from which I suffered as a young man," he wrote.

And J. David Bamberger, retired CEO of Church's Fried Chicken, credits his success in building that company to over $600 million in annual revenues to leadership lessons learned as a Kirby salesman.

John Kotter, professor of Organizational Behavior at the Harvard Business School, recognizes the development of leadership through DSOs based on his study of Mary Kay Cosmetics. "Leadership in a modest sense, i.e. leadership with a lower case (little) 'l' is far more prevalent and far more important than most people realize," he writes in his book *A Force for Change*. "Not flashy or dramatic, it rarely attracts much attention and often goes unnoticed. But it can be found in all leadership stories."

Kotter goes on to point out that there are many "little acts of leadership." He states: "In these cases, something unforeseen happens, often in the nature of a crisis. A person steps into the situation; figures out which direction things need to move; communicates that successfully to a few other people whose help is needed; and then energizes himself/herself and the others to make something happen under difficult conditions. Observers tend not to label this 'leadership' because the number of people involved is so small, because the vision's so modest and because the individuals do not fit our stereotype of leaders. But this most certainly is leadership."

Even in the first few weeks of your direct-selling career, if you elect to do so, you will be enhancing your leadership skills, one small step at a time.

In Shakespeare's *Hamlet*, Polonius says wisely, "This above all: to thine own self be true, And it must follow, as the night the day, Thou canst not then be false to any man." At the center of your success in direct selling will be the concept of being true to yourself. You must believe in yourself and the product or service you will be presenting. Believing in yourself and "doing unto others as you would have done unto you" is a powerful combination. It is far more meaningful than the advice of motivational speakers who focus on attitude alone, who would have you simply "think and grow rich" or succeed simply because you have "the power of positive thinking."

Chapter 5

Building Your Business

Top salespeople deliver what they promise. They think from a customer's point of view, act in the customer's best interest, and create and fulfill realistic customer expectations. They believe in relationship marketing.

Relationship marketing is establishing a good relationship between the buyer and the salesperson. In relationship marketing, equal importance is given to the buyer's and the salesperson's needs. Relationship marketing allows you to teach your customers—actually impart product knowledge—as well as provide good service and establish satisfied customers. At its best, it is a relationship based on needs, rapport, and trust. Relationship marketing is what customers want in the nineties.

Carl Sewell, president of Dallas's famous Sewell Village Cadillac dealership and author of the best-seller *Customers for Life*, writes: "One of the worst things you can do is charge a customer more than your estimate. Build in a cushion so you can always charge a little less."

As a direct seller, you will probably not be "estimating" the cost of repairs, so the cushion you must build in is honesty in your product or service claims. You should carefully state benefits as the company suggests, perhaps even understating them, while avoiding exaggerated claims that we hear too often with today's over stimulated marketing. Customers have become wise to wild claims and resent those who fashion their sales pitches around the denigration of others' products.

Theodore Levitt, who as the guru of marketers motivated me throughout three decades, said in the *Harvard Business Review* for January–February, 1980, that every product and service has four incarnations: generic, expected, augmented, and potential. The **generic** is the "fundamental, but rudimentary, substantive 'thing,' . . . it is, for the steel producer the steel itself . . . for a bank, it's loanable funds." You should know and understand the "generic" product or service that you plan to sell.

The **expected** product adds to the generic one all the traditional services customers expect, point out William H. Davidow and Bro Uttal in their book *Total Customer Service: The Ultimate Weapon*. These expectations include convenient delivery, attractive terms and conditions of sale, and adequate after-sale support. Again, you should understand these features and believe in them.

The **augmented** product adds to the expected one a bundle of benefits the customer doesn't expect, like instructions on how to properly apply makeup for the workplace or how to motivate a child to love learning. Since the augmented product exceeds the customer's expectations, it can produce lots of customer satisfaction. It's the augmented product that tends to build terrific product loyalty and repeat sales.

But Levitt insists that even the augmented product can, with familiarity, lose its power to increase satisfaction, which brings us to the **potential** product. Levitt explains: "To the potential buyer, a product is a complex cluster of value satisfactions. The generic thing is not itself the product; it is merely, as in poker, table stakes—the minimum that is necessary at the outset to give its producer the chance to play the game. It is the playing that gets the results, and in business, this means getting and keeping customers."

Davidow and Uttal applied Levitt's ideas to their definition of customer service in a way that is useful to direct sellers: *Customer service means all features, acts, and information that augment the customer's ability to realize the potential value of a core product or service.*

Your DSO will provide you with the basic training to get off to a perfect start. DSO plans vary as to their emphasis, and, of course, all have different product lines to learn. No matter whether sales are by party plan, a group sales situation, person-to-person, or some combination of techniques, the best way to build your business will be through contacting prospective customers and providing service to existing customers.

Your DSO's Support

Ask a lot of questions about the convenience of doing business with your choice of companies. Do they have telephone ordering? How quickly will your order be shipped to you (or where can you pick it up)? Do they frequently backorder products?

Mary Rose Schoinost of Watkins agrees about the importance of knowing your company. "When I was considering which direct selling company to affiliate with, I knew I wanted a company that was sound," she said. "I wanted a company that would work closely with its people. I wanted a company that would be able to send me product on demand— at all hours of the day. I wanted a company that I would be proud to represent."

The quality of service you receive from your DSO's support group often determines the quality of service you will be able to provide your customers. If you select a DSO that ships customer orders to you for delivery, this must be done promptly and efficiently. Perhaps even more important, if your DSO ships directly to your customer after the sale is made, you'll want strong assurances of reliability and accuracy, since your customer will blame you—not the company—if the order is late or incomplete.

Chris Harney of the Longaberger Company is proud of the way her company stands behind her when there are inventory shortages of popular baskets. "If Longaberger gets into an inventory mess—maybe we sell more of something than they think we are going to—they always back us up," she says. "They don't send people their money back and say, 'Sorry.' They say, 'We're going to do this for you, at this price.' And they'll take a loss on it. They do this to build a good image and make sure we look good in the eyes of the consumer."

A few companies have a plan by which you can maintain a modest inventory of frequently sold items for immediate delivery. This has an advantage in that the customer can begin to use the products immediately after she has learned to use them. It also saves the salesperson a delivery trip. This plan, therefore, provides more control over customer satisfaction. Most of the cost of customer satisfaction will probably be borne by your company, another great advantage of being in business for yourself but not by yourself.

Consumer Learning Prior to Purchase

Researcher Wes Hutchinson of the University of Florida is examining consumer learning in stores and through direct selling. The preliminary results of this project have uncovered some interesting facts. According to Hutchinson, consumers have a number of sources of information—friends, mass media, advertising, and salespeople, among others. All of these can be important in different situations. In some situations, learning occurs as a part of an intensive effort to gather information immediately prior to purchase. An example of this might be shopping for a television or an automobile. In other situations, learning occurs over a longer period of time as a part of regular product usage. For example, skiers learn more about the types and functions of ski equipment as they become more proficient at the sport and as they ski more frequently. Finally, some products seem to be associated with a "critical period" for learning at some point during one's life. For example, the teen years for women are characterized by intensive trial-and-error experimentation with cosmetics accompanied by direct peer feedback. This occurs both at school and with friends (especially "slumber parties," etc.). As women mature, have families, and enter the work force, their opportunities for this type of learning are extremely limited.

Each of these three types of learning suggest appropriate direct-selling strategies, says Hutchinson. If your customers engage in intensive learning immediately prior to purchase, you must be known to them as an expert so they will seek you out for information. If your customers are learning continually as they use the product, you must track them over time offering, information and advice as it is desired. Regular direct mail, telephone, and in-person support can all help. The third learning situation is especially difficult. One approach is to identify those customers currently in their critical learning period and communicate with them (hoping that your message will be passed on to others). An alternative successful approach is to "recreate" the critical period as part of your approach to selling. Party plan strategies, such as those used by Mary Kay Cosmetics and Tupperware, are examples of this. The party or skin care class provides potential customers with a learning environment that is normally unavailable to them because of their age or stage of life. It allows extensive exposure to products, demonstration of how they are used, and social feedback from other people attending the party. Such an opportunity for product comparisons and experimentation with products is rarely available in the usual retail environment.

Consumer Learning after Purchase

Arguably, the single most significant twentieth-century development in consumer policy is the demise of *caveat emptor* (let the buyer beware). However, an equally strong argument can be made that caveat *re*-emptor (let the repeat customer beware) still applies. That is, great effort has been made to protect, educate, and inform consumers prior to their initial purchase of a product. Once they have experienced the product, however, it is assumed that they immediately know the benefits the product provides and their own degree of satisfaction with those benefits for the price they paid. Unfortunately, says Hutchinson, "most research suggests that very little can be learned from one trial. Direct selling not only provides an excellent format for learning prior to purchase, the continuing relationship between buyer and seller allows the customer to augment their experiences in using the product with information and advice provided by the seller. This enhances the consumer's opportunity to learn and get more satisfaction from their purchases."

In group selling, for instance, the best way to meet the people who will become your future customers is often at your first parties, shows, or "classes." You are also trained to invite the guests or attendees at these group sales events to hold similar events in their own homes. One-on-one plans place heavy emphasis on various referral offers.

Regardless of the selling plan, you will more than likely be urged to start with people you know. "Setting up my business went very smoothly," said Jeanne Moseman of Cameo Coutures. "I called relatives and friends and told them what I had decided to do and asked if they would help me get started. The magic word was 'help.' Most people feel good about helping someone."

One warning about this is that some friends and relatives can be very discouraging with respect to a career in sales, and you must learn to simply ignore this "helpful" advice.

The world is full of people who would like to receive your products and personalized service. Talk to people you meet at your neighborhood associations, your child's sports league, in the checkout line at the grocery store, in your professional group, or while shopping.

Many DSOs will teach you to gain referrals through "networking," a word very much in vogue in today's world. Networking simply means deliberately meeting people who can mutually help each other in business. You might find it helpful to join business organizations like your local Chamber of Commerce, professional groups, your child's PTA, or groups whose members contain the kind of customers you would like to have. Networking is something you can do gradually—you needn't feel you have to approach everyone in one meeting. In fact, you'll be most effective if you become active in the organization over time, so members see you as someone to be respected and trusted. You can also network effectively in your everyday routine. However, networking is a two-way street. The people you network with will expect equal consideration from you. They often have a business you can patronize or recommend. Any time you are in contact with a new person is the perfect time to begin building your prospect list.

Sometimes a modest amount of advertising can help stimulate your initial customer list, though it is not usually efficient. You will find that most DSOs are very protective of their trademarks and must approve usage, since thousands of other independent contractors are depending on the quality and brand familiarity of that mark for their individual livelihoods.

In the late 1960s, I was traveling the United States recruiting and training for Vanda Beauty Counselor, then a new division of Tupperware's parent corporation, Dart Industries. I averaged well over 100,000 air miles a year and recruited and trained hundreds of people who themselves eventually recruited thousands of independent contractors. Time after time, almost without exception, people were astounded by the number of other people they knew when they prepared a list similar to the one that follows. I would make a game of filling out the list in a group setting (first names were sufficient), setting a time limit, and giving a small prize for the longest list. This list will help you see how many prospective customers you already have.

The Ongoing Relationship

Research at Mary Kay has shown that it costs five times as much to attract a new customer as it does to maintain an established one. The very best salespeople work with their customers in a way that creates a bond, an ongoing relationship.

Lois Cameron of Fuller Brush says, "The most rewarding thing about my direct-selling career is the fact that I am independent, sell a good product, and have people happy to see me when I arrive. It's nice to walk into a place and have customers who are happy to see me rather than have them looking out the door saying, 'Oh no, here she comes again!' I like people to say, 'Well, where have you been?'"

Here is a customer service quiz used with permission from a DSA member company. It has helped thousands of direct sellers better understand relationship marketing through customer service.

Place a check in those boxes where you agree with the statement:

☐ 1. It is more difficult to replace a customer than to keep one satisfied.

☐ 2. Customer service provides you with a steady income.

☐ 3. Customer service is important because it is a source for new recruits. (Recruiting is covered in Chapter 8. You may skip this question if you wish.)

☐ 4. Nothing can take the place of a smile.

☐ 5. Customer service is important because it generates referrals.

☐ 6. An excellent way to handle disappointment is to forget it and go right back to work.

☐ 7. Support customers' decisions and treat them with sensitivity— even if you disagree.

☐ 8. Customer service builds a stronger reorder business.

☐ 9. Often your attitude speaks louder than anything you say.

☐ 10. Customer service is the foundation of your business.

People I Know

... In My Family

Brothers/Sisters

_____

_____

Uncles/Aunts

_____

_____

Cousins

_____

_____

Nieces/Nephews

_____

_____

... Through My Children

Their teachers/Day care workers

_____

_____

Boy/Girl scout leaders

_____

_____

Classmates/playmates/Parents/PTA

_____

_____

Coaches

_____

_____

... At Work

Employees/Management

_____

_____

Fellow bus riders/carpoolers

_____

_____

Competitors

_____

From past jobs

_____

_____

Retired

_____

_____

Seasonal

_____

_____

... As Social Friends

Current neighbors/Old neighbors

_____

_____

Church friends

_____

_____

Fellow hobby enthusiasts

_____

_____

Friends from college/People in my clubs

_____

_____

Birthday/Holiday card list

_____

_____

Old friends/New friends/Acquaintances

_____

Personal telephone directory

_____

Social/Political

_____

... As Professionals

Doctors/Nurses/Lawyers/Dentists

_____

Accountants/Stockbrokers/Receptionists

_____

Postal workers

_____

... Who Sell to Me

Hairstylist/Realtor/Mechanic

_____

Grocer/clerks

_____

Plumbers/builders

_____

Dry cleaners/carpet cleaners

_____

Landlord/gardener

_____

All others I paid money to last year

_____

Others

_____

_____

If you agreed with most of these statements, you have a solid understanding of customer service. These questions apply to all categories of sales and service—whether the product sold is low cost or very expensive and whether it is consumable or durable.

Today's customers are paying close attention to product quality, value, and selection before making their purchases. Compare the product lines you are researching, and make certain they are of the highest quality, are safe and effective, are price competitive, and offer an outstanding value to the consumer. Look for a 100 percent, Total Customer Satisfaction guarantee. A company that will not provide a generous guarantee may have something to hide from its sales organization, as well as from its customers. (Guarantees of big ticket items may necessarily be more limited, protecting the consumer against mechanical defects.)

"If you want to keep their business, give customers all of what they ask for, without equivocation or quibble," famed retailer Stanley Marcus says in his book *Minding the Store.* "If you bargain with them, you're going to lose their goodwill." So the old adage, "The customer is always right," *is* right—most of the time, and especially with small issues, be they financial, service, or product complaints.

The key is, when something goes wrong—and eventually something will—your first action should be to apologize. Immediately say you are sorry. As simple as this seems, few of us do this instinctively. Most of us go on the defensive, a habit that's very hard to break. The best action is to do something about the problem then and there, the sooner the better.

Direct seller Gloria Gilstead has found this to be true. "Golden Pride/Rawleigh has a satisfaction guarantee, but usually if you follow up with customers on a regular basis, there are fewer complaints," she said. "It's sort of like complaint prevention—making sure the customer knows what she's buying ahead of time. Then there are no disappointments. And if there are, for any reason, I gladly refund their money or exchange the product. It's worth it if it helps you keep a customer."

We wish all customer comments would be pleasant and complimentary of us, our products, and our service, but this just can't always be the case. One of the greatest advantages of being in direct selling is that DSOs make it very easy for customers to complain. They are more likely to complain to a DSO than to a retail store. This is, believe it or not, good news for your business. Because unless you know that something is wrong, you or your company obviously can't fix it. This is a hard and sometimes painful lesson to learn.

More than thirty years ago, I helped establish Tupperware Home Parties' Customer Service Department. That was in the days before we learned Total Customer Service is the responsibility of everyone in the organization, employee and independent contractor alike. Tupperware was beginning to grow, and the volume of customer correspondence rose from an occasional letter to a steady flow. The Tupperware management had broadened its guarantee, and people were taking advantage of it. I'll always remember receiving a melted Tupper Seal in the mail, with a complaint claiming "defective product."

So the customer isn't "always right." There are some who will cheat, but I believe 99 percent are honest. And I believe even more in the long-term value of Total Customer Satisfaction. Tupperware, and most of the other direct selling legends, is strong today because of wide, broad, and deep customer loyalty built on excellent handling of customer complaints—even when the customer *isn't* right.

Ultimately, the only thing that will determine your success is what the customer wants—not what *you* want. "If you make *people* your business, it doesn't matter what you sell—you will always be successful," says Julie Sears of Home Interiors & Gifts. "Make people feel good about themselves."

As simple as this sounds, the vast majority of people entering any sales profession don't understand this. They are too wrapped up in themselves, and in what they want, to pay attention to the needs of their customers. The customers will tell you what they want in both products and service. Carl Sewell says, "By all means, ask customers what they want. But ask politely, and don't force them to answer. Present surveys in such a way that customers can ignore them if they don't want to participate."

However, be careful not to use "surveys" *you* make up as an opening to a sales presentation. This is often overdone and can be unethical. Learn to distinguish between legitimate market research, which should flow back to a single point in your organization for analysis, and surveys used simply to "start a conversation" or "sales pitch."

One way to look at your relationship with customers is to believe that each person who purchases products from you also purchases your service—your sincere desire to meet their needs.

Customer service is an essential component of successful direct selling. With over thirty-five years of experience, Robert Magarino of Stanhome knows the importance of customer service. "In direct selling, the main thing is to build a customer base—one by one," Robert says. "I make sure I take good care of my customers so that I can come back. I treat them well; I make sure they have no complaints at all. I work consistently; I plan my work, and then I work my plan."

A Customer Service Primer

How can you guarantee customer service that will satisfy? Try answering the questions that follow:

- ◆ Have you organized your files and developed a consistent customer service contact system?
- ◆ Have you called each of your customers within two to four weeks of their last purchase? (This is particularly appropriate for consumable product lines.)
- ◆ Do you promptly return all phone calls from customers (and have you installed a telephone answering device)?
- ◆ Do you keep your promises and deliver orders promptly?
- ◆ Do you take care of any problems without hesitation?
- ◆ Have you provided your customers with enough information?
- ◆ Have you provided your customers with samples, where appropriate?
- ◆ Do you remember your customer on her birthday and anniversary?
- ◆ Do you give each customer personal attention and make her feel special?
- ◆ Do you try to offer an acceptable exchange if a customer is not totally satisfied with a product? (The well-run DSO will unhesitatingly replace this product if it comes from your inventory.)
- ◆ Do you promptly and cheerfully refund the customer's money, under the terms of your DSO, when it is necessary to do so?
- ◆ Have you asked your customer other ways you can be of service to her?
- ◆ Do you have a personal customer service goal?

"We're really in the people business," says Barbara McMullen of Home Interiors & Gifts. "People are by far the most important factors that we work with. Accessories are just kind of secondary. I was fortunate to have some natural people skills, but then I learned more."

Every business has its challenges, and a direct-selling business is no exception. Understanding and handling objections is a major part of mastering your new business. Shirley Eismann of Tupperware puts it this way: "I overcame the word no in direct selling after I realized that the people

I was offering the opportunity to were not doing me a favor; I was doing them a favor! If they did not want to take the opportunity, that was fine. But I was going to be courageous enough to offer it to them!" One of the most difficult lessons a successful direct seller learns is that *objections are not rejections.* Remember that an initial negative response is frequently really a request for more information. When you offer that information you enable the customer to make a new decision. Most objections are, in fact, questions. And the person who controls the flow of questions controls the sale.

Objections Are Not Rejections

It's helpful to first establish common ground and agreement with your customer. For example, you can answer an objection by saying, "I know just how you feel, Jane. I felt the same way until I learned more." When you begin from the customer's viewpoint, you will keep her attention and be more likely to receive a positive response. Objections are signals that remind you to focus on the customer's individual needs and interests. Once you see them, you can personalize your presentation.

The important thing to remember is to not take no's personally; the person is not rejecting you. There is a tremendous difference between refusal and rejection. Separate the notion of personal rejection from that of impersonal refusal. Remember it is as honorable to sell as it is to buy. Your success is not dependent on one sale or the reactions of one individual. Many contacts over a period of time will ensure your success.

"When I first started direct selling, I feared that I wouldn't be successful and that people would say no," recalls Peggy Kidd of Stanhome. "But then I realized that I really didn't have anything to lose. If I didn't make the sale, at least I would gain experience. I also found that no's don't kill you."

In the insurance business, members of the once-famed "Million Dollar Roundtable" are those who averaged one success in every ten tries. Looked at one way, each of the top people in this industry failed nine out of ten times. But because they succeeded one out of ten, they were at the top of their profession. Most direct-selling organizations have a better yes-no ratio than one in ten, so true success will be that much easier and faster.

Barbara Armstrong-Allen of Art Finds International remembers: "When I first started out in direct selling, I had to toughen up just a little bit and not take things personally. I did have some trouble with that at first."

Mary Rose Schoinost of Watkins added, "You just have to push yourself out that door and say, 'There's nothing to it.' You just get yourself in that car and you get out there and try. And if you don't try, you will never know. One may turn you down, but the next one may invite you in and actually wine and dine you."

Fuller Brush's Oden Henson, who has been with the company for over thirty years, said, "I maintain my self-motivation by habit. I just get up in the morning and work. I feel like I have control of my destiny . . . there is no excuse for me to ever be broke."

Seven Keys to Overcoming Objections

1. Be silent. Listen. Resist the temptation to keep talking or to interrupt. For most of us, this is very difficult. But what your customer is saying is vitally important—especially to her. Never argue or put her on the defensive. Don't assume you know what she is going to say (even though you probably do). Don't interrupt her. You think many times faster than anyone can speak. Make use of this to silently anticipate what her real objection might be. If you anticipate correctly, you're ready to overcome it. If you guessed wrong, learn from your "mistake" and keep listening. Don't let grammar or speech differences interfere with your ability to listen.

2. Acknowledge the objection. Nod your head. Repeat what she has said. Ask her to explain the objection to you, to clarify what she is saying. Silently translate her objections to questions. Ask yourself, "What's missing here? What more does she need to learn?"

3. Empathize. A study published in the *Harvard Business Review* in the early 1960s identified the ability to empathize as one of two key determinants of sales success. (The other was ego!) No doubt, the ability to imagine yourself in another's place, to "walk in her moccasins," is a powerful asset. To understand another's feelings, desires, ideas, and emotions is to establish a link with the other person. Use the "feel, felt, found" method. "I know how you feel. I felt that way myself. And I found that. . . ."

4. Answer the objection. Your DSO will undoubtedly have an educational program that will help you respond intelligently to frequently encountered objections. But the key is to ask yourself, "How can I help this customer solve her problem?" When a person voices an objection or says she is simply

not interested, say, "May I ask you why?" Remember, the person's first objection is usually not the real reason. The real reason will come out when you ask "why?"

5. Sell the benefits. Once you have identified which benefits are most important to your prospect, promote them.

6. Offer a choice. Always end your statement with a choice between two positive alternatives. For example, ask, "Would you prefer morning or afternoon?" Never ask yes or no questions. Make sure of her answer and confirm it.

7. Know when to stop selling. This is the most difficult part. You wish to rush on with all the other benefits of your product or plan and overwhelm the customer with your service story. You just know it's "right" for her. But be silent. Listen. Say your piece and let your customer respond. Usually, it will be to accept one of your choices, and you have made a sale.

Bernie Gross, executive vice-president of a major New York advertising agency, tells of one of his art directors who didn't know when to be silent. Bernie and the art director had just sold a powerful advertising concept to a major client. The sale was made, and Bernie was packing up to go, knowing when to be silent. But the art director, full of pride for his brilliant, creative ideas, suddenly started pointing out additional features of the campaign, only to "spook" the client's management into postponing the decision to "review the new possibilities." They left without a decision.

"George," Bernie asked on the way home, "when we had dinner last night, and you ordered, what did the waiter do?" George replied, "Well, he wrote it down, then asked you what you wanted."

"And then, George, what did that waiter do?"

"He picked up his menus and left for the kitchen."

Bernie continued, "George, did he keep asking you what you wanted?"

"No."

"Then why did you this afternoon?"

Listen. Wait patiently with your order form. And when you get the order, thank her and leave.

Keeping Your Customers

Some customers of DSOs are lost through neglect. Failing to follow up with guidance, sharing, and genuine interest is like planting a crop and never taking time to harvest. You'll have nothing to show for your efforts. Be sure you are investing your time wisely with your DSO and are always focused on building a business relationship with each person who purchases your products or just sees your demonstration even without purchasing. If a person will spend fifty dollars the first time you see her, think of what she might spend over a period of years—over a lifetime. This is what is meant by the lifetime value of a customer.

In automobiles, it can be an astronomical amount. Carl Sewell estimates the lifetime value of his customers to be in excess of $300,000. For most direct sellers, the sum would be a lot less, but still substantial, especially when you consider the commission earnings potential from recruiting a very successful salesperson from your customer base. Estimated customer purchases per person per year just for cosmetics is around $600—and much more for other product categories.

Mary Kay and other companies offer computer-generated customer list services, even software packages that will help you keep track easily. Although you don't need a computer to be very successful in direct selling, many homes now do have and use them like any other mechanical convenience.

Your existing customers will become your best ongoing source of new customers. You will want to solve any problems quickly (as we discussed earlier), always deliver all orders promptly, provide full product knowledge, and keep in regular contact according to the needs of your customers. Above all, keep your promises. At this stage of your career, keeping customers happy will be your overriding concern. Following are some ways you can accomplish this vital task.

♦ **Keep in contact.** Rate your customers according to the amount of business you can expect from them. Spend more time and call more often on the customers who give you the most business, especially if you are in a repeat sales DSO. Even "big ticket" DSOs, such as those offering books, vacuum cleaners, and cookware, find their best prospects are their already-established customers. Besides phone calls, use birthday cards and other mailings to keep your customers aware that you are thinking of them.

Oden Henson of Fuller Brush concurs. "After a while in direct sales, you can identify those customers who you want to do business with and those who want to do business with you. You get to where you skip those who don't want to see you. Learn to spend your time with customers who appreciate your service. I decided early on that I wasn't going to let some negative person run me out of business."

♦ **Keep serving.** Make yourself indispensable. No customer will leave if it is to her advantage to stay with you. Keep customer records. This is your own databased marketing system, which will become invaluable in building your business—and perhaps your own organization. List special needs, likes and dislikes, special interests, family information, birthdays, and anniversaries. Do special favors for your customers to show them you care.

♦ **Be dependable.** When you make promises, keep them faithfully. It is the best way to prove you can be relied on—and that's of great importance to any customer.

♦ **Handle complaints immediately and fairly.** As discussed earlier, recognize complaints as a great opportunity to cement customers to you. Don't go out of your way to solicit complaints, but when complaints do occur, do *more* than the customer expects to correct the problem. It is usually very important that you let the company know of frequently occurring complaints, especially about products. Don't feel the company will be "upset" by this. A well-run DSO wants customer feedback, because quality improvement is a never-ending process. (Your DSO *should* go out of its way to solicit complaints through market research, 1-800 numbers, and prominently displayed guarantees.)

♦ **Show appreciation.** Everyone likes to feel important. Mary Kay Ash suggests you imagine every human being walking around with an invisible sign around his or her neck that reads, "MAKE ME FEEL IMPORTANT." Train yourself to respond to this "sign" instinctively and immediately. You will begin to build relationships with almost everyone you wish. Show your customers your appreciation through personal service. Working women require a special level of service, for they have serious time problems. You will build an immensely loyal clientele from your working customers by doing business on *their* terms, when and how they need your products and services.

Boosting Your Attitude

Many experts in sales and public speaking suggest that even if you are not feeling up to par or are nervous, just act enthusiastic and you will become enthusiastic. The mystic Gurdjieff suggested the "as if" method to help restore a positive attitude. You should behave "as if" something were true. Then make it happen. It's easy to be enthusiastic when everything is going smoothly, but the real test of one's poise and courage is to maintain enthusiasm under chaotic and challenging conditions.

Here are 10 attitude boosters:

- Believe in yourself, your product and your business.
- Smile! It will make you feel better.
- Call people by name.
- Be friendly and helpful.
- Become genuinely interested in others.
- Be generous with praise.
- Look at mistakes as opportunities for growth.
- Respect the opinions of others.
- Make others feel important.
- Above all, like yourself as a person, and to your own self be true.

This chapter has acquainted you with the basic building blocks of success in direct selling. Without actually experiencing some of the things we've suggested in this chapter, you're entitled to a little apprehension. But if you've basically understood and agreed with most of what you've just read, you are an excellent candidate to climb the first rung of the ladder of success in direct selling. You can do it!

Chapter 6

Managing Your Time

No matter what our background, age, ethnicity, financial worth, or status, we all have exactly the same amount of time. How you use your time is vital to your success and also to how you feel about yourself.

"I think the less time you are spending on your direct selling career, the less you are going to be fulfilled," says Norine Rodriguez of Cameo Coutures. "The more you put into the business, the more fulfilled you will be. It's your business, so the more you put into it, the more you're going to get out of it."

The key to success is careful planning. Once you begin setting goals and objectives, you'll be more in control and feel a greater sense of accomplishment. Goals give purpose to our efforts and provide essential direction. Remember, money is only one of the reasons for joining a DSO. Your goals must be very specific and include those things which are most important in your life, such as your family and their needs. Here are some suggestions to help you get started.

- Set one specific, achievable short-range goal. Do not make this a monetary target, but rather a tangible object that additional money would buy, for instance, a new dishwasher.
- Set a long-range goal, a major goal such as a new house, college education fund, or luxury yacht. Really want this goal.
- Be realistic. Do not set up a schedule that you can't achieve or that will take away from your spouse or family—or yourself. You will soon lose interest in achieving an unrealistic goal.
- Set a specific time frame. Write it down. Commit to your goal, and let others know about it.
- Establish priorities: what you want to do first, next, etc.
- Develop a plan of action.

Linda Rodgers, a direct seller with the Longaberger Company, believes in thinking big. "To be successful, you have to dream and think big," she says. "If you really want to soar in this career, you have to have the vision and the courage to set big goals. Don't be willing to settle for less than the best."

Geri Cray, a direct seller with Watkins for over a year, comments, "When I first started out with my direct-selling company, I had difficulty making myself stick to a schedule, and I still have that problem. When you are on your own and no one is pushing you, you have to push yourself. I still feel like I haven't pushed myself enough."

"When I first started with Art Finds International, I had to get into the 'work mode,'" says Jane Webster. "But the thing that kept me going was saying, 'This is much more fun than going back to an eight-to-five job and working for someone else . . . people telling me I had to be there at a certain time.' I never wanted to lose my independence."

Time management is particularly important to you as a direct seller. You are the boss. There will be no one there to make you take action or not waste time. You may be interested in a career in direct selling because you want a flexible schedule. But it takes good planning to achieve a flexible schedule and still earn what you need and want.

One of the most organized people I know is Mary Kay Ash. Her desk is always clean by nightfall, and she has learned never to handle the same piece of paper twice, an incredible skill to us ordinary mortals! More than 5,000 personalized letters go out from her office each month. But her real time management secret is a little pad imprinted with six numbered lines. She calls this her "six most important things to do list," and I've never known her not to fill it out for each and every day. It prioritizes her work for the next day and keeps her on track in an incredibly complex daily schedule. She is always headed in the most productive direction for that day.

Mary Kay's practice is to begin with the first item, deemed by her to be the most important for that day, and finish it before going on to the next. But Mary Kay urges those who use this system not to expect lists to solve all problems. Use them as a way to free yourself from drudgery and apprehension. It's amazing how just the listing of six items can give you peace of mind. What's more, I suspect that your subconscious works on some of the items while you are sleeping, for I often rise with answers or insights for my projects that day.

For those tasks which aren't priorities, but fall into the category of "round tuits," write each on a piece of paper and put them in a box. Also make up some slips with treats (read a book, go to a movie) and put them in the same box. Periodically draw one of the slips and do whatever it says. A round tuit? You'll get around to it one day!

Basic Goal Setting

The first step in goal setting is to establish clear and specific goals. Everyone has dreams. Turning those dreams into reality begins by setting a specific goal and then working towards it. I firmly believe you can achieve anything you want. But first you must decide what that is.

Keep your goals simple, realistic, and concrete. Although your goals should be far-reaching, make them obtainable. Then write them down. Effective goal-setting should be as much a visual or audio experience as a mental one. I suggest you actually post your goals where you and other members of your family will see and read them every day. You may also wish to tape your goal and listen to it daily.

In Tupperware years ago, we used to suggest that the dealer either take a photograph or cut out a picture of goals and create a goal poster, then share those goals with others. Those of you from sophisticated business or professional backgrounds might find this too simplistic—a kindergarten exercise. Nonetheless, it is a powerful way to stay motivated in the early days of your direct selling career. Don't knock it until you try it.

The next step is to set a deadline, especially for your short-term goal. Make a strong commitment to reach your short-term goal by a specific date. Then break your goal down into smaller segments. Focus on the number of customers you have to establish and serve to reach your goal, and also the number of other persons with whom you intend to share your new opportunity.

To start your own personal plan of action, write down the number of hours you plan to spend on actual sales and recruiting activities each week. You will also want to record any hours you plan to attend DSO functions (such as sales or training meetings) and the minimum amount of time needed to record the daily transactions associated with your business activities—most of which you will be doing as you go through the day. List all the major activities you can for the upcoming week. Some will include:

- Church and school activities
- Family time
- Other occupation (if you are working)
- Recreational activities
- Club or philanthropic work

- Personal time for shopping, errands
- Sales or "unit" meetings
- Training classes and workshops
- Customer contacts in person
- Customer contacts by telephone
- Product deliveries (if applicable in your DSO)

Based on this list, there is obviously no way you can schedule enough time to actually even start a modest, part-time direct-selling business, let alone build forward to a six-figure income—right? If you believe this, it's true. But ask yourself first, "What do those other 5 million people who are successful in direct selling have that I don't?!"

The Weekly Plan Sheet

Those who achieve success have established priorities, and most use some variation of what I call a "weekly plan sheet." You can draw the following weekly plan sheet for yourself in about 30 seconds. It's all you really need to first visualize what your week looks like, and it enables you to prioritize your activities to allow some time for sales.

Be sure to make time for yourself a top priority. Schedule at least one free day a week for yourself. The human body is productive and energetic only if it has enough rest. Time for yourself can give you an entirely new perspective on things. Mary Kay Ash has long believed in this and states her priorities as: "God first, family second, career third." She insists that in this order, "everything works"; out of this order, "nothing works."

Now let's go back to your goal. First, quantify it—that is, put a dollar amount on it. You'll also need a realistic forecast by yourself, your recruiter, or your DSO as to what you can expect to earn per hour at the fundamental sales level of your DSO. For the sake of easy calculation, let's assume this amount is $20 (net) per actual hour of selling time—not an unrealistic amount for most legitimate direct-selling plans.

Let's then assume the furniture you wish to buy will cost $2,000. Divided by $20, this furniture goal would take 100 hours of selling. If 5 hours can be invested in one week, your new couch will be sitting in your living room in just 20 weeks (100,5 = 20) or five months. I'm sure your goals are much higher, but they can be quantified as easily.

As you fill out your weekly plan sheet, inserting those hours you plan to actually sell, you will discover errands and activities that can be coordinated and combined to save time. Planning helps you organize and balance your time. Do this for your first few weeks, and you will feel you

Weekly Plan Sheet

Time	Sunday	Monday	Tuesday	Wednesday	Thursday	Friday	Saturday
8:00							
9:00							
10:00							
11:00							
12:00							
1:00							
2:00							
3:00							
4:00							
5:00							
6:00							
7:00							
8:00							
9:00							

are accomplishing more without feeling rushed or pressured. You might be interested in knowing that, based on statistics accumulated for twenty years in over one million "case studies," direct sellers who spend a full forty hours a week at their careers are almost universally successful. In other words, success is directly related to consistent, productive work (not "pretend work" such as paper shuffling and going to unnecessary meetings).

Troy Schlosser of Princess House says: "You don't get anything in this business unless you work hard at it. The harder you work, the more success you will have. . . . I always tell people, 'The best way to make your dreams come true is to wake up.' Every successful relationship is based on commitment and hard work—a successful marriage, a successful business. . . . People want the 'get-rich-quick' scheme, they buy lottery tickets and all of that—it just doesn't happen. If it did, everyone would do it."

Like your goals, post this weekly plan sheet in a prominent place in your home so your family will know where you will be during the week. A good idea is to include phone numbers with appointments, should you need to be contacted in an emergency.

Use your time wisely. Prioritize tasks you must do yourself, and delegate other activities you don't need to do personally. There will come a time when it will be better for you to hire someone to do the housework, because you will have found that your time is much more valuable on a per-hour basis.

There is no substitute for mastering the basics of your direct selling career—even, and especially, if you have had other sales experience. A common error is the assumption that you "know it all" because you have joined a DSO, say, from IBM, which admittedly has one of the finest sales training programs in the world despite the fact that they lost billions in revenues in the early 1990s. What works at IBM won't necessarily work at your DSO. One of my favorite direct-selling executives is Jack Wilder, formerly IBM's "golden boy" of sales, who joined Mary Kay Cosmetics in 1973. Years later, even after Wilder had left Mary Kay to join Shaklee as their vice-president of sales, he was calling me for advice on very basic direct-selling concepts. Wilder was brilliant, one of the best on-stage personalities I'd ever seen in action, but after many years in direct selling he still needed insights at the field sales level. It's important that you learn your business "from the ground up," no matter what your aspirations are for the future.

What I would urge you to do is forget, for the moment, that thousands of people in direct selling earn $25,000 or $50,000 or more per year. If you wish to reach these levels, you will. But only if you take the time now to take the first steps correctly. Earn those first few dollars the right way—the way your DSO suggests—for you will also be learning how to teach others to reach their goals. In most direct-selling plans, you can accelerate fairly rapidly after you've mastered the basics—but seldom before. And without the capacity to help others reach their goals, you will never reach the high income brackets.

At the end of each week, review your weekly summary sheet. Did you reach your goals for the week? Did you find time for additional business? Did you make the best use of your time? After reviewing your past week, begin planning your next week. You might, in fact, have to make up for lost time and work six hours instead of five. Make any adaptations necessary to be more productive.

Above all, stay determined to reach your goal. Maintain a good attitude. Once you have almost achieved your first short-term goal, immediately set a new one, appropriately a somewhat more ambitious one.

Here are a few helpful time management hints:

♦ Get an early start. Starting work just fifteen minutes earlier can make a big difference.

♦ Streamline paperwork. Handle correspondence, order-filling, and telephone calls promptly and efficiently. Get a three-minute egg timer for your calls; always answer quickly but politely, and be off the line in three minutes. Don't play "office" or "executive" by spending all your time on paperwork, a common failing of many in direct selling. Office time is lost time. You are rewarded most for activities that place you in contact with people.

♦ Keep a notebook and file box handy. Jot down reminders and ideas in the notebook, and throw those which are already written or printed (like newspaper clippings) into the box for later follow-up.

♦ Vary activities. This will keep your energy at a peak and your efficiency high.

Procrastination

The three major time wasters are distractions, waiting, and procrastination. The old adage, "Procrastination is the thief of time," is even truer today than in Edward Young's time two hundred years ago. We do put off until tomorrow what we can do today.

What tasks are you likely to avoid? Often, procrastination is really a fear of failure or of rejection. How many times have you put off a telephone follow-up call because you were afraid of the outcome? Or have you set such high standards for a task that you avoid doing it? Ease yourself in by doing one small part of a task at a time. Watch out for the warning signs of procrastination—"I'll do it as soon as I. . . ." Just begin; it doesn't matter where or how. (Mary Kay has established a "DIN-DIN" Club to remind everyone to "DO IT NOW—DO IT NOW!")

When you elect the direct option and work from your home for the first time, you will probably require a period of adjustment. In the first place, you're going to have to learn to put up with a new boss—you!

Large tasks don't have to be overwhelming. You eat an elephant one bite at a time. For instance, when you have a long list of business-building calls to make, cover the entire list with a blank sheet of paper so no names show. Give yourself a short time limit—fifteen to thirty minutes that you've scheduled for this purpose. During that time period, pull the blank sheet down to expose one name only, and say to yourself, "This is the only call I need to make right now." After that call is completed, you expose one more name and repeat the procedure. When the time period ends, you choose to continue or to stop. However, always end on a positive response. You'll carry that positive note with you for the rest of the day.

Janice Gordon of Mary Kay Cosmetics believes that putting people in charge of their own destiny is the greatest drawing card a direct-selling opportunity offers women in the workplace. "You can set goals and focus intently on reaching them," she says. "We all have days when we have the feeling we just can't get started. I find that feeling disappears one of two ways: the first business phone call I make in a day or a quick glance toward my goal chart."

Your Effective Selling Time

Your new situation may put your willpower to a severe test, and if you are easily distracted by other responsibilities or extracurricular activities that demand a lot of time—beware!

Here are some things for you to consider:

♦ How much are you going to earn, relative to the hours you invest? Make sure the DSO you have selected fairly represents earnings per hour as well as advancement possibilities. A reputable DSO will be able to document typical earnings situations that will parallel your own. You can and must estimate your earning potential at the outset.

♦   What is your effective selling time? It's easy to be overly
optimistic about your earnings potential unless you can re-
alistically schedule actual selling time. The typical person
will spend about 120 days a year on vacations, holidays, and
weekends, which "automatically" reduces days actually
available for face-to-face selling to 245. Of course, you can
elect to sell on Saturdays, for example. But for many, time
with family will override weekend selling. Many DSOs have
weekly sales meetings, to which you will usually elect to go,
and optional, occasional seminars, workshops, and other activities to help you improve your skills. These activities,
along with paperwork, illness, and other obligations can easily take another 20 days out of your selling year. Now you
are down to just 225 days to sell.

John I. Coppett and William Staples, of the University of Houston at
Clear Lake, give us a model for travel time calculation in their book,
Professional Selling: A Relationship Management Process.

Travel (In miles per year at 50 mph)	Travel Time (Computed in days)
5,000	12.5
10,000	25.0
15,000	37.5
20,000	50.0

Simply subtract the appropriate number of days from the base of
effective selling days, such as 25 from 225, and you are down to just 200
days. Then you must find a way to divide these 200 days by selling
activity. A typical home party takes two to three hours, with another two
to three hours of preparation, hostess coaching, telephoning, and other
follow-up for an average total of no more than five hours (most DSOs
would estimate between three and four hours total). If you want to sell
on a full-time basis (say thirty hours a week), your schedule could easily
accommodate six group selling situations (30,5) per five-day week. This
is above average, although many direct sellers accomplish this per week.
Most party-plan DSOs will have calculated a "party average" profit. Say
the national (better yet, regional or local) average profit is $100 per party.
Divide this by five hours and net average earnings per hour would be

$20. You have elected to work thirty hours in a five-day period, so $20 times thirty hours would equal $600.

The person in this example could reasonably count on forty five-day periods per year (200 days divided by five), and therefore forty times $600 or about $24,000 per year from this single source of income. This would not count reorder business, sources of commission income that may be available, or perks such as the use of an automobile.

The same calculations would apply to door-to-door selling. But no matter how you figure, your earnings will come back to the amount of time you have made available for effective face-to-face and telephone selling and, as you will see, recruiting as well.

Direct salespeople will often fool themselves into thinking they are working, perhaps because they go to sales meetings or shuffle papers, when in fact they are not utilizing effective selling time to sell.

Michael LeBoeuf, writing on "Managing Your Time, Managing Yourself," in Business Horizons, lists the typical time wasters for sales representatives:

- Telephone interruptions
- Drop-in visitors
- Lack of self-discipline
- Crises
- Meetings
- Lack of objectives, priorities, and deadlines
- Indecision and procrastination
- Attempting too much at once
- Leaving tasks unfinished
- Unclear communications

Having a weekly plan sheet or datebook is essential to avoid many of these time wasters. Many direct sellers also find that a telephone system is critical. Reproduced here is a useful telephone log, which you may feel free to copy and use to control your phone business. You may want to personalize this system to make it your own. You can develop a simple, easy-to-remember code for the "reason for call" column, such as "REF" for referral, "SO" for special occasion (birthday, anniversary), or "REO" for reorder.

No matter how you achieve it, managing your time becomes critical to a direct seller. Here is what Barbara Peasel of Stanhome has to say: "The minus of a direct-selling position is there is no guarantee of a regular paycheck. You have to put the time in and get the training to produce

Telephone Log

B=Busy
LM=Left Message

NA=No Answer
X=Complete

Name	Date	Reason for call	B	NA	LM	X	Comments/Referrals

and do what you need to do in order to earn. When you goof off and don't work, of course, the profits aren't there. In this business, you have to be 'on it' mentally and physically to go out and do your best."

Felicia Frierson of Mary Kay Cosmetics adds: "There is a saying, 'She's starving in the middle of an orchard!' This means that the person is hungry but is either too naive or lethargic to reach for a piece of fruit and feed herself. In much the same way, many of us don't realize what value or wealth we have in our ability to sell. For example, 'An apple a day keeps the doctor away.' Well, a sale a day keeps the 'blahs' away! Visualize yourself in an orchard and let the fruit represent the number of customers to whom you can make sales."

Evaluating the Direct Option

An oft-heard reason for failure, usually voiced after a salesperson has stopped making the necessary effort to create and maintain sales, is, "Well, I just didn't make as much money as I thought I would." In classic 20/20 hindsight, the salesperson believes a poor outcome was due to flaws in the DSO or in direct selling itself. In fact, he or she has gotten stuck in a self-fulfilling prophecy: I'm not making enough money, so why bother?

Then there are many who do give direct selling a good effort and find that they still don't seem to have achieved the level of income they would like. These people are on the edge of a tremendously important decision. They must take serious stock of their opportunity. They have at least three choices:

1. Continue on as they have been, steadily building a customer base to achieve whatever level of sales income it takes to make them comfortable.

2. Quit and go back to work for someone else. With only rare exceptions, people who elect this option improve their earnings potential. Those who have reached this point will have learned a great deal more than they can imagine or know until later in life. I was doing conservation work in the wilderness recently and for some reason, I mentioned my Kirby experience. It turned out that three of us in the same Jeep had started our business careers with Kirby and had gone on to become presidents of large companies.

3. Accept the challenge of building your own sales organization within the framework of your DSO. Surprisingly, only a small percentage will elect the last option. The field is

wide open to those who want to advance. And best of all, you
have already learned the fundamentals of what it takes to succeed.

If you have enjoyed helping others, if you have gained some self-
confidence and self-esteem, and if you are comfortable with the basics of
your business (even though you may not be earning enough right now),
then you may be ready for advancement in your DSO.

There are rewards beyond money in direct selling, and the reward
of helping others succeed is typically the motivating force behind the vast
majority of highly successful people in this industry.

Cheryl Montgomery of Mary Kay says, "I really do enjoy helping
others and seeing them get well and feel better about themselves, because
I've spent many years as a psychiatric nurse in a medical center. In helping
people within Mary Kay, the great rewards and loving care you give make
you feel so worthwhile and important."

Chapter 7

Managing Your Business

Many of the individuals who elect the direct option initially lack basic business management skills. Even those entering this industry from major corporations find that leading and managing a small business is often a far cry from functioning from within a cocoon in a large, structured, hierarchical corporation.

The majority elect the direct option with virtually no business skills. In a way, this is an advantage, for they carry with them minimal "baggage" of prior conceptions of business management. Generally, direct-selling organizations function best within a simple system, which we will discuss in this chapter.

It should be made clear that those who succeed most within DSOs are those who can both manage and lead. Only a very small percentage of individuals excel at both managing and leading. In fact, you will probably have to be in the top 2 percent of your DSO to be rewarded in the high five-or six-figure income levels. Your chances of achieving this are proportionally much greater than in any other occupational category with similar educational and professional-experience requirements. And typically, there is always room at the top for more large-income producers, which is usually not the case in the corporate world. Since only about 6 percent of direct sellers indicate they work over forty hours a week, your "competition" for the "top"—if you care to invest the time equivalent to what others consider a normal work week—would seem to be narrowed to one in three.

My observations of many groups of direct salespeople invariably show that one-third achieves at an extraordinary level, another one-third is on the way up, and the bottom third never becomes committed to the sustained effort it takes to be the best. In direct selling, you elect your third.

In a later chapter, we will make clear the distinction between leading and managing, for they are quite different skills. **Management** has to do with goal-setting, planning, budgeting, organizing, measuring, and bookkeeping functions. **Leadership** is quite different, and direct selling provides one of the finest ways to develop leadership skills. Once understood, the leadership function not only becomes second nature, but is also fun and infinitely rewarding.

To most sales-oriented individuals, the management function is one that is definitely not fun, but a "necessary evil." This is particularly true when you are in business for yourself and *by yourself,* for example, as the sole proprietor of your own shop. But even with a DSO, where the company furnishes some guidance and specific help, you can lose out because of your own poor management.

The two major components of managing your direct-selling business are time management and money management. These *can* be fun, and certainly can be part of your routine, which is what I stress to all new direct sellers. Mary Kay Ash has taught thousands of leaders how to handle their basic accounting functions by what she calls the "shoe-box" method—simple boxes for sales receipts and expense checks. Don't laugh. Kept up as you go along, such systems work surprisingly well.

It should be noted that some fail because they *over manage.* They spend their days thinking and planning, but never actually doing anything to create income, new customers, and new members of their sales organization. However, the majority of failures come from the ranks of people who can sell and recruit, but do so in a random, haphazard way. When and if they do make a little money, this, too, is handled in a random, haphazard way.

Basic Money Management

Now that you are on the way to achieving your goals, make sure you keep the money you are earning. Nothing will make your money management easier than to have a separate bank account for your business. You will get a true picture of your income by not mixing business and personal funds.

In addition, a separate bank account will help you know when you can take profits from your business and will make it easier for you to keep track of expenses. You may wish to have your checks imprinted with something like "special account," but do not use the name of your parent DSO. Your DSO has trademarked its basic business and product names, and it is important for the company (and you) that full trademark protection be maintained.

Deposit all your revenues, including cash sales and sales tax, in your business account. Sales slips should be retained to show the amount of sales tax you collected. Your deposits will become an official record of income for tax purposes. Using this account to pay business expenses also gives you a tax record of each item and greatly simplifies paperwork.

The downfall of new direct sellers is embezzlement—from themselves! This is usually not intentional. You may take a large sum from a business account to be spent on some personal want or need. More often, it's the siphoning away of seemingly insignificant amounts of cash for daily needs such as tips, food, groceries, or apparel. Pay only your *business* bills from your business account. Many direct-selling business transactions are in cash, which has a way of disappearing from your purse or wallet as the day wears on. Be sure you promptly deposit your cash receipts in your account before they disappear.

It is imperative to keep each set of transactions in separate files, with sales tickets and cash, checks, and credit card receipts carefully separated and attached to the respective files. An easy way to keep track of "petty cash" from your business account is to have a small sum, with the amount noted on a slip of paper, kept separately from your personal funds. This petty cash fund should be replenished with funds from your business account and reconciled with receipts. After your business is on a solid, profit-making basis, you will be able to write yourself a paycheck from this account.

The suggested business management styles of many DSOs may make it desirable to have a small amount of inventory on hand to serve your retail customers. Many direct sellers prefer to start their new businesses with a bank loan, which helps establish credit and reinforces money-management discipline. As sales revenues mount, the loan is paid back, and your business becomes financially stable—with a good credit rating should you need more working capital in the future.

"When getting started with my direct selling company, I put $1,300 on my credit card and went for broke," says Jennifer Taylor of Diamite. "If you're going to go for it, you might as well go. There's an excitement level about being in your own business. . . . Once I decided to do it, I just jumped right in. And in about three days I sold all my product and paid off my credit card."

It is also very helpful to establish a bank card such as MasterCard or Visa to be used exclusively in connection with your business. This makes it convenient to purchase supplies and other business requirements and gives you a good credit record. A few words of caution: keep the card account current, to minimize interest payments, and don't "embezzle" from this account, either. Keep your personal purchases on a personal credit card.

The simplest possible system is two "shoe boxes" or two large manila envelopes for each month—one for income, the other for expenses.

At the end of the year, the records you have collected in these envelopes will provide the information you need for calculating income tax.

In order to keep track of your monthly expenses, I suggest the use of a simple monthly expense sheet. Here is a very basic one which will serve your business well through your initial stages of growth.

This simple form will help you document the date and method of payment, the amount, what business category it falls into, and any notes you need to jog your memory at tax time.

Here are some tips to help minimize the amount of time you spend on the paperwork management of your business. Remember, the less time you spend on these functions, the more money you can make by being with your customers.

Handling Expenses

- ◆ Pay for business expenses with a check from your special business account or with your credit card used exclusively for business.
- ◆ Get a receipt. Write the items purchased on it, along with whether you paid in cash, by check, or charge to your credit card. Store all receipts in your monthly expense envelope.
- ◆ Note incidental cash expenditures without receipts (such as a business phone call from a public telephone) as they happen.
- ◆ Transfer this information onto your monthly expense sheet on a regular basis, either *as you incur the expense or weekly.* This is important. There is nothing more painful than having to spend hours struggling with a mass of paper that has become very "stale." Far more time is wasted trying to recall what this or that expense was.
- ◆ Keep a record of your automobile mileage in a log, journal, or diary. These expenses will be tax deductible at the end of the year.
- ◆ At the end of the month, enclose the bank statement for your business checking account and your credit card account in your business expense journal. Store these for tax time.

Tracking Income

Every DSO will have a sales ticket, and some furnish weekly summary sheets to aid in income record keeping. I can't urge you enough to perform each little bit of record keeping as it happens. Don't let it pile up.

Monthly Expense Sheet
Month of _____

Date	Paid by (CK, Cash, MC, VISA)	Payee	Amount	Invent.	Adver.	Car	Insur.	Office	Supplies	Taxes	Travel	Meals & Entertainment

Take a vow: *I will unfailingly deposit all income from my sales into my bank account.*

Each week, refer back to your goals. Did you spend the number of hours you planned on your direct selling business? Did you accomplish your income goal? This comparison between planned and actual will help you analyze the week's activities and help you form new plans to reach or exceed your goals. Doing this weekly helps you develop the good business habits you need to maximize your income and minimize your paperwork.

Tax Considerations

You may have some responsibility for remitting sales taxes, depending on your DSO. In almost every situation, you will have responsibility for collecting it from your retail customers. In many DSOs, sales tax based on the retail value of the product is remitted to the company at the time an order is placed. Normally, you recover this when you resell the product to your customers.

However, you will sometimes use your products for gifts to facilitate and promote your retail business (such as a "hostess gift" or a "gift-with-purchase"). When this happens, you may not be able to recoup the sales tax. So it's important to keep track of your non-recovered sales tax throughout the year. At tax time, you can simply add your non-recovered sales tax total with your other expenses on your federal and, if there is one, state income tax deduction schedules.

This very brief summary isn't intended as a substitute for professional tax advice: it is offered solely to allow individuals interested in the direct option to gain insight into the tax benefits of a career as an independent entrepreneur.

As an independent contractor, you are considered self-employed and may be entitled to special tax deductions. *Generally, it is preferable to have a CPA or a tax accountant prepare your return.* The cost of using a professional to prepare your tax return is usually modest. You should spend some time with the preparer to ensure that he or she fully understands your method of doing business and your self-employed status. This enables the accountant to seek and claim deductions that might not otherwise be evident. However, if you prepare your own return, you can obtain various free publications explaining tax laws from any Internal Revenue office.

The most important thing in preparing your return and assuring that you have the benefit of all proper deductions is to *keep adequate records of all income and expenses.* Such records are essential for preparing the return as well as for substantiating income and expenses if your return is audited by the Internal Revenue Service. An important point to note is that the more organized and "cleaner" the records you submit to the tax preparer, the more efficient the process will be. This usually results in less cost and more deductions—saving you money two ways.

Income and expenses incurred in your direct-selling business are normally reported on a special tax form, Schedule C, provided by the IRS. This form is especially designed for self-employed persons. Following are some points you should consider in calculating your net income for tax purposes.

Income

The calculation of the gross receipts made during the year is the first step in preparing your income tax return. This can often be done by totaling individual sales receipts or summaries you have made each month during the year.

Income might also include the value of prizes, awards, and car programs offered by your DSO, as well as other commissions paid to you during the year. Any commissions received as well as the fair market value of prizes and awards received during the year should be reported as other income. Your DSO is required to report to both you and the IRS if the amount of such incentives exceeds $600 for the year.

The total of these items comprises total income from which all costs and business expenses are deducted.

Deductions

Expenses. Many of your expenses may qualify as deductions, including:

- Commissions you pay others
- Bad debts (and your net cost of refunds to customers)
- Postage for business
- Conference or workshop expenses related to your business, including travel, meals, and lodging
- Advertising
- Business-related telephone and long distance calls
- Cost of samples
- Product insurance expenses
- Gasoline, oil, and other automobile expenses related to your business

- ◆   Accounting costs
- ◆   Stationery, business cards, and other printing
- ◆   Contract labor paid to someone to assist you
- ◆   Legal advice and expenses
- ◆   Dues to professional societies
- ◆   Interest on business debt
- ◆   Office supplies
- ◆   Customer entertainment (up to the amount currently allowed by the IRS). Be certain that the environment of the meeting place is conducive to business.

Cost of Goods Sold. The primary deduction from your gross receipts is your cost of merchandise sold during the year. DSO plans vary widely as to how this is recorded.

Some plans recommend you carry an inventory. With those plans, you would follow a calculation such as this:

Add: Wholesale value of your inventory at the beginning of the year.
Plus: Wholesale value of purchases during the year.
Less: Wholesale value of inventory at the end of the year.
Equals: Cost of goods during the year.

Obviously, in this calculation it is necessary that you determine the wholesale value of your inventory at the beginning and at the end of each year.

Other Deductions. With the addition of any commissions and prizes, the difference in the cost of your products and the money received for them is your **gross income.** Some of the following may then be subtracted to determine your **taxable income**.

- ◆   **Automobile expenses**. As a self-employed person working from your home, you are permitted to deduct the cost of operating your automobile for business-related reasons. Current IRS code allows two methods for determining the amount of expense deductible: the business portion of actual expenses incurred or a standard mileage rate. In the actual expense method, you must retain receipts or other documentation (canceled checks are generally not sufficient) for all automobile-related expenses. In the standard mileage rate method, in addition to mileage, documentation needs to be retained for interest, taxes, parking fees, and tolls. An automobile mileage log is the best evidence to support your business deductions in case of an audit. To be safe, the more documentation you have, especially distinguishing business from personal use, the better off you are in case of an audit.

There are certain limits on depreciation and investment tax credits for cars purchased after certain dates. To make sure you are taking the maximum deduction for your automobile, usually a major expenditure for direct sellers, I advise that you talk to your personal tax advisor.

- ◆ **Travel expenses**. Travel expenses, including meals, lodging, and incidental costs, are deductible while the taxpayer is away from home in the pursuit of a trade or business. The IRS says the expenses must be "ordinary and reasonable" in amount. As long as the purpose of the trip is primarily for business, travel expenses are deductible, even if some time is spent sightseeing or visiting. Such expenses, however, are not deductible if the trip is primarily personal in nature. In addition, trips outside the United States and its territories are rarely deductible, except to Canada, Mexico, and Bermuda. Be sure to consult the IRS before attempting to deduct international travel, as the code changes from year to year. A spouse's travel expenses are not deductible unless the spouse is also going for business reasons.

- ◆ **Entertainment expenses**. Generally, a high percentage of entertainment expenses are deductible if they are ordinary and necessary and if they are (a) directly related to or (b) associated with the active conduct of your business. In fact, in 1991 you could deduct 80 percent of such entertainment expenses. In addition, a percentage of the expenses for entertainment for generating goodwill is normally deductible if there is the possibility business will be produced by the entertainment. Remember, however, that no deduction is allowed for entertainment expenses that may be considered extravagant.

A percentage of business meals can be deducted if they are held in surroundings conducive to business discussion. In the case of meals and entertainment, documentation of the business purpose is generally necessary. This includes recording the name and relationship of the person entertained and the business discussed at the time.

Office-in-home expenses. The office-in-home deduction is available only when a specific portion of the home is used exclusively and regularly as the taxpayer's principal place of business or used for meetings or dealing with customers. This requirement is not met if the area (portion of the home) is used for both business and personal purposes. Deductions are also allowed for items allocatable to space in the home regularly used for inventory storage. Deductions for an office-in-home may not exceed your business profits. These deductions may not cause your business to show or increase a tax loss. In 1993, the IRS revised Publication 587, *Business Use of Your Home*. The IRS added two primary factors to the principal place of business test:

1. The relative importance of the activities performed at each business location.
2. The amount of time spent at each location on this business activity.

Here are two examples which will clarify these for you. However, you should consult your tax advisor to help you analyze whether you qualify for a home office deduction.

Example 1: Joe Smith is a salesperson. His only office is a room in his house used regularly and exclusively to set up appointments, store product samples, and write up orders and other reports for the companies whose products he sells.

Joe's business is selling products to customers at various locations in the area where he lives. To make these sales, he regularly visits the customers to explain product features and to take orders. Joe makes only a few sales from his home office. He spends an average of thirty hours a week visiting customers and twelve hours a week working at his home office. The essence of Joe's business as a salesperson requires him to meet with customers primarily at the customer's place of business. The home office activities are less important to Joe's business than the sales activities he performs when visiting customers. In addition, a comparison of the twelve hours per week spent in Joe's home office with the thirty hours per week spent visiting customers further supports the conclusion that Joe's home office is not his principal place of business. Therefore, he cannot deduct expenses for the business use of his home.

Example 2: Fred Jones, a salesperson, performs the same activities in his home office as Joe Smith, except that Fred makes most of his sales to customers by telephone or mail contact from his home office. Fred spends an average of thirty hours a week working at his home office and twelve hours a week visiting prospective customers to deliver products and take orders.

The essence of Fred's business as a salesperson requires him to make telephone or mail contact with customers primarily from his office, which is in his home. Actually visiting customers is less important to Fred's business than the sales activities he performs from his home office. In addition, a comparison of the thirty hours per week spent selling to customers from the home office with the twelve hours per week spent visiting customers further supports the conclusion by the IRS that Fred's home office is his principal place of business. Therefore, he can deduct expenses for the business use of his home.

Sadly, Fred Jones's' business is atypical of 99 percent of sales-related careers. For the typical salesperson, days spent confined to an office would ultimately destroy any chance of success. Yet proactive salespeople out seeing customers often need an office for their management duties as well: they just won't be able to receive tax deductions for it.

Child care credit. Individuals are entitled to a tax credit for qualifying child care expenses. Household and personal care expenses for a dependent under the age of fifteen or a dependent incapable of self-care qualify if incurred to allow the taxpayer to earn income. The credit is available to working married couples or couples where one spouse works full-time and the other works part-time or is a full-time student. The qualifying expenses cannot exceed the earnings of the spouse with the lower income. Credit is also available to a working, divorced, or separated parent if he or she has custody of a child under age fifteen.

Other Taxes

Tax regulations require you to supply your Social Security number to your DSO. Failure to do so may result in an IRS penalty. In addition, if a valid Social Security number is not on file, the company may be required to withhold a specified tax amount on payments, such as commissions and awards.

As a self-employed person, you are subject to a self-employment tax, which should be paid by you unless you are already paying adequate Social Security taxes by virtue of other employment.

If you exceed certain minimums, you are required to file a declaration of estimated income tax and pay quarterly installments of estimated state income tax, estimated federal income tax, and Social Security tax.

You should investigate this requirement carefully to determine whether it applies to your situation. As your earnings increase, you will be paying more taxes, but look at the good side. . . .

There are other important tax benefits of direct selling as well, particularly in the area of tax-deferred saving plans for self-employed individuals. Such plans allow you to defer taxes and many thousands of dollars each year, thus enabling you to build towards your own retirement plan.

CAUTION: As tax laws are constantly being amended or changed, you should seek advice from a competent tax accountant for application of this general information to your own federal, state, or local income tax return.

Managing a Unit of Independent Entrepreneurs

Mastering the management of your personal sales activities leads naturally and comfortably into the management practices you will need to be successful with your own "unit" of direct sellers. Each DSO's plan varies widely, and you should receive help with the plan you choose.

Maintaining Skills

Plan to continue actively selling and recruiting for most (if not all) of your career in direct sales. In my opinion, the true greats are still personally very active in the basics of their business. Michelle Buschini of World Book concurs. "To make sure I am successful in my business, I must do certain activities on a consistent basis," Michelle says. "My first priority is to have my personal sales in each week. In a direct-selling position, you must be out in front of prospects every week. Selling activity comes first."

I recently watched one of Mary Kay's million-dollar directors, while relaxing during a recognition trip at a luxury resort in Hawaii, recruit the wife of the hotel's general manager without batting an eye. It gets in your blood! If it doesn't, I can't guarantee that you will manage your way to success.

After mastering the basics of your particular DSO, never lose sight of them. Keep going back to fundamentals and keep insisting that the independent entrepreneurs you have attracted to your unit do likewise.

Moving the product is one such fundamental. Kevin Reitmeier of Kirby points out, "The most important thing we have to do as managers in direct sales is to show new recruits the product is being sold. Seeing is believing. If they don't see the product being sold with their own two eyes, they are going to continue to doubt until they fail."

There is a tremendous tendency to try to reinvent the wheel, to fall prey to what I call the "tempting tangents" that are all around you in your career as a direct seller. Innovation and innovative ways of serving customers can be great. But never change at the expense of building on fundamentals, whether for a standard presentation of encyclopedias or vacuum cleaners or a skin care class.

The great football coaches of history, including Tom Landry of the Dallas Cowboys and Vince Lombardi of the Green Bay Packers, were masters of fundamentals. They stressed blocking and tackling. An organized approach to "blocking and tackling" in managing your growing direct-selling business is very important. The time you spend on management activities will provide you with valuable information on which to base the decisions you will make. But learn to manage one step at a time, taking what you learned as a salesperson and in personal recruiting.

The biggest change for you as you advance in your direct-selling career will be learning to balance your time between your own personal selling and recruiting and in managing others. This balance will constantly shift as the number of people you are working with grows, but initially it's important that you keep a full schedule of whatever got you to a "management" position. Football coach Darrell Royal, when at the University of Texas, used the phrase "Dance with the one who brung you" to make this point. It especially applies to direct selling.

You will want to learn to help members of your "unit" set goals for themselves and give your working time to those who are successful at that. You should be communicating with all members of your unit—at meetings, through phone calls, or perhaps through a newsletter.

Husband-and-Wife Teams

Often, when you step from your own personal selling activities to building a unit and advancing to a position of leadership within your DSO, your spouse can make a tremendous difference—first, by supporting you; and in many cases, by actually joining you in the business. This is, in fact, common in many DSOs, especially with top leaders.

Gary Meyer, husband of top Princess House leader Lavonne Meyer, reflecting back twenty years, says, "In supporting Lavonne, on a scale of 1 to 10, I was somewhere around a -4. I did everything I could do to discourage her from being successful.

. . . Princess House looked like a threat to me and my role in the family. I didn't see it as an opportunity for Lavonne, I saw it as a threat to Gary. . . . I was very, very negative towards the business." But things have changed, and Gary's statement says it all, "The year I quit and retired early from Sears, my gross income would not have paid Lavonne's income tax for the year." In 1993, in addition to shutting down its venerable catalog business, Sears planned to close more than 100 stores, causing "trickle down misery" throughout much of grassroots America. It's fortunate for people such as the Meyers that direct options exist.

Gary McCoy, husband of Mary Kay National Sales Director Judie McCoy, says he got involved in the business "unintentionally." "The business," Gary recounts, "grew to a point where Judie was so busy that she needed help."

Gary's involvement has meant much to the McCoy family. "We found that we started working as a team, and instead of having just the mother figure and the father figure, we were really parenting with our children," Judie says. "It was great because when Gary was free to help, he could pick up the slack when I was out. It gradually evolved into a career where I don't think either one of us had a specific role. There was a lot to get done, and the family worked as a team to get it done."

One pitfall of couples in business together can be who gets the recognition. Egos are sometimes affected in the process. "Gary gives me the limelight," Judie says. "He allows me to be in the forefront."

Other DSOs place heavy emphasis on husband-and-wife teams, especially Tupperware's famous distributorships which, during the formative years of the company, were used almost exclusively. The traditional pattern was for the husband to oversee the management side—including a warehouse operation—while the wife handled field sales leadership, promotions, and recruiting. Furthermore, in companies such as Amway, recruiting was often a team effort with the husband taking the lead in many instances.

Mary Kay Director Kathy Helou gives credit to her husband Daniel for her success: "Daniel is the managing partner in the business, and I am the worker bee. I prefer to be outside. I'm rarely in my office, I'm out in the field all the time. I'm out there training, and that's what I love doing. I can inspire people to want to achieve more, which is a special ability I have been blessed with. Daniel is the managing person who loves to work on the computer, do newsletters, and put together training programs."

Top Mary Kay Director Sue Kirkpatrick's husband, Kirk, stresses the importance of learning all the different dimensions of the business, such as promotion, leadership, sales, and recruiting, as well as office management. Kirk zeros in on communication as the real key. "Working together as husband and wife, communication has been a challenge because we are always going in different directions," he says. "She is always trying to build one side of the business, and I am always trying to track it. But at the same time, we are working towards a common goal."

The direct option offers more opportunities for husband-and-wife businesses than any other form of retailing. Most of the stories I hear are of positive reinforcement of family values and an enhanced closeness within the marriage as a result of a husband-and-wife team. But there are also risks, especially those created by communication problems and ego conflicts. There may be situations where working together so closely abrades an already fragile relationship. Forming such a working relationship is not a decision to be taken lightly. One course of action is to allow the spouse to gradually learn about the business as it evolves, and perhaps the team will be formed naturally. In many of the situations I've observed, this is how the strongest teams are created.

Creating a Budget

Many managers of DSOs have only a dim sense of where their business is financially at any given time. They want to spend all their time on customers and unit members. But one chore you must do is making a budget.

To help you visualize this process, I've reproduced here a "Projected Budget" sheet, this one for a quarterly plan.

At first, projecting your budget will be rather hit or miss, but as you "try and try again" and gain experience, you'll be amazed at how accurate you become in forecasting your profitability—and at how challenged you are to improve. Approaching your business this way enables you to have a real feel for where you are financially at any moment and will definitely lead to improved profits.

One of the areas you will quickly get a feel for is that of promotional expenses. Again, we've found that superb "people-people" often lose their objectivity when it comes to promotional costs. They like to give nice awards and prizes and don't like to worry about the expense. But this often amounts to "buying" business you would normally get anyway and obviously leads to higher overhead.

It's helpful for you to think of your business expenses in two major categories—administrative expenses and sales expenses.

PROJECTED BUDGET
Quarterly Money Management Worksheet

Months of _____

Income	Month #1	Month #2	Month #3	Quarter
Personal sales				
Recruiting commission				
Other				

Expenses: Estimate your monthly expenses

Product Orders				
Postage				
Office supplies & equipment*				
Auto expense				
Printing				
Meeting room				
Awards & prizes				
Travel (transportation, meals, lodging)				
"Big events" travel*				
Insurance*				
Accounting fee*				
Telephone				

*Set aside 1/12 of these costs each month.

Money available = profit (income minus expenses)				
Federal/state taxes & Social Security				

Money available = profit (income minus expenses)

Administrative Expenses. These are the expenses necessary to run your business, regardless of the sales volume or number of sales-people involved. For example, meeting rooms or items such as a VCR, computer, or copy machine (usually used later in your career) are in this category.

Sales expenses. These expenses vary based on the amount of sales and the size of your organization, for example, postage, long-distance phone calls, out-of-town travel, and promotional contests.

Whether the expense is administrative or sales-related, always ask yourself, "What return can I expect on this investment, in terms of time as well as money?"

Any budget is worthless unless you review it every month. At the end of each month, add your actual income and expenses in each category and fill in the appropriate block. At the end of each quarter, set new goals based on the actual figures for the past three-months' experience.

For the next three months, repeat the process by continuing to write income and expense totals, month by month. About this time, you may begin to see certain income levels or expenses that are out of line. Rather than becoming aware of problems at the end of the year (when you can do little about them), you can begin to make changes immediately. Form a habit of following and understanding the flow of cash in your business. I can tell you as a former bank director and member of an executive loan committee, most of our problem accounts came from otherwise successful businesses that outgrew cash flows and never caught up. In a DSO, this should not happen if you are conscientiously depositing all receipts and not "embezzling" from yourself for those "extras" that your higher earnings put so temptingly within your reach. Resist temptation. Build your business. There will come a time where you can really indulge yourself, or, better yet, allow your DSO to send you on an exotic incentive trip—all expenses paid.

Once you have developed this habit of financial goal-setting and tracking over the course of a year, you will have sufficient information to begin developing semi-annual goals, then annual goals—and you will have mastered financial control of your business! Start now, so it will become a natural part of doing business, as natural as selling and recruiting.

At this point in *The Direct Option*, you should have gained some insight on what it means to establish a customer base, provide service to this base, and establish relationships. With this, you may well achieve all you want to in direct selling, and, if so, this actually concludes this book. There is no need to go further.

If you are interested in advancement, there is one important path to increased earnings: learning to share your opportunity with others. Whether it is called sponsoring or recruiting, this may be the next step for you in your direct selling career. So read on!

Chapter 8

Marketing Your Career

Almost every direct-selling organization includes "recruiting" or "sponsoring" as part of its business. The term sponsoring in multilevel structures has the advantage of being less militaristic in tone than "recruiting." Personally, I have disliked both terms as long as I've been in direct selling. "To sponsor" someone sounds as though it involves some sort of country club membership. And "to recruit" can be a scary concept. It conjures images of armed services recruiting, complete with high-pressure techniques. Or it connotes the type of professional recruiting done by personnel departments, obviously requiring years of training, hands-on experience, and a lengthy interview process. It makes me think of the slick company executives who visit college campuses with their highly polished presentations.

Perhaps you have this same imagery. Perhaps you also have a strong fear of rejection by those you might wish to "recruit" or "sponsor." And yet attracting others to your career and sharing your opportunity is the essential building block of advancement in the direct-selling option. It is one of the most fun, most rewarding things you will ever do. It is also one of the most natural things you can do: you have been "recruiting" all your life—you just didn't call it that.

After a stint in door-to-door sales and creating a marketing communications department (neither of which required any direct recruiting skills), I was propelled in the early 1960s into a job assignment that heavily involved recruiting—pioneering Tupperware's European expansion. On my first flight across the North Atlantic, I spent six solid hours studying the "manual," so I would be prepared to do that most difficult thing—recruit. On arrival at London's Heathrow Airport, I threw the manual in a wastebasket, deciding then and there that I would simply tell others what I knew and liked about Tupperware and its career opportunity. In a very important way, I am still doing that today, only now, of course, it's about the Mary Kay opportunity and that of direct selling as a career.

One of the first things I learned was to not overstate the opportunity, even unintentionally. In London, at my first recruiting session, I showed what was called a "Jubilee film," a movie of a major Tupperware event showing hundreds of women receiving wonderful awards, even cars. I also talked about typical earnings in the United States, since I had no firsthand U.K. earnings examples. To my astonishment, I soon found that my prospects simply didn't believe me. They thought the Tupperware plan was some sort of scam. I quickly learned to tone down my exuberance for Tupperware and its potential. I wasn't lying, but what I was saying did not at all relate to the experience and expectations of my prospects in that market.

Steve Smith of CUTCO/Vector had a similar experience. "In order to be able to recruit, I had to overcome the fact that I was overly enthusiastic," Steve says. "I got too excited sometimes about the great opportunity. I also had to overcome the 'too good to be true' image."

Recruiting often requires that we understate the DSO opportunity. Today, when talking to new prospects, I never talk about the yearly earnings of $300,000 to $600,000 our top people make. I talk in terms of what the newcomers can reasonably expect to earn per hour in their community, based on what is actually sold and earned locally.

Sadly, unethical recruiting and deliberately exaggerated earnings claims have become far too prevalent in direct selling. To counter this, the Direct Selling Association has instituted a Recruiting Code of Ethics to complement its already strong Consumer Code of Ethics (see Appendix A).

I also learned not to prejudge who would make good salespeople, but rather to tell everyone I met about the wonderful opportunities in the direct option. We do like to recruit people like ourselves—but be leery of prejudging how others will do just because of their appearance, language skills, race, age, or the fact that they are unlike you. In fact, one of the great lessons I learned while working in dozens of countries is that people are far more alike than different, and it is the "alike" that binds us together in a free enterprise, direct option environment. The one truly useful determinant is whether or not you think the person will represent you and your company with honesty and integrity.

At its heart, recruiting is no more difficult than sharing with someone else what you like about what you are doing. In essence, recruiting is marketing your career.

Susan Estes of Tupperware offers some tips on recruiting: "As far as finding potential new recruits, I always go back to the person who has the largest order because she obviously likes Tupperware, and she will probably want to help me out. Then I go to the person who has the lowest order . . . because she probably needs money."

It's very possible that, at first, you will hesitate to contact people to sell your product because you feel you might bother or intrude upon them. But you will discover that many people want your product, and even those who don't aren't personally rejecting you. Exactly the same situation exists when you are marketing your career to others. You have something of tremendous value to offer. Your career has been worth a lot to you, financially and personally. Many prospective recruits may not be able to see this value, at least not immediately, but remember that their no's reflect a lack of understanding or perhaps a personal situation they feel they can't afford to change just now. They are not rejecting you or your DSO.

Although the image of the direct-selling option has changed dramatically in recent years, there are still some who don't understand or appreciate the importance and richness of this career. Tina Kraft of Home Interiors contrasts this attitude with her own: "Some people look down at direct selling as if it's not a real job. I guess I just had the confidence in it to realize that it's the American way—free enterprise. Now I can't imagine being in any other career!"

A few years ago, I was a guest at two Harvard Business School classes on DSO incentives taught by Professor Robert Simon to second-year graduate students. In the first class, there was universal agreement as to the motivating value of the incentives used, one of which was the famous Mary Kay pink Cadillac.

The second class was a different matter. A young man, very anti–direct selling, attacked the use of incentives and, indeed, the whole value of this option. His negative comments drew some of his classmates with him into criticism. I knew I would have an uphill battle to open their minds to the positive potential of direct selling—until I noticed that a woman I knew named Gloria Mayfield had slipped quietly into the back of the room. Gloria was the administrative assistant to the dean of the Business School, had a master's degree from Harvard University, and was a mother of two children.

While working at Harvard (not to mention keeping up with her duties as a mother), Gloria had managed to win the use of a pink Cadillac from Mary Kay Cosmetics for exceptional unit sales performance. I knew she planned to resign her Harvard position that same week to put 100 percent of her time into her Mary Kay business. Gloria exemplified another benefit of direct sales, too, for as an African American, she demonstrated the opportunities for advancement available to minority groups.

My classroom strategy now became evident. I simply introduced Gloria, and she explained how she enjoyed a life-style she was only able to dream of before—one with flexibility, financial independence, and career fulfillment. Gloria told the class, "At Mary Kay you know you are good; the proof is in the prizes—such as my pink Cadillac—the recognition you receive from the company, and in your financial success."

By the time Gloria finished, my classroom antagonist had almost disappeared from sight behind his desk, in embarrassment. I merely had to smile, thank Gloria, and rest my case.

James Julian, an Amway distributor, states: "The only thing that hangs people up on the business is their lack of knowledge. I love it when people who have nothing, *status* themselves out of the business—especially without even seeing the plan!"

"I have to admit that I was a little uncomfortable with talking about career opportunity," says Kellie Woods with Mary Kay Cosmetics. "I think it was because I wasn't sure what my goals were. It was a little scary. Then one evening at a class, the hostess came up to me afterwards and said, 'You know, I should quit my job and do what you do.' What a break!" Kellie's experience is typical of many first-time recruiters. Our research, conducted year after year for the past twenty years, shows that roughly 50 percent of new direct salespeople have asked to join their DSOs.

Some college graduates or professionals hesitate to enter direct selling because they believe they will somehow lose the status associated with their college degree. In fact, in today's business environment, there are millions of degreed Americans performing menial tasks because a piece of sheepskin does not guarantee a job.

Resources

In marketing your career, you must realize that potential recruits are everywhere. Paula Parks of Princess House believes direct selling has a lot to offer. "I began recruiting because I knew that direct selling could be good for others," she says. "I recruit because of a person's need, not because of my need."

There are many resources, in addition to your customer base, which is built as you develop your retail business.

Some of the resources you can tap include:

- ♦ **Relatives:** Your mother, sisters, brothers, sons, daughters, and cousins all will enjoy learning more about what you do.
- ♦ **Referrals:** Ask for and follow up on referrals from your customers and friends. These can be great leads. Many direct sellers have learned to offer a thoughtful gift for such referrals.

♦ **Businesswomen and men:** These individuals are perhaps already successful, and, chances are, they will also become successful in your career. Don't be intimidated by their positions. Remember, you are doing them a great favor. Many have reached a ceiling in their current jobs and are seeking a way out and up in their lives. Your career offers that to any ambitious, persistent person.

♦ **Homemakers:** What better career opportunity for a mother with young children where she can determine her own hours and income?

♦ **Women active in community affairs:** These women are proven achievers and love to keep busy, so offer them the opportunity to own their own business.

♦ **Church friends:** Often wonderful prospects, they will appreciate the "go-give" philosophy of your DSO. Frequently, there are members of your church who need financial help, perhaps because of some tragedy in their lives. You should also make your career opportunity known to your pastor.

♦ **College students:** Almost every DSO is a good source of supplementary income for college students. Some opportunities such as those offered by CUTCO/Vector and Southwestern are tailored specifically to college-age persons.

♦ **Mature and retired individuals:** Often such persons have the time, motivation, and financial need to appreciate a new career in direct selling. As *I've* gotten older, I've learned that older persons—can be simply more interesting. These "more interesting" Americans often make outstanding direct salespeople, and many advance rapidly in their new careers because they have gained insights into people and how to motivate them. Many have hard-earned leadership skills which they can multiply in value in the right DSO.

♦ **Handicapped persons:** Our national association, the DSA, publishes statistics that show the direct option is ideal for those with handicaps. I have known of blind people becoming very successful in DSOs, and of those with speech and/or hearing handicaps selling through highly visual demonstrations. Lack of mobility can impede growth in some DSOs, but often handicapped individuals can be helped in their selling situations by family members. Of course, much retail selling and recruiting can be done by phone, an ideal situation for many handicapped persons.

Marian Kestler, a Mary Kay beauty consultant, encountered problems in pursuing other careers due to her physical handicap, but found she could be successful in direct selling. "I have a teaching degree but couldn't get hired due to my handicap," Marian says. "I had been using Mary Kay products for a long time, and the next thing I knew, I was selling them. This is the first company in a long time that has really given me a chance to show how well I can do. My handicap hasn't been a problem.

♦ **Minority groups:** Many DSOs provide sales aids and literature in languages other than English. Kitchen Fair, Mary Kay, and Tupperware, for example, have many materials translated into Spanish. The direct-selling option can be a very rich one for new immigrants, as they earn while they learn and make new friends in America. They often become very adept at recruiting within their ethnic group. Even within groups with language barriers, such as Asian Americans, recruiting growth can be very rapid. Leaders with bilingual skills can open the door of opportunity for their networks.

♦ **The under-educated:** So much of a good DSO's teaching style relies on in-person training that an individual who has not achieved academically can often start anew. Direct selling first teaches self-confidence, and that leads to self-sufficiency. If basic literacy is mastered so order forms and other necessary paperwork can be completed, the under-educated can carve out new careers. Many use the extra income and flex-time to improve their basic academic skills and so do "double duty" with their direct option, emerging as educated, productive members of society—sometimes wealthy as well!

Use Your Intuition

Maria Arapakis, sensitive author of *Softpower*, claims that everyone has an intuitive guidance system, but not everyone uses it. "Despite our legendary 'woman's instinct' and female 'sixth sense,' many of us have lost touch with (and lost trust in) our intuitive powers," she says. "Women are not the only ones out of touch with intuition. In contemporary Western societies, intuition is a pathetically under-utilized force for males and females alike."

Your intuition, when permitted to function, can allow you to see beyond today and beyond the outward appearance of your prospective recruit. A word of caution—don't be an amateur psychologist. What I'm suggesting is simply to learn to be aware of others, their personalities, and their needs so you can direct your message to what they most want to hear and accept. Never let your own ego block your reading of someone else's. You can't be an effective recruiter if you allow your ego to always be in the forefront.

Personality Types

There are many lists of "personality types" floating around in the selling industry, most of which are confusing and even misleading if you are trying to pigeonhole a person into a "type." At their root, all such systems really revolve around different forms of personality types. Let's focus on just four such ego expressions, more to prepare you for different responses than to lead you to "force fit" a "type" to an approach. Most people switch from type to type anyway, so don't look for clear distinctions—just indicators or clues to cue your responses.

Dominant Personality
- Will ask brief questions
- May interrupt to get you to the point
- Is always in a hurry
- Looks at her or his watch often
- Is restless
- Usually wants a career that can advance to management rapidly
- Makes quick decisions
- Loves respect and prominence

Suggested approach: Show this prospect a lot of facts and figures. Carefully point out the career opportunities at each stage and how each step can be made in the shortest possible time.

Influential Personality
- Talks a lot
- Asks many questions
- Goes into great detail if you ask a question
- Is enthusiastic
- Is fun-loving
- Is friendly
- Loves recognition

Suggested approach: Invite this person to one of your unit meetings, and introduce with great fanfare. Point out winners in your DSO's publications, as well as the grand way in which they are recognized.

Steady Personality

- ◆ Loves status quo
- ◆ Family-oriented (will tell you all about them)
- ◆ Is reserved but friendly
- ◆ Will do anything to help
- ◆ Likes to be part of the group
- ◆ Lovable
- ◆ Slow to make a decision, but loyal to that decision once it's made.

Suggested approach: Invite this person to a meeting of your DSO, or one of your own unit, and point out the camaraderie to be found there. Many DSOs have philosophies that fit this individual perfectly, such as Mary Kay's "God first, family second and career third." Such priorities help this level-headed prospect decide to join your plan.

Compliant Personality

- ◆ Loves details
- ◆ Asks questions
- ◆ Wants all the literature you can give her or him
- ◆ Critical, analytical, but gets the job done
- ◆ A perfectionist
- ◆ Tends to criticize herself or himself

Suggested approach: Build the individual's self-esteem, and you'll have a winner. Be sure to stress the training you and your DSO provide. Schedule training immediately, before she or he loses confidence.

Regardless of the personality type you perceive, it's vital that you avoid confrontation. Don't challenge—empathize. Always keep the prospect's needs in mind. James Julian of Amway states, "The most rewarding thing to me about sponsoring is to see someone who really needs the money—a family that really needs the money, a guy who's really deserving—accept the opportunity."

The Recruiting Process

One of the most fundamental barriers in recruiting is complacency. "The only minus of a direct selling position is getting people to believe in themselves again," James Julian says. "People are too comfortable, and they're afraid to step outside their comfort zones."

To overcome any barrier, it's productive to think of recruiting in seven stages.

Stage 1—Introduction to the Product

Your new customer's view of what you do is vitally important to the success of recruiting her. Your sales presentation should be professional, yet relaxed; thorough, yet brief; educational, yet fun.

Margarita Garcia of Kitchen Fair is a good example of a former customer turned direct seller. "I tried the product for about eight months," Margarita says. "After I found out I liked the product, I decided to sell it. I didn't want to go into the business without using the product myself. That was really important to me."

Stage 2—Satisfaction with the Product

The way in which you follow through to achieve total customer satisfaction is often critical to recruiting success, because you will not only be assuring satisfaction with the product, you'll be assuring satisfaction with *you.* When you have achieved rapport through product performance and personal service, you might try calling the prospect and using this approach, time honored with top DSOs: "I just haven't been able to get you off my mind. You really seem to love the product, and I can't help thinking that you would be great doing what I do. I would love to spend about thirty minutes with you at your convenience to see if my DSO is something you would be interested in either now or in the future. Which would be better for you, the first part of the week or the last?"

This approach could backfire if used by a male recruiter to a female prospect. In fact, the first time I heard it taught, it was by an attractive male executive at Tupperware to a large audience of female dealers, who had a large laugh at the executive's expense when he said the words, "I just haven't been able to get you off my mind!"

Beth Corson, an Amway distributor, asks prospects for a portion of their time to show them "the picture." Beth said, "I tell potential recruits if they were going to look at or buy a beautiful Van Gogh painting, and I only showed them the right-hand corner, they probably would not go for it. But if I showed them the entire painting, that would make the difference. That's the way I want to explain the business to them. They have to see the entire picture. So I've never asked anyone to 'join me in the business.' I just ask them to 'look at the picture.'"

Stage 3—Curiosity about the Company

This step may occur along with step one or two or during a product delivery. You can set this up by leaving behind literature about your DSO or perhaps a video that markets your career. Remember, marketing your career is a numbers game, and wide distribution of literature and other recruiting aids usually pays off in at least creating curiosity about your DSO. If you cannot create curiosity, always be sure to ask for referrals. Follow up with referrals immediately. Here is a suggested approach:

> This is Joan Smith with Company X. Do you have a minute?
>
> Yesterday I spoke with a friend of yours, Sally Jones, who happens to be a good customer of mine. I mentioned to her that I am looking for a few key people who would be good at doing what I do. I asked who she knew who had a good rapport with people, and you were the first person she mentioned. Based on that recommendation, I felt compelled to call you. Could you use some extra income if you found something you would enjoy doing?
>
> Because your recommendation comes so highly, I'd really like an opportunity to meet with you and talk about my DSO in more detail—with no obligation, of course.
>
> Tell me, is there any reason why we couldn't get together for thirty minutes or so just to see if my DSO is something you could be interested in, either now or in the future? Which would be the best time—the first part of the week or the last?

In building your retail sales, you will have undoubtedly developed quite a list of customers. If you have not asked all of these customers for referrals, you may be missing out on the best source of recruits. Customers make excellent sources for recruiting prospects, because they have been through stages one and two already. If you have overlooked this source of recruits, you may wish to give them a call, following this approach:

> This is Joan Smith. You know, I've been with my DSO for some time now and just realized that I have done you an injustice by never really telling you in detail what I do. I say injustice because I have a special gift for all my customers who

recommend someone to me who is accepted by my DSO and becomes active. You certainly are the kind of person I look for, and even though I know you might not be interested right now, if I could give you more details, then perhaps you could refer me to someone who is. Would you consider being one of my guests at my next DSO meeting?

Stage 4—Knowledge about the Company

The important thing here is to be sure the prospective recruit receives reliable, thorough information about your DSO. Take her or him to DSO functions, and use your DSO's recommended recruiting interview.

Stage 5—Desire to Fill a Personal Need through Your DSO

Although a prospective recruit may have a real need in her life, your efforts can at first fall on deaf ears unless she truly wants to make a change.

Sue Kirkpatrick of Mary Kay says: "There are always going to be unhappy people; it's up to them whether they decide to do anything about it or not. You have to be comfortable with the fact that you're not going to recruit everybody. You can only help someone who wants to be helped."

It is a real challenge to create a desire in people to make something of their lives. Desire comes from within, and without it, your good intentions can be wasted. This is a stage for prospective recruits that can change at any time. If dealt with fairly and with respect, such a prospect can be recontacted at a later date if she feels she is not ready for the opportunity now.

However, sometimes a potential recruit may really be interested in the opportunity but doesn't feel she has the qualifications. As in selling, a response that seems negative is often a request for more information. In Chapter 5, we detailed a seven-step program to help overcome objections, and these same steps apply to recruiting. In brief, they are:

1. Be silent/Listen
2. Acknowledge the objection
3. Empathize with the objection or problem
4. Answer the objection
5. Sell the benefits
6. Offer a choice
7. Know when to stop selling

Don't give up because someone says no the first time. Recognize that someone might be saying, "This opportunity is not right for me at this moment."

Here are some of the most common "excuses" and suggested responses:

> *Excuse:* "I could never sell."
>
> *Response:* "I know just how you feel. I felt the same way, but one of the first things I found in my DSO was that we don't sell—we teach! You know, we are constantly sharing new discoveries with our friends. It certainly makes sense not only to share the benefits of an excellent product and program, but also to get paid for it. People love to buy, but they don't like being sold. Are you willing to learn? If you are, I can teach you."
>
> *Excuse:* "I'm too busy."
>
> *Response:* "I'm a busy person, too. That's why I chose you. You see, busy people provide the best service. They are usually the most organized."
>
> *Excuse:* "I have to ask my husband."
>
> *Response:* "I know just how you feel. I felt the same way when my recruiter talked to me about this career. I went home and talked to my husband about it. I found that I kept wanting him to make the decision. He kept saying, 'It's entirely up to you; you are the one who'll be doing it.' Would your husband make your decision or would he encourage you to make your own?"
>
> *Excuse:* "I'm already working at a career I enjoy."
>
> *Response:* "Great! Could you use some extra money? How do you know you won't like this as well? You owe it to yourself to at least hear all the facts. If you're looking for income security, you can make additional income on a part-time basis and keep your job until you feel comfortable and established in your new career. That's one of the great things about this DSO—you are independent and can set your own hours."
>
> *Excuse:* "I have an eight-to-five job which I must keep."
>
> *Response:* "This opportunity allows you to make a choice between a job or a career. You can work as much or as little as you wish. And how many eight-to-five jobs reward you with recognition, prizes, and virtually unlimited earning potential? Are you being paid what you're worth or what someone else

thinks your job is worth? With our DSO, you can be your own boss. You can work as much or as little as you want, and you can arrange your own schedule. Everyone has the same opportunity; you are only limited by your goals and dreams." (In Mary Kay, seven out of ten independent beauty consultants are also employed, either full-or part-time.)

Excuse: "I don't have the time."

Response: "I know how you feel. I felt the same way, but I found that once I started writing down what I did, I had plenty of time left for my career. Let's take a 'weekly plan sheet' and mark down everything you have planned for next week. See how much extra time you have? That's one of the great advantages to a career in this DSO—you work your own hours.

"I have personally completed hundreds of such weekly plan sheets, and it is extremely rare that a person, even when pressed to list errands, going out to dinner with friends, or church activities, doesn't have some time left for career activities."

Excuse: "I'm too shy."

Response: "I understand how you feel. I felt the same way, but I found that once I had completed my initial training, I was feeling more confident. You know, being in a DSO is one of the best self-improvement courses available today."

Excuse: "I know someone who was with your DSO and quit."

Response: "Do you judge yourself by other people's successes or failures? There are many reasons why a career in my DSO may not have been right for your friend. But I've found what may not suit one person may be perfect for another. And I know you'd be great! Are you willing to let yourself be successful?"

Excuse: "I'm not a self starter. I need a structured environment to function."

Response: "I know how you feel. I felt the same way, but I found that even in an office job, I was always trying to make those structured hours fit my schedule. And you know, that's one of the things I like most about my career. Now if I need to go to the doctor or run an errand, I don't have to worry about my boss getting angry.

"But you know, you can develop your own structure. I needed to myself. Just work out your own weekly plan each and every week to include your business activities during a normal business day. I'll bet you will like being your own boss and setting your own hours, rather than having someone else tell you when you have to work! Don't you agree?"

Excuse: "I really don't know anyone."

Response: "That's no problem. This career will give you an opportunity to meet so many people. All you need to know is one person; that's how it starts. One person tells another, and so on. I'll tell you what, let's try to list those people you do know."

Excuse: "I don't want to obligate my friends."

Response: "I know how you feel. I felt the same way, but I found that once they tried the product, they thanked me for sharing it with them."

It's important to be sincere in responding to your prospect's questions so you gain her trust. You will want to learn to ask questions which draw her or him out, and then listen *actively*. You don't want to overwhelm your prospect with too much information.

Julie Sears of Home Interiors & Gifts emphasizes the importance of asking potential customers and recruits a lot of questions. "I ask people about themselves," she says. "I focus on *them*. I find out what their needs are. I have made it my business to learn about people and what makes them tick. I try to understand where they're coming from."

Active listening requires a real effort to pay attention to not only the spoken word, but the unspoken as well. Eye contact, body language, and expressions all "speak" loudly as to the person's real level of interest—or lack of it.

Sherry Suib Cohen, author of the best-seller *Tender Power*, says, "Communicate, don't explicate." Cohen describes real listening as follows:

It's not selective hearing, paying attention to just what's nice and not threatening.

It's not finishing other people's sentences.

It's not figuring out your answers before you hear the other person's entire comment.

It's not thinking you have to solve the other person's problems; sometimes people just want an audience, not a panacea.

Cohen goes on to stress that when it is your turn to talk, don't lecture, but rather disclose. That's why I've often suggested you use the "feel, felt, found" method, but use it sincerely. You must have really felt those same emotions when you were learning to sell and recruit.

Stage 6—Excitement about the Opportunity

This step really speaks for itself. You must display this excitement, and when your prospect does, you are very likely to receive a yes to your invitation to join your DSO.

Stage 7—Decision with Motivation to Do It Now

You must ultimately "close" by asking your prospective recruit to make a decision after you've taken her through the previous six stages. This process may have taken thirty minutes or a year. Attracting others to your career will come automatically to you, but it doesn't happen automatically. You must continually be asking and taking many people through the seven stages. Use your selling abilities where you can, but be sure to use your patience and acceptance of their desires where you can't.

Marketing your career to others is the only basis on which you can build to the higher levels of income in direct selling. It will ultimately be successful only if your marketing efforts have been truthful, sincere, and have placed the other person's interests, desires, and needs first. When done in this spirit, it will provide you with far more than money alone. I know that I really have helped others become self-sufficient and have thus earned "the paycheck of the heart." That is one of the greatest joys available to direct sellers.

Mary Kay Consultant Judy Hilleary expresses it this way, "Recruiting is so rewarding. To be able to offer someone an opportunity to grow and to develop her personality as well as upgrade her quality of life is very satisfying."

Once you have marketed your career to a number of others, you must begin to develop your leadership skills. The speed of the leader is the speed of the pack. But don't shy away now. You are very close to incredible success. In direct selling, *leadership can be learned.*

Chapter 9

You *Can* Lead

Yes, you can lead! But the odds are you don't see yourself as a leader. You may think of popular business heroes such as Jack Welch of GE, Lee Iacocca of Chrysler, the late Sam Walton of Wal-Mart, Victor Kiam II of Remington Products, Inc. (Remington Shavers and Lady Remington), or Mary Kay Ash of Mary Kay Cosmetics and think, "I could never be such a charismatic, powerful, popular, awe-inspiring leader."

Hogwash! If you have developed a unit of direct sellers, you are already a leader of some substance and can (from this moment on) deliberately enhance your leadership skills. One of the greatest things about direct selling is that it is one of the best careers in which to develop leadership skills. The ethic of leadership is encouraged daily, even hourly, in DSOs, especially those composed of independent contractors. But it's not just an ethic of "business leadership," it's an ethic of life as well.

Cheryl Lightle, president of Creative Memories, puts it this way: "In our industry, we deal with many people who have not realized their potential or have not had an avenue for it to develop. Traditional leadership requires what I believe to be a lot of unnecessary expenditure of energy—like pulling a rock uphill. Direct sellers create an environment in which people can develop their own leadership skills. When this happens, the results can be dynamic; and everyone involved is a winner."

Success Can't Be Managed

You cannot *manage* your way to success. In fact, to think of yourself as a "business executive" or a "manager" is the surest way I know of to be a failure in direct selling.

At Mary Kay Cosmetics, we call it "executive-itis." For years, until we understood this phenomenon, we used to conduct classes for what we call "Directors-In-Qualification (DIQs)" focusing on business management skills. These week-long events tended to produce individuals who, from that moment on, thought of themselves only as managers or as people who ran their own company and were president, CFO, and sales manager—all in one. It's no wonder we had so many people "graduating" from this session thinking of themselves as executives. They began working from behind a desk and immediately quit doing the things that had made them leaders in the first place—personal selling, recruiting, and leading by example. The *real* leaders in our field sales organization kept telling us we were sidetracking leadership development, and we were. Needless to say, we've now corrected the program and today rely far more heavily on the inspiration—the "I" stories—of leaders from the field, rather than advice from managers from the home office.

Warren Bennis, author of *Why Leaders Can't Lead,* contends, "The great leaders are gone and with them our dreams."Bennis stakes his entire faith on the emergence of an awesome, powerful leader, such as his example, Martin Luther King, Jr.—surely a great leader and one of my heroes, whom I met during the Civil Rights movement of the 1960s. "Deep in all of us there is still and always will be a need to believe, and one day a leader will appear who will express that need and fulfill it," Bennis writes. I could not disagree with him more. He has missed the essence of leadership and, in fact, completely missed why the United States has provided so much *real* leadership over the past 200 years. Despite the criticism of the world's press (including our own) concerning our nation's current stature, I believe that we still know more about creating leadership than any nation on earth. We may not have a single, awesome leader, but we do have tens of thousands of confident individuals who can lead our nation back to greatness. Many of these leaders will get their start in a DSO.

Unfortunately, Bennis is not alone in longing for the great leader. In many parts of the world, especially Europe, it is continuously stated that leaders are "born, not made." Although the arrogant robber barons of the nineteenth century, such as Rockefeller, Morgan, and Carnegie, considered themselves leaders, they were merely men who controlled by greed, intimidation, fear, and raw power. There are many people today who believe this is what leadership is all about. In the great greed wars of the 1980s, new-age robber barons emerged from their Wall Street "sewers" to conduct endless raids, takeovers, and leveraged buyouts—driven by avarice and an unshakable belief in their idiosyncratic view of what was right. They destroyed companies and people because there were few real leaders to oppose them.

A New Model for Leadership

Professor John Kotter of Harvard Business School believes our thinking is so ingrained in the traditional leader-follower model, that many people have difficulty imagining even two leaders in any situation. "Yet for the same reason that it is possible to have four leadership roles in one case, it is possible to have 40 or 400," he says.

One of the examples that Kotter uses is that of the Mary Kay independent field sales organization. "Without a lot of people like this, Mary Kay could not exist," he writes in *A Force for Change*. "These are 'ordinary women' who work part time as beauty consultants and try to build up their own direct-selling organizations. It is no small chore to attract people, train them, help them set realistic goals and motivate them. Without leadership, this does not happen. Some of these individuals probably think this task is something that pertains only to Mary Kay herself, not to them. But what they provide is most certainly leadership, and it is collectively of enormous importance."

In my experience, leadership formation within the independent contractor ranks of DSOs is commonplace. Savvy DSO executives have long ago given up a pretense of "leading" their field sales organizations. Some have acknowledged a "dual leadership" structure with sales leadership readily conceded to independent entrepreneurs.

One of the great benefits of direct selling is the opportunity for self-actualization, self-development, self-esteem, self-confidence, and, most important, self-sufficiency. Achieving these goals is the best preparation for leadership, because you are ready to help others become self-sufficient.

"It is your experiences and how you learn to adapt and adjust to your experiences," states Ronda Ulrich, Mary Kay national sales director, "that helps you become a leader. I truly believe that leadership development is ultimately self-development. The biggest thing that helps someone aspiring to be a leader is that they want to grow in their people skills. They are always in a self-development mode. Effective leaders are constantly learning—*constantly*."

Another of Mary Kay's national sales directors, Judie McCoy, adds: "To really develop leadership qualities in other people, you need to recognize their talents and encourage them to become the best they can become. I believe that in corporate America, molding people is more important than developing people. My unit is a potpourri of personalities from all different walks of life, and I encourage people to retain their individuality. My leadership style is to encourage independence in people. I enjoy watching people take off and do their thing, and I just love the fact that I can sit back and applaud them and say, 'Isn't it great that she is different from me in style, yet look what she has accomplished.' Then we can come together in our relationship at this level and build out of mutual respect; not because we are alike, but because we are respectful of each other as individuals.

The bookstores, and perhaps your shelves at home, are awash with the new literature of leadership. What has fascinated me over the past three decades has been the ever-changing definition of leadership in business and political thinking and the constant, unchanging pattern of leadership within the independent sales forces of direct-selling organizations.

The attempt to define, describe, and codify what leadership is has defied the best philosophers and thinkers the world has produced. It was Max Weber, the German sociologist, who applied the word *charisma* to anyone with some "extraordinary personal quality, actual or alleged." Nicole Woolsey Biggart says in *Charismatic Capitalism* that "DSOs are best understood as charismatic forms of organizations, and the practices and arrangements distinctive to the industry flow from that."

There is some historical merit to Biggart's observation of the power of charisma within DSOs, for many were founded by charismatic people such as Rich DeVos, Jay Van Andel, Art Williams, Forrest Shaklee, Mary Crowley, and Mary Kay Ash. But charisma is not a prime requisite for leadership, and many DSOs are proving that today. Kotter does not believe, nor do I, nor does Mary Kay Ash, that charisma is the key to leadership at all. He defines four attributes of leadership: intelligence, drive, mental health, and integrity.

In *A Force for Change*, Kotter uses Mary Kay as an example. "Ask people why Mary Kay is such a good leader, and they often refer to her charisma. Ask them why they think she is charismatic, and they refer to the way she speaks to groups of people and how they respond to her; that is, they point to her naturally charismatic speaking style—something she was certainly born with. But ask Mary Kay about this, and her response emphasizes something different. 'People are often amazed at how I can talk about the firm so naturally and spontaneously without any notes,' she says. 'What they don't realize is that it has taken me years to get to the point where I can do this as well as I do. Oh, I'm sure I have some natural ability, but that's only one part of it.'"

If you think you can never, ever become a leader because you lack charisma, think again. Focus on the very simple leadership traits Kotter identifies. Not even all of these have to be present in abundance. You don't have to be a Nobel Prize winner to be intelligent. And you are certainly considered mentally healthy even if your life and relationships aren't perfect. However, drive and integrity are the two leadership traits that cannot be compromised. The common denominator of all leaders of morally sound endeavors is integrity; all possess it. (It's possible to "lead" in an evil sense, as Hitler did, without a shred of integrity, but this form of "leadership" is entirely different, most often ego-driven demagoguery.) Finally, although you can be a minor-league leader with only average drive, reaching the major leagues requires a lot of drive, determination, and persistence.

"To succeed in direct selling you have to be willing to put in the hours—long hours," says Kevin Reitmeier of Kirby. "That's what it takes—unless a stroke of luck comes your way or you win the lottery. It's going to take a lot of hard work, dedication and commitment to get where you want to go. There's no question about it. It *does* take a lot of energy."

Harvard's Abraham Zaleznik, commenting upon leadership development for the World Economic Forum in Davos, Switzerland, cited the pragmatic philosopher William James, who distinguished between "once-born and twice-born personalities." He viewed the once-born person as being in harmony with his or her environment, basically resistant to change. This person gains much self-esteem from a sense of belonging to a community that nurtures and shelters. But the twice-born person, James believed, has encountered disappointment. This individual, therefore, becomes a more objective thinker and becomes detached from the perspective of the community. This person turns inward, searching for identity. Finally, this individual begins to understand her talent and begins to use and cultivate it. This person struggles to realize what is in her heart. This combination of drive and vision makes her a great candidate for leadership.

Mary Kay top director Kathy Z. Rasmussen agrees with this assessment of how top leaders may develop. "At my first top Director event in 1981, I really wanted to find out what the common ground was of leaders in my DSO. After several days of watching and studying and listening one on one, the only thing I could identify was that most of these women had overcome adversity, especially in their personal lives."

It is Rasmussen's theory that overcoming adversity helped these leaders handle rejection. "That seemed to be the common ground," she says. "They were all sizes, shapes, ages, and nationalities; but they were people who, when the going got tough, they got going. They were able to persevere."

Rasmussen also sounds a warning for those electing to move into leadership in direct selling. "Something that is rarely addressed in DSOs is the cycles that most businesses have. . . . If you think your company, be it a small business or a large organization, is always going to be up, then you are in for a rude awakening. Every organization is going to have cycles—good and bad times. But the good thing about bad times—it's always going to get better if you hang in there!"

Ronda Ulrich adds that effective leaders really don't think much about failure. "They're always in a learning mode vs. a failure mode. Their vision is so focused, so totally focused, that it becomes a passion."

But how does one become passionate enough for leadership? Ronda has an answer, "Do the things that you don't feel like doing. When you start acting upon the things that you know you should be doing with determination and persistence, you're going to have the passion!" Ronda believes passion can be deliberately acquired, and I agree with her.

Beyond Kotter's basic traits, and Rasmussen's thoughts on having to overcome adversity, the leadership characteristic mentioned most often is flexibility. It's axiomatic that, in direct selling, you must learn to adapt—to "go with the flow." Rasmussen puts it this way: "Flexibility is the key to leadership and to developing other leaders. You create an organization that allows for people within your DSO to be different from one another, as long as they are moral and ethical."

Interestingly, however, none of us in DSOs have ever really been able to pre-identify leadership potential among ourselves. For instance, when asked if she could pick leaders out because they were intelligent, Rasmussen quickly responds, "Don't you wish you could; you could give everyone an IQ test and off you'd go. But leadership has little to do with native intelligence or even developed ability. It really has to do with your willingness to *fail* forward to success—to pick yourself up every time."

Leadership Requirements

1. Have a Vision of Your Future

You have to have a vision for where your business is going. As Kathy Rasmussen says, "If your vision is only for tomorrow, then you are going to do things differently than if your vision is 'Where do I want to be three or twenty years from now?' You have to be really careful that things you do today don't hold you back from your long-term goal. I think that when people don't grow in a DSO, it's because they don't have a long-range vision."

For the past thirty years, I have tried to have a personal five-year plan. In truth, I've now had about eight five-year "vision statements," which is a bit more than the years I've been in this business. Visions, once converted into actual strategies for life or business, need to have reality checkpoints built in. But in becoming a leader, the first essential step is to create that vision, then write it down for all to see.

Once the vision is agreed upon and written down, keep it constantly in mind. When asked what separates the top performers in Mary Kay from the others, National Sales Director Nan Stroud responds: "We never yo-

yoed. We never went away and came back. No matter what was going on in our lives, we never yo-yoed. We were driven by a passion and a vision."

As well as having your personal vision statement, you will share in that of your DSO. According to a 1991 survey, 98 percent of Mary Kay directors and 85 percent of consultants surveyed were aware of the company's vision statement.

2. Use the Butterfly Principle

In large organizations, the next leadership step is aligning people to your vision. In a DSO, this process is much more successful if you learn to help others align themselves to *their* vision. This then establishes a host of allies who will ultimately help you achieve *your* vision.

The important thing to always keep in mind is that most DSOs are composed of independent contractors, so "alignment" must always be viewed from the perspective of the individual. Mary Kay National Sales Director Carolyn Ward says, "An acorn cannot grow in the shadow of an oak. It's important to be an oak, but you have to know when to pull the branches in."

And National Sales Director Maxine Sandvig adds, "To be effective, a leader must successfully influence the way people influence themselves. The test of a leader is not what she can do, but what her people can do without her."

Lauren Debonis of Discovery Toys agrees: "It's so easy to get into mother management instead of mentor management. You give people what they need, but it has to come from within them to go off and want to do it and be able to do it. You can only do so much. And if you think you can do it for them, you're kidding yourself." It often comes down to quashing negativity and providing encouragement. A sales leader I know has a giant plastic fly, called the "But Fly," that sits on the shoulder of anyone in her meetings who uses the word "but" as an excuse for why she hasn't done something. The "but" offender wears this reminder until another person "wins" it.

A person in the pastures of South Texas in the fall may see a flight of Monarch butterflies enter a field from the north. The colorful cloud will move purposefully through the field toward the south. But as hundreds or thousands of butterflies cross by the observer, she may note that individual butterflies are flying in all different directions—up, down, east, west, even north (which is backwards). This totally random movement within the swarm of butterflies symbolizes for me the freedom of action of independent entrepreneurs. When the flight has moved on, the observer will note that all the butterflies have moved south, through the field, and on to a remote place they've never seen in the rain forests of Mexico.

Some powerful Leader is at work here, with a vision for the butterflies, aligning them and communicating with them, urging them to continue on to that precise point—the only point on earth that will preserve their species. Their Leader cares about them.

In the process of gaining allies, of helping others establish visions that align somewhat with your own, the element of caring must always be present. In your own DSO, you must spend much time communicating your sincere concern for the members of your "team" or "unit" and help them learn to align others to their own dreams. "The higher the leader climbs, the more a philosophy of teaching others to lead themselves is important," Maxine Sandvig points out. "As Kahlil Gibran says in *The Prophet*, 'The teacher does not bid you enter the house of his wisdom, but rather leads you to the threshold of your own mind.' It's akin to watching the successes of your children more closely than your own."

3. Be Ethical

Leaders must build trust through a strong sense of moral commitment and a strong sense of values. "Under-promise and overdeliver," as automobile dealer Carl Sewell says, applies to people commitments as well as to product claims.

Ethical business conduct, even within a small organization, may not be easy and can be costly. But I believe it is good business. Furthermore, I believe ethical conduct can be measured. CPAs have given us ways to measure goodwill for the balance sheet, but loyalty is an important measurable asset also. Loyalty to and from the sales organization as well as from customers is probably the greatest asset a DSO can have. Loyalty and trust in a DSO are built on everyday ethical conduct, such as handling customer complaints, because independent entrepreneurs are not tied to the organization by a paycheck or in any of the usual ways.

I believe in the fundamental sense of fairness that Americans have pretty consistently exhibited over the years. From such a base, it is possible for ethics to be learned. Here are a few little bits from my personal ethical mosaic, which I've built, piece by piece, from what I've learned throughout my life and career:

Even on minor daily problems, quickly take responsibility —take the high ground. Don't let them fester. Festering problems develop into bad situations, whereas quick reactions can save the day and maybe even minimize the cost of your decision.

Pay attention to these details. Use these little things to establish an ethical mosaic of your own.

If you can't change a potentially unethical situation, *get out of it*. If you operate from an ethical base, don't change when others lack ethics.

Never knock the competition. We stress this "rule" for our employees and sales force, and it works. Every "knock" is a boost for the other fellow.

It isn't enough to do the legal thing. Do the right thing. It feels good, your staff can sleep at night, and so can you. It pays, too—everyone has more energy for the real job. Don't take ethics for granted. Read, attend seminars, talk to your friends, your bosses, and your peers about ethical issues.

Finally, never forget that it isn't enough to have a code of ethics; you also need the competence and the guts to follow it. It's what I've come to think of as caring competence.

All of the companies discussed in *The Direct Option*, as members of the DSA, are committed to supporting the Association's Code of Ethics. (See Appendix A.) The Code recognized the obligations and moral and legal responsibilities of association members to consumers and set forth the basic fair and ethical principles and practices to which DSA companies pledge their allegiance. In 1992, the Code was enlarged to include provisions that made it apply to "consumers of the industry's opportunity," thus encompassing ethical conduct in recruiting practices.

4. Create Self-Motivation

Constantly motivating and inspiring your sales organization is the sine qua non of success in a DSO. But it's far more than "hoopla," as it's been called. In truth, Tupperware's Jubilees, Shaklee's Leadership Conventions, and Mary Kay's Seminars are spectacular events, and there are many like them in direct selling. Such meetings are one of the things for which the industry is famous.

But these meetings are more than just fanfare, as Barb Lehman of Watkins points out: "It's really nice to get up on that stage. And I think the nicest thing about it is that all of your peers respect you, because they know how you got there. It's not like being born rich. Nobody gets there who doesn't work hard—that's just the type of business this is. And it's really nice. It's something that you're proud of when you get there.

. . . I think everybody needs a little bit of that."

But, in fact, the job of motivation goes on year-round, with special emphasis placed on helping others become self-motivated. This is the real challenge of leadership—to somehow help others turn that mental switch "on" and acquire the motivation to succeed. Some of the most important ways this happens in a DSO are through setting examples and presenting personal testimonials (often called "I" stories). To me, these "I" stories are one of the most personally motivating parts of my job and invariably "recharge my batteries." It really doesn't take a huge success story, either, for success is relative.

Joel Broadbent of the Southwestern Company shares: "I believe in the old saying that you become like the people you associate with and the books you read. I try to influence myself by being with people who have done what I have done and who are going where I want to go. I also try to read as many motivational books as possible to keep my positive frame of mind."

Motivation doesn't require the public speaking skills of a tremendously charismatic individual. Most great leaders motivate with a constant stream of little things—notes, a word of recognition at the right moment, or a helping hand for someone in trouble or discouraged.

"I motivate my recruits by giving them good training and positive strokes, picking them up when they are down and offering new ideas to them," says Shirley Eismann of Tupperware. "Another very important thing I do with my recruits is walk them through the challenges they have so that small problems don't become mountains in their minds."

Ronda Ulrich adds: "You can have anything that you want if you make people feel important—anything. It is more powerful as a motivator than money, prizes and cars, or wonderful working conditions." She continues: "All it takes is forgetting yourself and just being interested in others. This is essential to becoming an effective leader."

If you would like to be a leader, direct selling provides endless opportunities to learn how, more than any other career choice.

The traditional corporate hierarchy is a leadership concept gone hopelessly wrong. You really can't lead a company that insulates executives from workplace realities and isolates those who are closest to the job from the decision-making process. The fact that American companies tend to be underled and overmanaged accounts for what some experts describe as a leadership vacuum so intense "implosion is imminent." Lack of leadership is one of the most critical issues facing the United States today and is in itself a compelling reason corporate America ought to be studying and learning from DSOs.

If hierarchically organized companies expect to make it in the twenty-first century, they have to create a corporate environment conducive to leadership. This means shifting from a top-down, totally controlled management culture to a decentralized culture totally committed to customers and employees—companies that will look very similar to the way most DSOs are structured today.

There are many examples of leadership gone wrong in American industry—one of the most notable being that of John Akers, ousted CEO at IBM, who led his huge hierarchy down the wrong road in the 1980s and early 1990s to large losses of money and careers in a company that once said it would never have layoffs. In contrast, Jeff Stiefler, CEO of IDS Financial Services, led his hundred-year-old company by turning his organizational chart upside down to put the customer and sales force on top. The resultant emphasis on sales and service transformed IDS, in the past traditionally resented by the field sales force as arrogant and unresponsive, into an organization known for its supportive style. In 1992, IDS set new records with revenues of $2.9 billion and profits of $297 million to lead the financial planning industry.

5. Set Unit Goals

Creating a fantastic direct-selling unit takes the cooperative efforts of a group of independent entrepreneurs working together with enthusiasm toward a common goal. To do this, paradoxically, you must help your organization's members create goals and keep them moving by:

+ Listening to their *individual* aspirations,
+ Focusing enthusiasm toward *individual* goals, and
+ Visibly recognizing *personal* achievements through meetings and newsletters.

Helping others set goals may be more challenging than you'd expect. Peggy Kidd of Stanhome explains: "When I first became responsible for working with new recruits, I found that a lot of people don't really have anything they want to accomplish. They would prefer to just let life happen rather than try to become something on their own. People have so much ability, and yet so often they don't do anything about it."

One of Mary Kay's favorite sayings is, "People will support that which they help to create." Inform members in your organization of your plans; let them have a part in making those plans. Each person must have pride and confidence in his or her contributions. Let your attitude reflect your appreciation and pride in your people.

When you set your budget, you established your goals and priorities. The next step is to translate those goals into overall goals your organization can identify with. These should build spirit, unity, and identity among your members. Members will have both individual and group goals and will want to work hard to help achieve all of them.

The whole is the sum of its parts. Once the overall organizational goal is established, break it down into individual goals for your members. Find out what motivates each individual and encourage each person to work toward her or his goal. Help others develop personal career goals. In addition, help your members develop an easy-to-follow, step-by-step plan to hit their targets. Ask for commitment to work toward the objective. Most important, let each individual know you are there to help and that you want her or him to succeed.

Deborah Balka of Cameo Coutures comments, "I've learned in direct selling if I recruit someone, my goals are not her goals. And I have to learn what her goals are. I can only help her achieve what her goals are, not mine. And usually if I help her achieve her goals, that all works in with mine."

Goal-Setting Checklist

♦ Schedule a private conference with each individual, limited to one hour.
♦ Prepare a list of questions before the conference which will help the individual determine his or her goals. (For example: How are you enjoying your career? What have the benefits been to your family? If you have areas you would like to improve, what are they? What are long-term goals for yourself and for your family?)
♦ Listen intently to the answers.
♦ Review personal goals.
♦ Establish a program and a timetable.
♦ Develop a follow-up program to review the individual's progress and reevaluate the personal timetable.
♦ Recognize progress in front of others and as often as possible.
♦ Establish new and higher goals as the individual achieves the original ones.

There are no shortcuts to building a successful direct-selling career. You will be the key to its success, both as a manager and as a leader.

Here is a scale used by Professor John Kotter to show the differences between leaders and managers. If you were a fantastic leader with absolutely no managerial skills, you would be located at the upper left-hand corner. If you were a terrific manager but had no leadership skills, you would be at the lower, far-right, corner.

Just for the fun of it, mark an "X" as to where you believe you are today. If you *do* elect the direct option, go back to this chart periodically and determine whether you are making progress. Are you learning to manage better? Have your leadership skills improved? I have had the thrill of watching people move into the upper right-hand "box" over the years.

As they have done so, I have watched them succeed—in the full meaning of that word.

Leadership/Management Scale

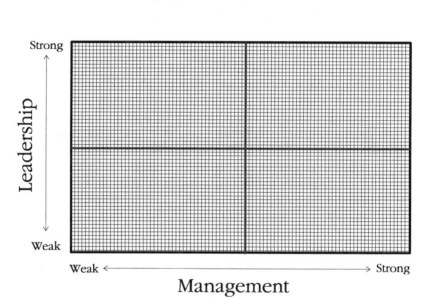

Chapter 10

It's Where You Finish

In Chapter 1, you were introduced to a number of direct sellers. We explained that while most of the examples in that chapter had been drawn from one company, they still reflected typical DSO experiences. The women who were mentioned were all from Mary Kay Cosmetics, and each had appeared on stage at Mary Kay's Seminar the same year. In fact, I interviewed them during an event called a "Royalty Reception" at Mary Kay Ash's home just prior to a Seminar program. After Mary Kay had personally greeted and visited each of the scores of women who had earned the right to be at this event, I conducted interviews from a random sample—anyone who was willing to take a few moments away from the fun and ceremonies to say a few words about her background.

Everyone there had achieved something remarkable during the prior year. For each, the culmination of their success was Seminar. These women were the best in class out of more than 250,000 independent entrepreneurs in the Mary Kay organization. At Seminar, these women would proudly appear on stage as Queen of Sales or Recruiting or as a member of one of our prestigious "Queen's Courts" on what we call "Awards Night." They qualified by being the top achievers in their respective categories of individual or unit sales, or they were members of our highest group, the National Sales Directors (NSDs). Mary Kay Cosmetics' NSDs (about seventy-five women) average approximately $200,000 in annual income, with the highest in the $700,000 range.

Before sharing the stories of some of these winners, I want to emphasize that every top DSO has a similar recognition program, whether it's called Jamboree or Jubilee or Seminar. And almost every top DSO has success stories similar to those highlighted in *The Direct Option*. Mary Kay was merely the most available and accessible source of information for me.

Most DSOs will proudly describe their top recognition events, contests, and incentive travel programs as either part of attracting you to their organization or, soon after you join, to inspire you to greater achievements. I use Mary Kay only as an illustration, not to "sell" you on one particular organization. The purpose of this book has been to acquaint you with many DSO options, and most have their own spectacular programs of recognition.

As we have stressed elsewhere, the high-income and recruiting achievers usually fall in the top 1 or 2 percent of any given DSO. And for most, it typically takes time to achieve this ranking. Getting rich and famous quickly is *not* what *The Direct Option* is all about. But it can happen to "ordinary" people with extraordinary dedication and, relative to other career ladders to wealth and fame, it can and often does happen in a relatively short time period. Professional careers such as medicine, law, business, and academia usually take six to eight years of undergraduate and postgraduate academic work, then internship, assistantship, or managerial apprenticeship for a number of years to achieve top income and recognition levels equivalent to those of top performers in direct selling. But success in a DSO does not happen overnight.

Ruell Cone, a Mary Kay national sales director, says her story is one "of drive, determination, pride, and perseverance . . . of the Consultants and Directors who helped me become a National!" Ruell, as does any truly successful individual in direct selling, credits her success to others. "It is most of all their burning desire to make their dreams come true . . . it is the story of their great courage, their dedication, and their commitment to excellence," she says. "You can make all your dreams come true because the seeds of greatness are within you—you have the power to make it happen," she adds.

Alma Gaines of Little Rock says, "This has truly been the most fantastic twenty-five years I could ever hope for. My husband Bill never regretted the $25 we spent on my first demonstration case! Because of the opportunity I accepted in 1964, my family has benefited tremendously. We were able to send our daughter to the college of her choice, and Bill has been able to do so many things that he wanted to do." Bill now helps Alma. "We make a great team," she says. "I have grown so much personally. I have self-confidence. I know I can dream big and achieve it."

And Nancy Tietjen, a $3 million–dollar commission earner, can now bask in the sunny garden of her mansion in Scottsdale, Arizona, after enduring many harsh Minnesota winters as a shotgun shell packer. "Sometimes," says Nancy, "we see successful people and think, 'Oh, they were just lucky, or it's fate, or they were there at the right time,' but I believe success in life can be predicted with absolute certainty. . . . You just have to plan your work and work your plan." Nancy has been lucky in the sense that Darrell Royal, former University of Texas football coach, meant when he said, "Luck is where opportunity meets preparation." Or as columnist Earl Wilson put it, "Success is simply a matter of luck. Ask any failure."

Take Rubye Lee, who initially didn't have the courage to speak to more than two people at a time but today is another $3 million NSD. On her way to outstanding success, Rubye remembers she wanted a lot for her unit—and that its members wanted a lot, also. "I threw myself into building those people," she says. "And guess what happened? Something magical! I became so involved in their goals and aspirations, so enthusiastic, that I forgot about my fears and inhibitions. My confidence grew with their growth." Shy, retiring, soft-spoken Rubye can and does inspire thousands with her story, as well as her determined, quiet, but very evident enthusiasm.

Or Gayle Carmichael of Los Angeles, California, who couldn't afford air conditioning for her red-faced babies in the heat of a Louisiana summer: She now has topped $3 million in earnings. Those who know Gayle know her to be a resolute person whose strongly held beliefs have helped mold the company's direction. She, like Abraham Lincoln, always bears in mind that, "Your own resolution to success is more important than any other one thing."

"During my years in building my organization, I have been supported by so many wonderful people; and I know I would not be where I am today without them," she says. "Most of all, I'd like to tell each person in my DSO to continue to 'keep the dream alive and well' and, therefore, feed my enthusiasm."

One of the great lessons of *The Direct Option* is that we have learned from hundreds of individuals who have, for whatever reason, been inspired to dream and keep their dreams alive by the accomplishments of others. These winners have been able to visualize their dreams and have been able to hold on to those dreams no matter what confronted them.

Gayle Carmichael is a great example of holding on. Thinking back on her career, she recalls, "I had my ups and downs—but I kept saying to myself, 'There are a lot of people who are doing this very successfully, there's no reason why I can't do the same.'"

When we met Holly Zick in Chapter 1, she told about her days of struggling to provide for her family. One son needed braces and another needed glasses. Today, Holly says, "Todd has beautiful straight teeth, and when he smiles I know it was all worthwhile. Shawn is an honor student and avid skier who sees his way clearly in the world."

But Holly's route to over $2 million in commissions was never easy. She recalls, "I had been given two pieces of advice early in my career. One was to always have a dream in my heart—and I did—and the other was no matter what happens—keep moving. I kept right on going. I was on my way and nothing was going to stop me."

.   Holly also helped pioneer Mary Kay Canada, a challenge she remembers well. "With demonstration case and recruiting notebook in hand, I was off to another country to build a Canadian organization," she says. "Another risk, another challenge—but 'keep on moving' was my motto."

All successful careers, in fact all of life itself, are a blend of discouragement and achievement. The trick is to keep focused on your dream and the immediate task at hand. Perhaps the most inspiring reminder to me of the power of focusing on the positive rather than the negative, of the good that we are doing, is Mary Kay NSD Rena Tarbet, another million-dollar commission achiever. You'll recall from Chapter 1 that in the 1970s Rena was diagnosed as being terminally ill with cancer. Her treatment, as it often is with this disease, was painful and debilitating. Yet you may also recall her words—"True happiness is from within and does not depend on outward circumstances."

Today, Rena is well on her way to another million dollars in earnings and in bringing joy and laughter to thousands. "I will always be eternally grateful for the positive attitude that Mary Kay instilled in me," she says.

Mary Kay NSD Shirley Hutton, the consistent top achiever in an organization of more than 250,000 and the first director to top $5 million in commissions, reflects on how she does it in her aptly named best-seller, *Pay Yourself What You're Worth*. She writes: "My objective was success from the day I agreed to join Mary Kay. . . . I could have easily surrendered my career as the sun went down on another day of ten noes and one yes, but I didn't. Every yes counted. They added up meteorically and made me a record holder with Mary Kay Cosmetics."

Every day that passes, Shirley sets a new record for earnings in my DSO. And, at about $700,000 a year, she'll be hard to catch. One day, someone will. In the meantime, Shirley is indeed paying herself what she is worth. So can you in the direct option of your choice.

Recognition, Recognition, Recognition

The in-store retailers often cite the 3L's—"Location, Location, Location" as the primary source of success. And in all forms of retailing, including direct mail and direct selling, in the 1990s and beyond, "Service, Service, Service" has come into its own. But for the leadership of a direct-selling unit or DSO, "Recognition, Recognition, Recognition" is the underlying key to success. Self-sufficient people are happiest when they are helping others become more self-sufficient or when their self-esteem is being boosted by some form of recognition, by word or deed, by trophy or prize, by private praise or public honor.

The experienced direct seller will usually recognize an accomplishment as quickly as possible through word of praise or a special gift, even if the DSO is going to later award a prize or recognition on a fancy stage with spotlights and music.

Recognize "on the spot" with the right words; but always be sure recognition is truly earned. Insincere praise is usually detected and can often backfire, eroding the trust you have built up with individuals. The best way to ensure that your praise and recognition are always on the mark is to really *care* about your associates. If you have read the many comments from top direct sellers in this book, you have seen they truly believe Mary Kay's famous saying, "All you send into the lives of others comes back into your own." The million-dollar leaders we have met all share this belief, and universally attribute their success to others. The first reaction, the first words out of a superstar's mouth when receiving major recognition, is invariably something like, "I couldn't have done it without the fantastic members of my . . . !"

As a superstar yourself, the "perks" will be astounding, far beyond those offered in most careers. The most important perk is self-sufficiency, the firm knowledge that you can maintain your chosen life-style no matter what—that you are not subject to the whims of any "boss," save yourself.

You will also find you are respected in your community; and because of the people skills you've developed, you will often be called upon to help with community and charitable projects. Few academic courses can teach the problem-solving power leaders develop within DSOs. So-called experts invariably approach people problems with masses of statistical information (and we've used a lot in this book). But, in fact, most problems are quickly solved if the person handling the problem has spent some time leading a direct-selling unit or company. Remember, virtually every member of such an organization is independent and therefore, thank goodness, can't be told or ordered to do something. To accomplish anything, the visionary leader must align by suggestion, by example, and by recognition. The leader must find ways to help others become self-motivated towards a solution.

There are those who would question the viability of direct selling for the 1990s and the twenty-first century. These doubters think in terms of how old the industry is. Perhaps they think that because it is old, it must be obsolete. In *Charismatic Capitalism*, Nicole Woolsey Biggart states, "The conditions that supported the growth of direct selling in this country are to some degree transitory, of course."

Biggart's "transitory, of course" is a little unclear, as the industry has spanned the entire history of America, coming into its own in the Great Depression and growing through boom and bust. The direct option is as transitory as the United States.

But Biggart goes on to say, "DSOs are attractive because so few employers accommodate the social preferences and family realities of women workers," and that the industry benefits from "the unequal, rationalized and uncertain conditions of bureaucratic employment."

That's exactly why the direct option is a model for the new millennium. Incredibly, the United States has become more bureaucratic at the end of the twentieth century, moving more towards big government and over-regulation of small business. Meanwhile, traditional, large corporation employers struggle with economic conditions that created more—not less—job stress for most workers.

Addressing an audience at St. John's University in 1985, former president Ronald Reagan said, "We have lived through the age of big industry and the age of the giant corporations, but I believe this is the age of the entrepreneurs, the age of the individual. That's where American prosperity is coming from now, and that's where it's going to come from in the future."

Megatrends 2000 authors John Naisbitt and Patricia Aburdene agree with Reagan. "The great unifying theme at the conclusion of the 20th century is the triumph of the individual," they write. "The 1990s are characterized by a new respect for the individual as the foundation of society and the basic unit of change. 'Mass' movements are a misnomer. The environmental movement, the women's movement, the antinuclear movement were built one consciousness at a time by an individual persuaded of the possibility of a new reality."

Whatever your political or futurist persuasion, Reagan, Naisbitt, and Aburdene are right. The new millennium will be the age of the individual. *Money* magazine estimates there are nearly 600,000 American millionaires, and some 60,000 new millionaires are created each year. Most reach this status through their own efforts—not by inheritance—the magazine states. You have met some of them in *The Direct Option* and there are many hundreds, perhaps thousands, more in the direct-selling industry.

The Direct Option is a book about choices.

Choose your own direct option with care and patience. But make your choice today. Act. And persevere. Don't give up.

Dallas entrepreneurial billionaire H. Ross Perot says, "Failures are skinned knees—painful, but superficial, and they heal quickly." Mary Kay Ash talks about having the most skinned-up knees in the group.

Remember, it's not where you start. It's where you finish. And in the direct option, there is really no way you cannot finish ahead, certainly ahead of where you are now—maybe even on top of the world. For even if you don't become one of those 60,000 new millionaires each year, you will learn lifetime skills.

In recalling her first encounter with Frank Stanley Beveridge, founder of Stanley Home Products (Stanhome), Mary Kay Ash says: "At my first meeting, at the Adolphus Hotel in Dallas in 1938, the Stanley instructors said three things. First, 'Get a railroad track to run on.' Then, 'Hitch your wagon to a star.' I had hitched to Stanley star Laveda O'Brien, from whom I learned much. And the third thing they said was, 'Tell somebody what you're going to do.'

"So I marched up to Frank Stanley Beveridge, and I said, 'Mr. Beveridge, next year I'm going to be Queen.' And he should have laughed—if he had known he was talking to someone with a $7 party average. But he didn't. He took my hand, and he looked me in the eye and he said, 'You know, somehow I think you will.' And those five words propelled me to Queen the next year and literally changed my life."

Those five words and the constant refrain of her mother, "You can do it," did more than propel Mary Kay to success in a single contest. They helped her achieve monumental success personally, professionally, and financially. With a little encouragement and your own belief, you, too, can do it.

Chapter 11

The Winning Team: Profiles of Successful Direct-Selling Organizations

How would you answer the question, "What is the ideal job?" When asked, thousands of direct sellers answered, "Making money doing what I enjoy doing!" Perhaps they know something you need to know.

Young or old, of any ethnic background, educated or not, wealthy or not, you can choose the direct option. Deliberately choosing the direct option, as opposed to "stumbling into" the career opportunities offered by many companies, will take careful consideration of your options. A good starting point is the product itself—do you like and identify with the particular product grouping that is offered by the DSO?

From the companies profiled in this chapter, you will have an extensive list of products to choose from. It is imperative that you choose a product line you like and understand. You will quickly master the sales presentations involved if you have some affinity for the products themselves.

"Let the little voice inside you talk to you," advises Lauren Debonis of Discovery Toys. "Use your intuition. Is there something that really tugs at your heart? When you feel that you want to stand up on top of the tallest building and shout to the world, 'I have the greatest thing in the world that you need to see or try or hear about!' that's the company you should go with."

All of the plans presented have a significant upside potential that can lead to high six-figure incomes. But the essential thing for you to do *now* is to narrow your choice of companies by the product line offered, and call the favored companies for more information. Often, DSOs are listed in the Yellow Pages, and you may want to contact a local independent representative.

It's also a good idea to ask friends and acquaintances for their impressions of product lines, because brand familiarity can often ease your entry into the market. However, even with the companies profiled here, you may not find wide consumer awareness since many don't advertise heavily. This should not be viewed as a handicap, particularly considering the highly innovative products and service you'll be offering.

"The product line was the ultimate reason I chose the company I went with," says Dawn Rehbock of Encyclopaedia Britannica. "I didn't compare it to anything else. Nothing else mattered. The reason I went with Britannica was the way people responded to the product. . . . It's a wonderful thing. Aristotle said, 'But man by nature desires to know,' and that's what this product is all about."

After looking at the product, consider the culture. Do you identify with the people in that particular DSO, and do you share their philosophies and beliefs? And of course, can you visualize yourself making money within their given marketing plan, as well as achieving other important personal goals, such as self-sufficiency?

Pete Matz, a very successful Amway distributor with twenty-three years of experience, was not satisfied with the nine-to-five living he could make as a nuclear physicist in the corporate world. Pete looked for a business where he didn't have constraints or restraints. "Direct selling was something I could get started in immediately," Pete recollects. "It gave me direction in my life. I didn't feel like I was just marking time on a job. I was able to start moving toward a direction of having my own business."

Pete soon realized that the potential of the direct-selling industry was, in his words, "very, very large—larger than I realized. I also saw it as a growth industry, and I began to enjoy the work much more than I anticipated." Today, Pete runs distributorships all over the world—Korea, Thailand, Guatemala, and Hungary are some of the markets he has developed as an independent contractor.

DSOs provide the product, the training, and all the basic support services you need to succeed. You do not already have to have any of the business skills such as law, finance, or management. With every DSO, you *learn as you go* and *earn as you learn*—usually with no or minimal risk—even if you later find you made the wrong decision in your selection of product or company. The direct option is unique in that it takes much of the fear out of the initial decision. You almost cannot lose.

Company Profiles

The companies I have selected to profile here are representative of the companies that comprise the DSA. They represent all the popular product categories offered by direct sellers and all the typical sales plans. New, smaller companies as well as those which have been in business for over 100 years are included. Additional companies are listed in Appendix A to further broaden your choice. More information can be obtained by contacting the DSA headquarters (address in the appendix), since new members are constantly being added and information for those profiled may have changed following publication date. For now, let's review the major product categories offered by DSOs.

The typical initial investment (usually for a demonstration case) of the companies listed ranges from zero to less than $100. Ease of entry is a hallmark of virtually every DSO, and legitimate companies always offer a "buy-back" policy which further protects the individual. The terms of such buy-back policies vary by company, but many are typical of Mary Kay Cosmetics' 90 percent guarantee for up to a year after purchase. (The 10 percent differential should not be viewed as income to the DSO. It barely covers freight and handling to return the merchandise—obviously not a profit-making exercise.)

Cosmetics, Fragrances, Skin Care, and Clothing (35 Percent of All DSO Sales)

This category includes clothing, cosmetics, fragrances, skin care, jewelry, and shoes. If you like to teach, are interested in beauty and fashion, and enjoy makeup application, you should explore this category. Some of the largest DSOs are in this category, and several major companies offer cosmetic and skin products in addition to their main lines. For example, Amway, which falls into the household care category, also offers a selection of cosmetics, as does the Jafra division of Gillette. Avon products, the largest DSO and one of the world's largest cosmetics companies, belongs to this category, with estimated 1991 worldwide sales of $3.5 billion.

Established in 1896 as the California Perfume Company, Avon has had a major impact on direct selling for many decades. Although Avon elected not to be profiled, it is a publicly held company, so current financial and other business information is readily available.

In my opinion, Avon has been one of the positive factors in direct selling's modern era of growth because of its ethical treatment of representatives and customers. The company has been a consistent supporter of the DSA, and former vice-president Tom McGrath played a major role in establishing the industry's non-profit educational foundation, the Direct Selling Education Foundation, in 1973.

MARY KAY COSMETICS, INC. Dallas, Texas (800) MARY KAY
Products: Skin Care, Cosmetics, Personal Care
Annual Retail Sales Estimate: $1 Billion
Methods of Sale: person-to-person, party plan

Amount of Initial Investment for Salesperson: less than $100
Year Founded: 1963
DSA Member since 1970

The pre-eminent company in skin care and color cosmetics for all skin types is Mary Kay Cosmetics, the largest party plan company in America, with the greatest direct-selling share of skin care sales, significantly greater than Avon's U.S. skin care total.

Mary Kay founded her company on Friday, September 13, 1963, with just nine independent beauty consultants including her daughter Marylyn and two employees—her sons Richard R. Rogers and Ben Rogers. Richard Rogers is now chairman of the board and one of the truly dynamic executives in the direct-selling industry. Today, there are approximately a quarter of a million women around the world who are independent contractors selling the Mary Kay brand.

In addition, the company is internationally known for the quality of its products and the level of service provided by the independent sales organization. The core of the Mary Kay product line—the product category it is best known for—is skin care. Among female facial skin care users who can identify a single best brand of skin care, Mary Kay ranks number one by a wide margin. The company also has a policy of offering a limited line of products so the consultant can provide on-the-spot delivery and can be thoroughly educated on each and every item in the line.

Founder Mary Kay Ash has become a legend in the industry. In fact, she and her company have done more to provide economic opportunity for women than any other individual organization in the world. Mary Kay's autobiography, *Mary Kay*, had sold over 1 million copies by 1992. The company actually started when Mary Kay retired from a twenty-five-year career in direct selling, somewhat disenchanted because opportunities for advancement had been denied her as a woman in business. "No one took women seriously back then," Mary Kay says today. "Every time I'd propose something, all the male executives would say, 'Oh, there she goes—thinking like a woman again.'" During my early years with Mary Kay, she would, in her own sweet way, remind me from time to time that I was "thinking like a man again." And she was usually right—her insight was typically what was needed to fine-tune our field sales programs for our almost all-female organization.

After her "retirement" in 1963, Mary Kay began writing down all the things she disliked about her former work experience and all the things she could think of to improve. When she was finished, she had created a vision for the future that is even more appropriate today than in 1963. Those notes set forth the fundamental operating principles and philosophies of the $1 billion cosmetic giant that bears her name. Mary Kay herself has been recognized worldwide as a leader in giving women economic power. "Even in the fifties and sixties, I knew that keeping a good house and being a good wife and mother were not enough for some women. Women needed someone to give them the chance to prove their potential."

Mary Kay's vision of a great company dedicated to the needs of both the consumer and the sales organization remains relevant today and is incorporated in the company's ongoing vision statement:

The Mary Kay Vision

To be preeminent in the manufacturing, distribution, and marketing of personal care products through our independent sales force.

To provide our sales force an unparalleled opportunity for financial independence, career achievement, and personal fulfillment.

To achieve total customer satisfaction worldwide by focusing on quality, value, convenience, innovation, and personal service.

Recognition, incentives, and personal fulfillment were three clear points in Mary Kay's plan. She wanted to give women the chance to hear the applause of thousands for a job well done. Mary Kay asked, "When was the last time anyone got up and cheered a woman for a clean floor or sparkling dishes?" And she still believes that self-confidence, enthusiasm, and success are bred from recognition, praise, and the right incentives.

Mary Kay learned her lessons about the power of incentives and recognition events in the 1930s when she was selling household cleaning supplies with Stanley Home Products (now Stanhome). One year Stanley awarded an alligator handbag to the "Queen of Sales" at a regional event. Mary Kay set her goal to be the Queen the following year and win a similar handbag. The following year, she achieved the top status, only to receive a fishing tool—a flounder light! "Since flounder gigging was not high on my list of leisure activities, right then and there I decided that if it were up to me, I would award 'Cinderella prizes'—the kinds of things that women want desperately but won't spend money on for themselves, like jewelry, luxurious accessories, home furnishings, and travel to exciting places."

Mary Kay's legendary recognition event known as Seminar had its roots in Stanley's then well-known "Pilgrimage," a homecoming held annually at Stanley's headquarters in Westfield, Massachusetts. Although I've heard glowing reports of this event from my former Tupperware coworker Gary McDonald, a Stanley dealer in the 1940s, Mary Kay remembers it more for things "not to do." For instance, after riding a bus for days from Texas to Massachusetts, she found a much-anticipated tour of Frank Stanley Beveridge's home was, in fact, a walk around the outer gardens with no "Mr. Bev" in sight.

For many years, Mary Kay personally greeted hundreds of top performers in her Dallas home at each of the company's Seminars, where more than 25,000 beauty consultants gather for a three-day extravaganza of recognition, education, idea exchange, and fun in Dallas each summer. It's been called a cross between the Miss America pageant, a Broadway show, and the Academy Awards. On Awards Night, the Dallas Convention Center turns into a fantasy land where dreams come true onstage for hundreds of top achievers.

In 1967, with the company growing steadily, Mary Kay rewarded herself with a new car—a Cadillac. She marched into her local Cadillac dealership, picked out a shiny new Sedan de Ville, and told the dealer to paint it the shade of her lip and eye compact, the famous "Mary Kay pink." When the dealer told her she was crazy, Mary Kay persisted. "I ignored his warnings, and the first Mary Kay pink Cadillac was born," recalls Mary Kay today. "Some people, even now, 'put down' the pink Cadillac," she says. "But I ask, 'What color Cadillac did your company award *you?*' And then they usually try to change the subject."

The Mary Kay pink Cadillac is famous around the world. Recently, I toured China, Moscow, and the wilds of Patagonia and was asked everywhere if I drove a pink Cadillac. My response was always the same, "No—I haven't earned one." The car is more than transportation—it's powerful recognition for those who *have* achieved. Today there are more than 1,000 pink Cadillac winners in the United States.

A demonstration case, called a Showcase, is all that is required to start in Mary Kay. This case costs under $100, although the cost of the actual products is valued at many times that amount. However, the company is eager to provide its new Independent Beauty Consultants with very complete product demonstration aids and teaching-oriented materials at a reasonable cost.

Independent beauty consultants purchase merchandise at discounts from suggested retail prices. The discount can range from 40 percent up to 55 percent or even 60 percent during special promotional offers, making the consultant's gross profit on her retail sales quite handsome. Most sales are from skin care classes or individual facials until consultants build larger customer bases, where reorders become a very important source of profits.

The Mary Kay plan is not multilevel. Everyone in the organization buys at the same discount rate directly from the company. There is a comprehensive ladder of success which allows a consultant to achieve the status of team manager by maintaining personal and team sales requirements and by having a specified number of personal recruits, each active and qualified by recording minimum sales. A team manager may then qualify as a sales director and may continue up the career path to achieve the status of senior director and executive senior director. She may later become a national sales director, with each step offering greater income opportunity. These positions are awarded the use of cars and receive top commissions for recruiting, educating, and motivating others. Women who want more control of their lives and flexibility in their careers can choose a proven track to enhanced earnings based on the size, strength, and quality of the independent sales organizations they build.

Mary Kay Cosmetics is an example of a direct-selling company that has changed with the times. Advanced income potential, innovative sales aids and leadership techniques, a flexible marketing plan, world-class product quality, and proven performance have earned the company a place in history and ensured women around the world a uniquely fulfilling and successful career option.

DUDLEY PRODUCTS, INC. Greensboro, North Carolina (919) 668-3000 or (800) 334-4150
Products: Cosmetics, Fragrances, Hair Care, Skin Care
Method of Sales: person-to-person
Amount of Initial Investment for Salesperson: none
Year Founded: 1967
DSA Member since 1975

One of America's largest manufacturers of ethnic hair care goods, Dudley Products, Inc., is the second-largest supplier to African-American hair salons in the United States and is expected to become the leader in the 1990s.

Founder Joe Dudley tells graduates from his Dudley Cosmetology University, "You are the salvation for many people. You are the people that must make the difference. There are promising times ahead for young, black Americans." More than 3,000 people have graduated from his school in Kernsville, North Carolina, since Dudley opened it in 1989.

"I am, I can, and I will," is the powerful philosophy that Joe and Eunice Dudley live by each day at Dudley Products. They send a special message to young people growing up in America today: "It is important that you understand that no one has the power to control your destiny but you. With the right attitude and the will to succeed, nothing can hold you back but you. But you must learn to set goals and be persistent in working toward those goals. We could give our own children money, but we couldn't *give* them initiative, courage, loyalty, integrity, or insight into the needs of mankind. Those are things they must learn for themselves as they go through life. Those are the values we must instill in all of our young people."

One of eleven children, Joe Louis Dudley grew up in a three-room farmhouse in the small rural town of Aurora, North Carolina. He was kept back in the first grade; suffering a speech defect, he was labeled mentally retarded. But his mother, Clara, never stopped believing in him.

Dudley started his highly successful business twenty-four years ago. The company has focused on the African-American women's hair care market, which constitutes 35 percent of all hair care products sold. The rate of growth of this market is about double that of the general hair care market in the 1990s.

Dudley Products, like all established DSOs, has developed a company which eliminates the costly middleman. About 80 percent of the ethnic hair care business is controlled by ten distribution companies, and Dudley's plan bypasses them.

This no-middleman plan enables Dudley to recruit, train, and motivate the more than 30,000 independent cosmetologists who sell his products. Although it is relatively easy to get started with Dudley Products, training is required to achieve cosmetology status. From chemists to stylists, Dudley Products employs top-flight personnel to assure the quality of their relaxers, shampoos, colors, curl and body wave systems, hair sprays, dressings, and bath and fragrance products.

The company also recognizes the importance of a thorough education and is committed to doing its part to ensure that deserving young people have the opportunity to reach their goals. Each year, Dudley Products awards college scholarships to outstanding high school seniors through its "Adopt-A-School" program. The winners are awarded four-year renewable, full-tuition scholarships to major in business at either North Carolina A&T State University or Bennett College of Greensboro, North Carolina.

In 1991, Dudley Products won the DSA's second Vision For Tomorrow award for its programs for young Americans. As that year's chairman for the DSA's Annual Meeting, I had the thrill of presenting this distinguished award to Joe Dudley and, in a surprise announcement at our Awards Banquet, also revealed that he had won one of President Bush's Points of Light Initiative Foundation Awards. It was a triumphant night for the man once labeled "retarded" by his schoolteacher.

Decorative Accessories (18 Percent of All DSO Sales)

The second most popular category is decorative accessories, a category ideally suited to people with a flair for decoration and home furnishings. The consumer of the 1990s is focused on the home—its style, furniture, dishware, appliances, and special home accessories such as oil paintings, limited-edition prints, and other such products. This will mean a continuing boom in this area of the market, well-suited to a DSO because in-home demonstration is so effective.

HOME INTERIORS & GIFTS, INC. Dallas, Texas (214) 386-1000
Products: Decorative Accessories and Gifts for All Seasons
Annual Retail Sales Estimate: $600 million
Methods of Sale: person-to-person, party plan
Amount of Initial Investment for Salesperson: $250
Year Founded: 1957
DSA Member since 1970

This leading company was founded in 1957 by one of the industry's best-loved pioneers, Mary C. Crowley. The story of the company is phenomenal by any standard, but the real story is in the philosophies of its founder and how these philosophies have been carried forward since her death from cancer in 1986.

Crowley's pastor, Dr. W. A. Criswell, remembers: "Several times she said to me, 'This is the way my will reads: I, Mary Crowley, being in possession of all my senses and in my right mind, gave away everything I had.' She gave away millions and millions; in every area of her life you'll see her largess."

Crowley's direct-selling career was linked to that of Mary Kay Ash, the founder of Mary Kay Cosmetics. These founding mothers, along with Jan Day of Jafra, owe their initial training to Stanley Home Products, now Stanhome.

Mary Kay Ash invited Crowley to become a Stanley dealer in 1949. "Pretty soon I was making more at night holding Stanley parties than I was in the daytime keeping books," Crowley said in a 1985 interview. "I thought, 'This is for me!'" Crowley went on to succeed in Stanley as well as World Gift and then launched her own company in 1957, starting with little else but her strong religious convictions and a hard-won loan from Dallas banker R. L. Thornton.

Home Interiors & Gifts has helped many people achieve exciting, rewarding lives as displayers. More than 30,000 displayers present coordinated accessories for the home, including sconces, ornamental plaques, decorator pictures, figurines, planters, shelves, table accessories, and mirrors. They still follow Crowley's original training, based on the "BUS" concept. BUS stands for balance, unity, and scale, and is the key to good design. The company provides professional training to displayers, who are taught the art of accessorizing and how to add beauty, charm, and personality to any room in the home. Displayers are also taught how to sell to and serve their customers effectively. Home Interiors & Gifts prides itself on its ability to help others achieve personal development, expand their creative abilities, and gain self-confidence as well as skills in communication and in working with people.

Sales are made through the party plan, and the company has a fine hostess service plan which assures bookings and an ongoing source of business. Furthermore, there are incentives and advancement programs for those who want to continue to excel in Home Interiors & Gifts.

Crowley, like Mary Kay Ash, contributed much to the economic liberation of women. Crowley has stated, "I want to be a good role model. I have attempted to do that, but I am not what the world now considers to be a 'feminist.' I am much more interested in liberty than equal rights. I think women want to be loved, they want to be needed, and they want the freedom to develop."

LONGABERGER COMPANY. Dresden, Ohio (614) 754-6300
Products: Decorative Accessories, Housewares, Kitchenware
Annual Retail Sales Estimate: $100 million (1990 actual); $140 million (1991 estimate)
Method of Sale: party plan
Amount of Initial Investment for Salesperson: $325
Year Founded: 1973
DSA Member since 1988

The Longaberger Baskets story began in the rolling, forested hills of southeastern Ohio. At the turn of the century, the Dresden Basket Factory made large ware baskets for the region's pottery industry. The basket factory, like many businesses, was severely affected by the Depression. So the owners elected to sell it to one of their long-time employees, John Wendell Longaberger, for $1,900.

Basket weaving nearly became a lost art in America (almost going the way of the buggy whip). But J. W. Longaberger persevered, combing the nearby woods for hardwood maples from which the basic weaves were made. He also began creating specially designed baskets for homemakers in the village.

In 1972, Longaberger's son Dave (who had experience in direct selling with the Fuller Brush Company) saw the opportunity for American-made baskets and revived the family business. Today, the Longaberger Company has thousands of associates selling across the United States.

In 1990, the Longaberger Company won the DSA's first Vision for Tomorrow award for the incredible renovation of the small village of Dresden. The Longaberger heritage thrives in this village and in homes throughout America, where Longaberger associates tell the company's story and present the handcrafted wares.

Since 1977, Longaberger products have been sold directly to customers in their homes. The company believes its products are best marketed among family, friends, and neighbors in the home of a hostess. The hostess is the link between the associate and the potential customer. The hostess, guided by the associate, invites family, friends, and neighbors to her home, serves refreshments, and makes everyone feel welcome. After a show, the hostess receives her choice of several benefits.

Payments are collected on orders at the time of the show, with the associate retaining a 25 percent commission and sending the rest to the company (less booking rewards). The baskets and other products are shipped directly to the hostess via United Postal Service.

A Longaberger associate is an entrepreneur operating his or her own business. Once an associate gains six new recruits, each active and qualified by recording minimum sales, she may become a branch advisor. She can then qualify as a regional advisor and later become a sales director, with each step offering greater income opportunity.

Tami Longaberger Kaido, president of Marketing and Sales, sums up the company's philosophy: "We believe that there are many different ways of measuring 'success,' and each individual has his or her own idea of what 'success' is. When new Sales Consultants join our company, we try to help them be successful by *their* definition." Tami Kaido was named chairman of the Direct Selling Association in 1993, a fitting milestone at her DSO's twentieth anniversary.

ART FINDS, INTERNATIONAL. Miramar, Florida (305) 431-2277
Products: Art Annual
Retail Sales Estimate: $10 million

Method of Sale: party plan
Amount of Initial Investment for Salesperson: $149
Year Founded: 1977
DSA Member since 1987

Art Finds, International is the name of the company resulting from the merger in 1991 of Collectors Corner and State of the Art. Art Finds, International was selected as a more meaningful and descriptive name for the business. The company buys art from around the world.

State of the Art was started in 1977 by Bob Kuechenberg, a Miami Dolphins all-pro lineman. Collectors Corner was founded in 1977 by Joe and Eileen Seed. Both companies believed that people have a genuine love and appreciation for art but did not have an acceptable or available outlet from which to acquire it. They also believed that most people are intimidated by galleries that dictate taste, selection, and cost to their patrons.

Charles (Chuck) E. Swanson, retired president of Encyclopaedia Britannica and a Direct Selling Hall of Fame member, acquired Collectors Corner in 1986 and State of the Art in 1990. Swanson is the company's chairman and chief executive officer. Art Finds has become a $10 million art sales company through its direct-selling, service-oriented sales style. The company's philosophy is to take the intimidation out of art and make it fun—to open a window to the public by exposing, educating, entertaining, and inspiring people to enrich their lives with art. Art Finds also believes customers have the right to determine their own taste in art.

The company has sold over two million pieces. A major key to the company's strength is its gigantic collection, exceeding 100,000 pieces. This large selection supports an ingenious telephone coaching system through which clients dictate their art and color interests to their art consultant, determining the style and type of art which will be displayed at the show they attend.

Art Finds has one of the highest sales averages per show in direct selling—over $600. It has established a strong niche by providing its customers with high-quality products at reasonable prices and at the same time offering its independent contractors a high-income earning opportunity.

Art consultants are able to advance in the company through recruiting. They receive an override on all first-line recruits. Once consultants have qualified for the first managerial level, assistant unit leadership, an additional override is earned based on the commissions of each first-line recruit in their direct down line.

PRINCESS HOUSE, INC. North Dighton, Massachusetts (508) 823-0713 or (800) 453-7600

Products: Fine Crystal, Decorative and Gift Items

Annual Retail Sales Estimate: $118 million (1991)

Method of Sale: party plan

Amount of Initial Investment for Salesperson: initial deposit under $100

Year Founded: 1964, a wholly-owned subsidiary of Colgate-Palmolive since 1978.

DSA Member since 1972

Princess House, Inc.'s products include handblown and handcut crystal, as well as unique collectibles, porcelain and metal giftware, and cookware and dinnerware designed for today's fast-paced life-styles. The handblown crystal Princess Heritage Collection includes stemware, pitchers, candlesticks, vases, condiment sets, serving bowls, and a variety of other accessory pieces.

Lead crystal items, acquired from all over the world, are created of 24 percent full lead crystal. These include vases, candle-holders, lamps, and collectibles such as paperweights, vanity gift sets, and animals. Princess House produces two distinctive collections of full lead crystal which feature highly reflective, deeply cut, jewel-like facets. Another collection is an exclusive line of crystal dinnerware and serving accessories.

All Princess House products are sold exclusively through home demonstrations led by independent, professional consultants. At a Princess House home party, a hostess or host arranges for an independent consultant to give a product demonstration for a group of friends or neighbors. The party combines shopping and socializing in a pleasant, relaxed environment. Princess House parties are very elegant and are often held by candlelight. In addition to viewing products, party guests learn the latest in decorating and entertaining. In this approach, Princess House is right on target for the continuing trends of the 1990s in home entertaining and decorating.

Princess House products (like most other direct-option companies) continue to sell well in all economic climates for several reasons: the goods are of very high quality, yet reasonably priced; people are spending more and more time at home; people continue to purchase products such as those offered by many DSOs (including Princess House) for birthdays, weddings, and anniversaries—the important gift-buying events; and, of course, shopping at home is convenient, pleasant, and provides the buyer with service and attention superior to most retail outlets.

The national average of sales per Princess House party is well over $250, one of the highest in the industry. Consultants may request that shipment be made directly to the hostess, making pick-up more convenient for their customers. Consultants never have to deliver products, nor do they have to stock inventory. Salespeople, therefore, average $15 to $20 an hour.

"Princess House welcomes all types of individuals as Consultants and Organizers," says Princess House president Steve Zrike. "The most important group to us, however, is working mothers who are looking for an alternative to the inflexible, often unsatisfying opportunities offered in the traditional marketplace," he adds. "Not only can working mothers earn substantial incomes selling Princess House's elegantly functional product line, they can do it without compromising the family values so important to them. That's why our Mission reads as follows:

"'To improve the *quality of life* of every family we serve through the Princess House party plan opportunity:

by providing consumers with exclusive quality products of the highest value through a convenient distribution system;

by providing Consultants/Organizers with the most personally satisfying and financially rewarding opportunity in direct sales.'"

Nutritional Products, Beverages, Foods, Water Filters, Water Purifiers (9 Percent of All DSO Sales)

Nutritional products, weight management products, food supplements, and specialized food products (such as spices) have long been a focus for direct selling. Some of the oldest companies in the industry, such as Watkins (founded in 1868), are still marketing spices as well as household products through a DSO.

Health and wellness are key concerns for American society. Many direct-selling companies offer products and programs aimed at helping people make life-style changes with fitness in mind. In addition, many of those offering nutritional supplements and related products also offer a mix of household and personal care products. Nutritional products and food supplements are well suited to direct selling because customers need proper demonstration and orientation to maximize the benefits of these products.

WATKINS INCORPORATED. Winona, Minnesota (507) 457-3300 or
  (800) 533-8018
Products: Spices/Extracts, Food/Beverage Products, Health Aids and
  Wellness Products, Household Items
Annual Retail Sales Estimate: $65 million U.S.
Methods of Sale: person-to-person, party plan, direct mail, retail,
  fairs, and exhibits
Amount of Initial Investment for Salesperson: $72
Year Founded: 1868
DSA Charter Member 1910

Watkins Incorporated, one of the oldest direct-selling companies,
carries a full range of spices, food-related products, liniments, salves, and
other personal care products. For many years, the National Association of
Direct Selling Companies (NADSC) held its annual meeting at Winona,
Minnesota, because of the prominence of Watkins.

Watkins was built on the ideal of sharing and caring for one another.
More than a century of product quality and knowledge supports the sales
efforts of the more than 35,000 dealers for the company. Watkins's tradition of quality and excellence began in 1868 when a determined young
man named Joseph R. Watkins acquired the rights to a line of products,
including a popular liniment. In 1885, Watkins moved his company to
Winona, where river steamboats and railroads permitted easy access to
materials. Watkins found great success in his home-selling method—a
method little known and used at that time.

Today, Watkins is a business for people who want to improve the
quality of their lives and attain personal goals through dedication and
perseverance. To start at Watkins, dealers purchase a Quick Start Assort-
ment, which contains over $100 worth of the company's best-selling prod-
ucts as well as a sales literature packet. Dealers are urged to become
familiar with the products by using them, so they can communicate with
their customers from first-hand knowledge. Watkins products are sold on
an appointment basis or through a Watkins Great Get-Together (WGGT).
The WGGT is the Watkins version of a typical party plan presentation.

The dealer/distributor retail profit plan is based on a sales campaign
schedule. Each sales campaign is four weeks in duration, and there are
thirteen campaigns in a year. A dealer's final profit is determined by total
retail purchases throughout each campaign. By increasing the total retail
sales in each campaign, a dealer can become a distributor entitled to
higher commissions. A distributor is also entitled to Watkins's Breakaway
Bonus Program, which pays varying amounts of commission based on
organizational levels developed downline.

DIAMITE CORPORATION. Milpitas, California (408) 945-1000 or
(800) DIAMITE (number available for active distributors)
Products: Nutritional Supplements, Diet Products, Skin Care, Water
Filters, Home Care Products
Annual Retail Sales Estimate: $50 million–$100 million
Method of Sale: person-to-person
Amount of Initial Investment for Salesperson: $54
Year Founded: 1975
DSA Member since 1981

Diamite focuses on nutritional, personal care, and home care products and has thousands of associates throughout America. Diamite's mission statement is "A company dedicated to enhancing the quality of people's lives—physically, personally, spiritually and financially."

The Diamite sales and marketing plan centers on retail sales, but earnings are enhanced by a profit plan that encourages development as a group manager. After becoming a group manager, an individual strives to become a group coordinator who earns personal profits of 50 percent and a sales achievement bonus of up to 20 percent.

The Diamite organization, which reached 45,000 salespeople in the early 1990s, provides an even greater earnings opportunity to individuals who advance to team coordinator, team director, diamond director and double diamond director, where incomes can exceed $250,000 a year. The company also offers a VIP bonus program that provides medical insurance, dental insurance, life insurance, a retirement plan, a travel bonus, and other awards programs.

Diamite's key product line is a unique system of diet supplementation that combines the best of Western nutritional information and technology with the best of Eastern herbal alternatives. Diamite also offers a full line of skin care products, a tested and proven water treatment system, and a full line of home care products.

President Rudy Revak shows his pride in what Diamite is accomplishing when he says, "Diamite is truly enhancing the quality of people's lives through its products: physically, by helping people feel better than they have ever felt before; personally, by helping people change and grow and develop as individuals through its training programs; spiritually, because of Diamite's basic principles of caring and sharing and helping people to help themselves and financially, by helping people earn extra income or develop new careers. Diamite helps people reach some of the greatest dreams they have ever been able to dream."

SHAKLEE CORPORATION. San Francisco, California (415) 954-3000 or (800) SHAKLEE

Products: Nutritional Supplements, Household Products, Personal Care Products, Water Treatment Systems

Annual Retail Sales Estimate: Up to $500 million

Methods of Sale: person-to-person, direct mail

Amount of Initial Investment for Salesperson: $5 Year

Founded: 1956

DSA Member since 1964

Shaklee is a multilevel marketing company which sells nutritional supplements, natural personal care products, earth-friendly household cleaners, and home water treatment systems. The company is built on a philosophy of being "in harmony with nature," the company's slogan. The nutritional supplements and effective non-polluting products attract people whose commitment extends beyond merely selling products to a concern for helping others improve their lives through good health and a better environment.

New distributors have no territorial restrictions and average a profit of 35 percent. The company provides continuous training by sales supervisors, mostly done in the field with support, guidance, and personal attention for new business builders. The company provides access to sales programs, product innovations, sales materials, and insurance plans.

Since its founding in 1956 by Dr. Forrest Shaklee, Sr., and his sons, Forrest, Jr., and Raleigh Lee, the business has expanded rapidly. In the last three decades, Shaklee has grown from a family-run venture to a Fortune 500 company listed on the New York Stock Exchange (NYSE), with operations in Japan, Canada, Malaysia, and Puerto Rico. In 1989, Shaklee Corporation was purchased by Yamanouchi Pharmaceutical Co., Ltd., one of the most profitable pharmaceutical companies in Japan.

Today, Shaklee's corporate headquarters in California overlooks San Francisco Bay and there are three Field Service Centers, in New Jersey, Illinois, and Southern California. Also located in the Bay area is a science and technology facility where the company's product development and research are performed. Shaklee has operated one of the world's largest nutritional supplement manufacturing facilities since 1979. Located in Norman, Oklahoma, this plant maintains rigid quality controls and utilizes the industry's most modern production methods to develop the finest natural nutritional supplements.

About 70 percent of Shaklee's product line is in the food supplements category. Shaklee is also particularly proud of its cleaning line, featuring one of the company's first products, Basic-H, a concentrated biodegradable multipurpose cleaner. In addition, Shaklee offered a "career with a conscience" with environmentally safe products long before it was trendy to be "green."

"Shaklee is a company still operating by the wisdom and insight of its founder, Dr. Forrest C. Shaklee," says David M. Chamberlain, chairman of Shaklee Corporation. "His belief in nature and the environment is reflected in our product philosophy, 'In harmony with nature.' And his compassion for people guides our Golden Rule business policies."

Everyone at Shaklee starts as a distributor. The only requirement is to stay active by ordering at least once a quarter. As distributors build larger organizations by sponsoring other distributors, they can progress to assistant supervisors, then supervisors. Top ranks in the Shaklee sales force are coordinators, keys, and masters.

Along with the earning opportunity offering financial freedom, many Shaklee distributors are also awarded cars. The company's annual conventions are typically held in first-class international resorts. Top sales leaders get fully paid transportation and accommodations to places like Hong Kong, Vienna, Madrid, Hawaii, and New Zealand.

Shaklee is also known for its support and nutritional consultation with world-class athletes and extraordinary projects. Shaklee served as a nutritional consultant for the U.S. Ski Team, which won more medals at the 1984 Winter Olympics than any other team. In addition, five Mount Everest expeditions have looked to Shaklee for nutritional programs and products. Shaklee also supplied "Official High Energy Foods" for the 1990 International Transantarctica Expedition, and sponsored the successful Voyage Round the World Flight and the Daedalus Project world record for human-powered flight. Furthermore, Shaklee is the title sponsor of the top amateur cycling team in the United States, Team Shaklee, which has set two world records never before held by Americans and has won more than 250 races throughout the United States.

GOLDEN PRIDE/RAWLEIGH. West Palm Beach, Florida (407) 640-5700

Products: Home Remedies, Food Supplements, Specialty Foods, Spices

Annual Retail Sales Estimate: $25 million

Method of Sale: person-to-person

Amount of Initial Investment for Salesperson: $25 (application fee)

Year Founded: 1889

DSA Charter Member since 1910

From the horse and buggy days to the conquest of outer space, high quality, specialized foods, home remedies, food supplements, and household products have had a marketplace. In 1889, W. T. Rawleigh recognized these needs and began a successful door-to-door sales business of home remedies, spices, and flavorings. His efforts gave birth to a sales staff operating as independent contractors.

The W. T. Rawleigh Company was established with the home and family as top priority. In order to continue to serve these priorities, the product line was expanded to include food supplements and nutritional and household products. In 1989, the W. T. Rawleigh Company was purchased by Harry W. Hersey, president and owner of Golden Pride, Inc. The merging of the companies retained the heritage of over 100 years and preserved the traditions of both companies, even to the extent of changing the corporate name and logo to reflect the identity of both companies.

According to Hersey, family pride and tradition continue. Hersey says, "To meet the needs of the nineties and the twenty-first century, the major emphasis is on an exclusive product line focusing on health and well-being. These natural products provide an excellent opportunity for in-home product presentations and one-on-one sales."

Golden Pride/Rawleigh retail sales provide income opportunities for all distributors, further enhanced by the marketing plan. Training is also provided to all distributors.

Like most DSOs, Golden Pride/Rawleigh utilizes major contests to help promote sales and interest in opportunity with the company. Trips to the Caribbean, South America, Jamaica, Mexico, and Bermuda have, according to Hersey, stimulated tremendous growth.

Committed to "Serving your family since 1889," Golden Pride/Rawleigh offers a unique combination of yesterday's heritage with a focus on today's needs.

Vacuum Cleaners, Home Appliances (11 Percent of All DSO Sales)

Following World War I, America enjoyed a surge in industrial output and new product development, which included the first home labor-saving devices—revolutionary products such as refrigerators, washing machines, cookware, and vacuum cleaners. Virtually all of the original major appliances were sold by direct sellers as they introduced the new products and taught women how to use them. They started a complete revolution in the American home, freeing women from many time-consuming tasks.

In fact, several of the companies that began in the 1920s are still in business today, including Kirby, West Bend, and Electrolux, which became the world's symbol for vacuum cleaners. Today, Electrolux (known as "Lux" in Europe) is a multi-billion dollar company in Europe, with a significant percentage of vacuum cleaners still sold much as they were in America in the 1920s—door to door through direct sellers. (The U.S. Electrolux organization, owned by Sara Lee, is not affiliated with the giant Sweden-based European company.)

Most home appliances today are sold in stores, although vacuum cleaners still have a significant share of the market through DSOs.

KIRBY COMPANY. Cleveland, Ohio (216) 228-2400
Products: Vacuum Cleaners
Annual Wholesale Sales Estimate: Up to $500 million
Method of Sale: person-to-person
Amount of Initial Investment for Salesperson: none
Year Founded: 1914
DSA Member since 1951

The Kirby Company, a division of Scott Fetzer, manufactures high-quality vacuum cleaners and accessories at plants in Texas and Ohio. The company's world headquarters are located in Cleveland. The parent company, Berkshire Hathaway, also owns World Book Encyclopedia. Kirby has been in business for over seventy-five years and sells its products to independent factory distributors for resale to consumers by means of in-home, person-to-person demonstrations.

The company has factory distributors operating in thirty-nine countries. These distributors have virtually all come up "through the ranks." They are first recruited as independent dealers (as I was in the early 1950s) through newspaper ads or personal contacts by distributors.

Dealers are then developed to become consistent volume sales producers. The training is continuous, and dealers come to sales meetings every morning of every working day. Within about a year, dealers have learned enough selling techniques and business principles to help teach others. In my opinion, Kirby has one of the most thorough and intensive training programs in the entire direct-selling industry, one that builds a high skill level and great discipline.

The next step for independent dealers is opening their own Kirby office, which is still under the domain of the factory distributor. These

"Distributors-In-Training" are positioned so they can learn the basics of recruiting, training, and developing others to operate a profitable business. Area distributors have much the same responsibilities as factory distributors and are on their way to promotion to this level.

A new factory distributor will most likely relocate to an area outside the marketing area of his or her promoting distributor. This evolution is called the "Kirby Road to Success," and distributors who recruit people and extend this level of opportunity receive monetary rewards from the company based on the purchases of their appointed new distributors.

Success at Kirby is based entirely on the individual and is at the heart of a marketing plan that has been successful for generations. Many of the top executives of the company were once successful distributors. In fact, the president and CEO of Kirby in the early 1990s had been one of the most successful independent distributors in the company's history.

One of the most important features of Kirby is the quality of its products; millions of consumers can testify to machines that almost literally "never wear out." As with other DSOs, delivering superior quality and service to consumers of the world has really paid off for Kirby and its worldwide network of dealers and distributors.

Household Cleaning Products, House, Auto, and Animal Care Products (3 Percent of All DSO Sales)

Just three companies reviewed in this section account for over 10 percent of industry sales by themselves—the Fuller Brush Company, Stanhome, and Amway Corporation. All three companies (especially Amway), have very broad product lines that spread throughout most other categories. These companies, however, will be discussed in this category because they started with household care products. These companies have contributed significantly to the history and growth of direct selling.

Household cleaning products, providing they are of excellent quality and value, are a logical choice for a direct seller because these products are needed and used in every home. It was on this premise that Fuller Brush became the world's largest direct-selling company for a while early in the century.

FULLER BRUSH COMPANY. Boulder, Colorado (303) 440-9448 or
   (800) 523-3794
Products: Cleaning, Housewares, Kitchenware
Annual Retail Sales Estimate: $25 million–$50 million
Methods of Sale: person-to-person, direct mail, retail
Amount of Initial Investment for Salesperson: $30

Year Founded: 1906
DSA Member since 1948

Alfred C. Fuller of New Britain, Colorado, was one of the true pioneers of direct selling. Fuller picked and sold strawberries as a child in the summer and was quoted as saying, "I think my later organization of Fuller Brush men as independent dealers who are businessmen in their own communities, draw no salary from the company, and earn only on the fruits of their own sales, was germinated in a Nova Scotia strawberry patch."

Fuller was reputed to be inarticulate, shy, and easily put off. What served him well, as it does every successful direct seller, was persistence. "Eighteen years of rugged Nova Scotia farm life had made me impervious to discouragement," he said. His sincerity opened many doors, and he was convinced that his mission was to lessen the drudgery of domestic life. Fuller was familiar with his brushes and could emphasize that he was not simply selling a brush, but a valuable service. This sense of mission—providing a welcome service (instead of just "selling someone something")—is a hallmark of many successful DSOs.

When Fuller founded his company in 1906, he believed that product superiority was the key. "The trick was not to make her buy, but to show her what the brush could do." He often preached, "Know the product well. Persuade the homemaker to hold the item and observe it in use. It will sell itself. Getting in [to the home] is the trick; after that, anyone worth his sample case can get a sale."

One of Fuller's earliest policies was that no potential dealer should be rejected because of physical handicap. This was to set a standard in direct selling practiced to this day. The industry today has a large number of physically challenged persons. Fuller's motto stated, "With equal opportunity to all and due consideration for each person involved in every transaction, a business will succeed." In the 1990s, the company is significantly increasing its efforts to develop opportunities within the Hispanic and African-American communities.

On April 10, 1906, Fuller married Evelyn Ells, who had some retail sales experience. One day, Evelyn borrowed Fuller's samples, outsold him, and claimed her rightful commission. This makes Evelyn one of the true female pioneers in direct sales, along with P. F. E. Albee of the California Perfume Company (Avon).

In 1912, Fuller hired a fellow Nova Scotian, Frank Stanley Beveridge, to help recruit college students. Beveridge remained with Fuller until 1929, when he left to organize Stanley Home Products (now Stanhome)

In 1948, the year Red Skelton starred as "The Fuller Brush Man," the company first introduced the concept of "Fullerettes"—a sales team of women to sell new lines of cosmetics. The Fullerette concept failed but was restarted in 1960. Nicole Woolsey Biggart, writing in *Charismatic Capitalism*, quoted Fuller on those early years: "This was the age of women's emancipation. As she swept out into a world wider than her own home, she sought shortcuts in her housekeeping, for which Fuller products were a ready answer. As women entered office and factory employment, maids became scarce, forcing women to do their own housework. A wife who was indifferent to the brushes and mops her servant used was particular about the quality of her own. The times were with us." In some ways the trend of direct selling to women continues, as the number of women entering the work force has steadily increased since Fuller's time and the time available for shopping has sharply decreased.

Fuller's company grew virtually overnight from its local base to cover the national market. The company was extremely well-managed. During each year of the Depression it achieved constant sales and recruiting growth, a remarkable accomplishment.

Today, women comprise more than 90 percent of Fuller's representatives. The company expects a continued emphasis on women but anticipates that its enhanced earnings programs will also attract many more couples. The company is planning to change its image in the 1990s, including its catalog, where consumers will see a new look, new prices, and a new focus on helpful, problem-solving information. In addition, the company will restore its tradition of service. Future Fuller representatives will participate in rigorous training programs developed by the new Fuller Home Care Institute. Furthermore, Fuller Brush has introduced a network marketing plan and commission structure designed to provide financial and personal success.

The company currently offers products through direct sales, direct mail, and a limited number of retail outlets. In the future, plans call for distribution channels to integrate and expand to provide consumers access to Fuller products and services whenever and however they want it. New plans are under way to expand access via 1-800 phone ordering, shopping mall electronic kiosks, and television home shopping.

AMWAY CORPORATION. Ada, Michigan (616) 676-6000 or (800) 544-7167 (U.S.)

Products: Cleaning, Autocare, Cookware, Cosmetics, Encyclopedias, Fashion Accessories, Food/Beverage Products, Fragrances, Health and Fitness, Home Appliances, Jewelry, Nutritional Supplements, Security Systems/Devices, Skin Care, Water Filters. There are over 400 items bearing the Amway name.

Annual Retail Sales Estimate: Over $3.5 billion

Method of Sale: person-to-person

Amount of Initial Investment for Salesperson: $35 required; the company also offers a "full" sales kit for about $100

Year Founded: 1959

DSA Member since 1962

In 1959, Richard M. DeVos and Jay Van Andel, armed with a new household cleaning product called Frisk (purchased from a Detroit chemist) and a revolutionary new marketing plan, created a new business entity—an innovation in direct sales called Amway. Within a year, Amway moved to a former Masonic Hall in Ada, Michigan, and then to an abandoned gas station, where the company began to manufacture LOC and other products, including the famous household cleaner SA8. Amway's first products were unlike anything on the market. They were biodegradable before anyone knew what biodegradable meant.

Amway began as the dream of two men. Today, well over 1 million distributors worldwide share that dream. Through their own efforts and by developing and using their own talents, Amway distributors make choices about their quality of life. They, like many other members of DSOs, have found a way to make their dreams come true. Rich DeVos retired in 1993, and his son Dick DeVos assumed the position of president.

According to *Forbes* magazine, "The Amway business has come to symbolize for great numbers of people their chance to get out of their rut." *Forbes* reported Amway's sales force to be about 500,000 in the United States, 500,000 in Japan and "several hundred thousand more in places like Germany, Mexico, Korea and Malaysia."

The remarkable diversity of Amway's sales force is a reflection of the company's philosophy as well as the philosophy of direct selling in general. Amway respects each individual and is committed to his or her success. The company's system of awards gives distributors who achieve certain goals personal recognition as well as financial bonuses.

The DeVos and Van Andel families are each worth close to $3 billion. Van Andel has stated the company's basic philosophy: "Freedom and free enterprise are like Siamese twins. One cannot live without the other. Allowing people the freedom to work for themselves and compete in a free marketplace has been the best and most productive economic approach ever devised."

In 1981, former president Gerald Ford and other dignitaries joined Amway's co-founders in dedicating a $10 million Research and Development Center at the Ada complex, which had grown to gigantic dimensions (well over 2 million square feet at the Ada complex and a total of 6 million feet worldwide). Amway has attracted many supporters and admirers, including former president Ronald Reagan and comedian Bob Hope, who has served as an Amway spokesman.

The Amway sales and marketing plan has remained essentially the same through the years, a tried and proven method of product distribution. As various levels of distributors have met and surpassed existing goals, Amway has developed new ways to compensate and recognize them. Amway will offer its "passport to freedom" as long as there are people who strive for it.

Rich DeVos, speaking when he was Amway's president, summed up his vision: "Too many people consider a country's economic system irrelevant to its politics, religious life and other cultural characteristics. That's a dangerous error. The economic system of a nation is the backdrop against which all else unfolds. It sets the stage for the entire life of a country."

STANLEY HOME PRODUCTS DIVISION OF STANHOME INC.

Westfield, Massachusetts (413) 562-3631 or (800) 628-9032
Products: Cleaning, Cosmetics
Annual Retail Sales Estimate: $50 million–$100 million
Method of Sales: party plan
Amount of Initial Investment for Salesperson: $20–$100
Year Founded: 1931
DSA Member since 1941

The name Stanley, now Stanhome, has become a household word, and its products are recognized as being synonymous with quality. Today, the Stanley Home Products Division of Stanhome has approximately 27,000 dealers in the United States. Building on these roots, Stanhome has expanded into direct selling on the international level and, through diversification, has also become a major giftware and direct response marketer. The company is a member of the New York Stock Exchange and the Fortune 500.

Today's world is fast-paced, and the time spent cleaning the home must be kept to a minimum. The modern homemaker still wants to know how to better manage the home and make it look its best at all times. A Stanhome dealer is equipped to offer such help and advice through great sales aids and training—and a reputation spanning several decades of quality and service.

Under its founding name, Stanley Home Products, Inc., Stanhome was the parent of all party-plan companies and the training ground for some of the industry's leaders. Jan Day of Jafra, Brownie Wise of Tupperware, Mary Crowley of Home Interiors & Gifts, and Mary Kay Ash of Mary Kay Cosmetics all learned from the person who created the party plan, Frank Stanley Beveridge. In fact, most party-plan companies owe their basic selling structure to him.

Beveridge began his career with Fuller Brush. In 1931, he formed Stanley Home Products, and the first Stanley salesmen went from door to door. Beveridge taught his dealers that each sales call was a lesson in homecleaning and maintenance, lessons in salesmanship learned from his Fuller experience. Beveridge told his dealers, "There is something of real value in the home. You're not simply selling brushes and chemicals, you are also selling what they will do. You are selling clean walls, clean ceilings, clean teeth. You are selling health and sanitation." These were powerful lessons, learned well by the major companies that were spawned from Beveridge's seminal work.

But such teaching-oriented demonstrations took time, and Beveridge was apparently already researching early "party plan" concepts when he was approached by Norman Squires, then a dealer with the Wearever Aluminum Waterless Cooking Company. Squires is given credit for developing the "club sales" party plan at Wearever and then taking the plan in the early 1930s to Stanley Home Products, where he found a ready audience. Squires then formed his own company, called Hostess Home Accessories, Inc., which was bought by a former Dupont chemist named Earl Tupper in 1950—one year before the formation of Tupperware Home Parties, Inc.

As Beveridge developed from a shy boyhood, he came to realize that the way to achieve personal success and business satisfaction was to "better your best." His philosophy is as viable today as it was when he founded the company in the depths of the Great Depression in 1931.

A major effect of the Stanley Hostess Party Plan was the opening of the door of opportunity for women. Women in the 1930s were not generally accepted as door-to-door salespeople. Furthermore, because door-to-door selling was time-consuming, homemakers found it a very difficult career to pursue.

But the party plan changed all that. The homemaker was able to schedule parties around the needs and activities of her family. She had the opportunity to visit with her friends while supplementing her family's income. The homemaker proved to be the perfect Stanley Dealer—one homemaker talking to another homemaker about the products she knew and used herself. The Stanley party proved to be a great way to shop, entertain, and sell, as it is today. It is an extension of the desire of Beveridge to serve the needs of dealers and consumers alike.

Beveridge said, "What we have tried to do in Stanley is to say, 'Here is an opportunity. Go out and work; go out and give of yourself; go out and give of service; go out and give of helpfulness; and you won't have to ask anyone for anything because it will be multiplied all the time. And the more you give, the more you'll have! And that's the way to do business!'"

Cookware, Tableware, Cutlery, Kitchen Accessories, Kitchenware (10 Percent of All DSO Sales)

The independent contractors of direct-selling companies in this category are close in lineage to the original "Yankee peddlers" who were so much a part of the founding of America. These early salespeople brought goods and services, with a heavy concentration of household items, to a population scattered over millions of square miles. They also brought news and information, becoming a part of the frontier's social fabric. In much of America today, these same social factors exist.

Today, as years ago, these independent salespeople are bringing the state of the art in cookware, cutlery, and plastic housewares to the consumers of America. They also bring value-added information as they teach consumers how to use the newest kitchen and home tools.

CUTCO/Vector Corporation. Olean, New York (716) 372-3111 or (800) 828-0448
Products: Cutlery, Cookware
Annual Retail Sales Estimate: $50 million–$100 million
Methods of Sale: person-to-person, direct mail (to prior customers only), fairs, and exhibits
Amount of Initial Investment for Salesperson: $120
Year Founded: 1949
DSA Member since 1949

CUTCO was founded in 1949 as a joint venture between Alcoa and Case Cutlery and as a manufacturing source for CUTCO Cutlery. The nationwide segment of CUTCO is Vector Marketing Corporation, the sister company. Both are wholly owned subsidiaries of Alcas Corporation, which today is privately held. Vector Marketing has more than 150 offices nationwide, each with its own direct-sales organization selling CUTCO products exclusively through more than 16,000 independent salespeople.

A central part of the CUTCO/Vector opportunity is the high-quality CUTCO product line. Famed for its cutlery quality, CUTCO has no reservations in identifying its products as "the world's finest cutlery." As important as CUTCO's product quality has been to the company's success, the Vector selling program and the opportunities it offers to its field force are viewed as being equally important. The Vector sales force is an enthusiastic, high-energy organization composed primarily of college students.

CUTCO and college have gone together for hundreds of thousands of college students over the years. Many of these student salespeople are now prominent business and civic leaders who look back on their experience as having a very positive impact on their careers. The relationship between a college student and Vector is a win-win situation: Vector gets to work with bright, talented young people, and the students receive a good income opportunity, a flexible schedule that can accommodate the pressures of college, and invaluable experience in dealing with people and presenting ideas. To further enhance sales opportunities, Vector also conducts three Scholarship Competitions annually.

Vector also offers an exciting series of management opportunities to its sales team. The manager team consists of positions from assistant managers and branch managers (both available to students still in college), to district managers, division managers, and zone managers, which represent an attractive career ladder for those who choose to join the Vector management team after graduation. In fact, the entire management team (including Don Freda, Vector's president and CEO) worked their way up through the organization.

Although the Vector opportunity, both short-term and long-term, becomes obvious once a person has joined Vector, it is difficult to persuade many college students (particularly those who have never had a prior selling job) that they really can sell. Therefore, Vector offers a unique "guaranteed commission" for beginning sales representatives. This "guarantee" aspect provides beginning Vector salespeople with confidence they will receive compensation for effort expended. Of course, certain qualifications must be met to qualify for the guarantee. For example, salespeople must complete a minimum number of one-on-one presentations to qualified potential customers. Although most salespeople exceed their "guaranteed commissions," Vector finds they feel "it's nice to know it's there."

Erick Laine, chairman of the board of Alcas Corporation (the parent company), says, "I cannot imagine a more gratifying way to do business; to manufacture a fine product that we *know* will give the customer a lifetime of satisfaction, and to take it to market in a manner that provides thousands of young people a great income opportunity and a fabulous learning experience at the same time." Laine has been an inspirational leader within the industry, and particularly in his work with the Direct Selling Education Foundation.

KITCHEN FAIR (REGAL WARE, INC.). Jacksonville, Arkansas (501) 982-7446 or (800) 643-8259

Products: Cookware, Decorative Accessories, Housewares, Kitchenware

Annual Retail Sales Estimate: $10 million–$20 million

Method of Sale: party plan

Amount of Initial Investment for Salesperson: $20–$50

Year Founded: 1982

DSA Member since 1982

Kitchen Fair is a company founded upon the precepts of opportunity and shared earnings and is based on over sixty years of stability and business experience from its parent, Regal Ware, Inc. Kitchen Fair's exclusive home demonstration sales program and unique direct-selling interest-free payment plan enable the entering consultant to earn financial rewards, travel, recognition, friendship, security, and, most important, to achieve self-fulfillment. Kitchen Fair, unlike most U.S. businesses, offers all of its training and other programs in English and Spanish and therefore has a high percentage of Hispanic consultants and managers.

Kitchen Fair features a unique, creative program with a distinctive array of more than 100 quality products, including durable handcrafted cookware, kitchen accessories, and home decorative items. Many of the products feature striking colors and artistic as well as functional designs that develop a strong repeat business for the consultant.

Consultants earn a basic commission on sales at exclusive showings to groups in homes, in the workplace, and in organizations. The company estimates that for every $100 in sales, the consultant will earn $25 or, based on national averages, $85 or more per hour of actual selling time.

Consultants also receive a performance bonus, paid monthly based on a percentage of orders entered, and a "sponsorship bonus" is paid to those qualified.

Additional steps to success include qualifying as a manager through sponsorship of five consultants (and, of course, approval of the home office). Other steps include achieving a senior manager level as well as group and executive director positions, featuring car allowances and exceptional compensation programs.

Kitchen Fair president Gary Stephen stresses that this is a business for the whole family. "[Family] support is extremely important to your overall success, and your family will share in your success through the added income and valuable prizes you receive, which the family can share."

Kitchen Fair executives also stress that the two guiding principles of the company's success have been simplicity and excitement. A simple and highly rewarding marketing plan makes it easy for new consultants to experience success. In addition, Kitchen Fair's creative monthly programs enable customers and consultants alike to maintain a high level of excitement.

TUPPERWARE HOME PARTIES. Orlando, Florida (407) 847-3111 or (800) 858-7221

Products: Housewares, Kitchenware, Toys, Games, Microwave Cookware, Decorative Accessories

Worldwide Net Sales (1990): More than $1 billion

Methods of Sale: party plan, person-to-person, fairs, and exhibits

Amount of Initial Investment for Salesperson: $85 (can be earned)

Year Founded: 1951

DSA Member since 1951

Three generations of busy mothers have cared for their families using Tupperware products. But when Earl Tupper first introduced his flexible plastic products to America in 1945, the response was less than overwhelming. Plastic, as a practical, commercially useful material, was in its infancy.

So how did the vision of a self-proclaimed Yankee trader and inventor create a company whose products are in more than 90 percent of all American households and are sold by independent Tupperware consultants through the party plan in more than forty countries around the world?

Tupper was a true pioneer. He not only found a practical way to make a new plastic that was tough, lightweight, flexible, and nonbreakable, but also devised the virtually air-and liquid-tight Tupperware seal. However, Tupper found he couldn't sell these revolutionary products in stores. It took the direct option to pioneer the products via home parties. In 1951, Tupper hired Brownie Wise to create a direct-selling system for

Tupperware, and in April of that year, founded Tupperware Home Parties, Inc.

Tupperware has been an American institution now for over forty years. Although I had sold vacuum cleaners in college with Kirby, Tupperware was the company which launched my direct-selling career, well over thirty years ago. Even then, in the late 1950s and without much advertising, Tupperware had established huge brand awareness. Today, everyone knows the Tupperware name, and almost everyone has at least some idea what a Tupperware party is. The market penetration of Tupperware is so phenomenal that it has become part of our culture. There are approximately 100,000 Tupperware consultants in the United States. In fact, Tupperware can be credited with launching the plastics revolution of the early 1950s.

Wise knew how to make a career in Tupperware fun and exciting. She and Direct Selling Hall of Fame member Gary J. McDonald knew how to inspire people to excel. From their personal experience with Stanley's Pilgrimage, they invented the famous Tupperware Jubilee, a model for many sales conventions held throughout the direct-selling industry today.

One of the many Tupperware distributors I remember with fondness from those "pioneer days" was Tom Damigella of Boston. Damigella was a former Stanley dealer and actually started selling Tupperware through his party plan organization in 1948. He bought directly from Earl Tupper, and his success led Tupper to buy Hostess Home Accessories from Norman Squires in 1950 (see Stanley Home Products profile). Damigella, Harvey Hollenbush, and Brownie Wise were among the earliest Tupperware distributors. Even into the early 1990s, Damigella was still going strong as a Tupperware distributor.

The feeling of genuine care and concern as well as the service level which the sales force provides to its customers started early on. The sales force structure includes independent Tupperware consultants, who demonstrate and sell the products and recruit new consultants; independent managers, who maintain their personal sales and recruiting efforts while supporting consultants in their unit; and distributors of Tupperware products. In 1987, the distributors were converted to independent franchisees.

Since only consultants can become managers and only managers can become distributors, the organization is made up of highly motivated, knowledgeable, and well-compensated people. There is a saying in Tupperware, "You build the people, and the people will build the business." This typifies the approach managers take to developing the sales and service skills of their consultants.

The benefits of a career in Tupperware, as in most DSOs, include flexible hours coupled with unlimited income potential. Consultants earn approximately $12 an hour and can qualify for cash or gifts through contests. There is no barrier to entry, and the necessary tools require only a modest cash outlay. The opportunity kit, with a retail value of almost $200, costs about $85.

Managers earn $20,000 to $50,000 a year and can qualify for the use of a car as well as bonus points for gifts, cash, or trips. Managers provide leadership to consultants they have recruited—consultants look to managers for guidance, training, and expertise. In return, managers receive an override percentage of consultants' sales in addition to income from their personal sales.

As life-styles have changed, Tupperware brand products have changed as well. For instance, to maximize space in homes, recreational vehicles, and boats, Tupperware introduced the Modular Mates container systems in 1982, an innovative line of freezer containers in 1989, and its TupperWave cookware system, a revolutionary new line of microwave cookware, in 1990.

Life-style changes have not only affected America's eating habits and food storage needs, but also its discretionary time. As noted, fewer women are home during the day. Therefore, fewer women feel they can spend two hours at a traditional Tupperware party. In response, Tupperware has adapted the party to fit today's busy life-styles. The classic Tupperware party has been joined by a shorter version. The "Office Party," "Stop 'n' Shop Party," "Rush Hour Party," and "Kitchen Planning Party" have been tailored to today's consumer. Special microwave cooking classes as well as food freezing classes have even been adapted for today's life-styles.

Tupperware's hallmarks—attention to excellence and ingenuity in product design—will undoubtedly continue as innovative products and product lines are introduced. Tupperware president Rick Goings places tremendous emphasis on maintaining the rigid standards of high quality that founder Tupper established. Tupperware products have a full lifetime warranty against chipping, cracking, peeling, and breaking in normal noncommercial use. And the sense of caring between Tupperware and its consultants as well as between consultants and customers will continue to be nurtured as it has been for over forty years.

Leisure, Educational Products (8 Percent of All DSO Sales)

One of the most rewarding categories is one that offers educational opportunities and enhances the leisure-time activities of millions of Americans. America has lagged far behind other developed nations in the quality of education, and several companies in this category provide an important service by actually teaching consumers the importance of learning—both for themselves and for their children.

Christopher Shea, writing in 1993 in the *Chronicle of Higher Education*, summarizes the beliefs of many educators:

- ◆ Children are not reading much, and what they do read does not offer them the challenge they need to become better readers.
- ◆ They are watching too much television.
- ◆ Educators are not "comfortable" with the idea of spending more time with high-achieving students—they fear creation of an "academic elite."
- ◆ The effort educators have made to improve the achievement of average students has brought down the level of top students at the same time it has raised the level of students at the bottom.
- ◆ Standards in secondary schools are low, and they are getting worse.

Statistics released in 1993 confirm this summary. About a third of students now entering college need remedial education. But, perhaps worse, fewer students scored above 600 in the Scholastic Aptitude Test (SAT) for 1992 than in 1972: 116,630 in 1972, only 75,243 in 1992. Concerned parents equipped with the excellent products and educational training offered by DSOs *can* make a difference.

Distinguished historian and professor at Yale University Paul Kennedy, writing in *Preparing for the Twenty-first Century*, states, "The forces for change facing the world could be so far reaching, complex, and interactive that they call for nothing less than the re-education of mankind. [Education] implies a deep understanding of why our world is changing, of how other people and cultures feel about those changes, of what we have in common—as well as what divides cultures, classes and nations."

The Yale University professor adds, "Enhancing the role of education is inextricably linked to an even greater issue, namely the position of women in both developing and developed countries."

In the 1920s, Encyclopaedia Britannica was owned by Sears, Roebuck and Co. But despite this company's tremendous retailing clout (it would become the world's largest retailer), encyclopedias were not effectively sold in-store. It took direct selling to bring these valuable learning tools to the American public. In addition, educational toys and books for children also benefit by a teaching-oriented direct-selling approach, because a "show and tell" demonstration adds value to the products and helps the "teacher" (usually a mother) better use the toys and books to educate her children. Educational issues and family values have great implications for a parent considering a DSO, since such a career offers many opportunities to increase the quality of time spent together and involves children in work activities. Those who choose an educationally oriented DSO can benefit even more.

ENCYCLOPAEDIA BRITANNICA NORTH AMERICA. Chicago, Illinois (312) 347-7000

Products: Educational Products and Services, Encyclopedias

Annual Retail Sales Estimate: $650 million (in 1990)

Methods of Sale: person-to-person, direct mail, retail settings such as fairs, exhibits, and malls

Amount of Initial Investment for Salesperson: $65

Year Founded: 1768 (direct selling began in 1915)

DSA Member since 1971

The *Encyclopaedia Britannica* is one of the most prestigious reference book sets in the world. When people want an informative, useful, easy-to-understand reference, they look to Britannica. There is an annual revision program to make the encyclopedia as up-to-date and easy-to-use as possible. Electronic versions are also available, obviously the wave of the future.

The company itself is more than 200 years old. It is one of the world's most successful companies, producing the oldest continuously published reference work in the English language. It provides thorough training to direct sellers, including carefully planned videotapes, clinics, and advanced training backed by detailed written materials and sales aids. The earliest reference to direct selling in the company's archives was dated October, 1915.

Encyclopaedia Britannica provides a continual flow of prospects, generated by exhibit counters, local marketing, national advertising, and extensive direct mail programs. It also offers medical and life insurance, a retirement program, and other benefits.

The company's sales representatives are trained to succeed with a program that has become a model for the direct-selling industry. The representatives are taught how to sell through clinics that feature the most state-of-the-art sales techniques available and through informative videotapes. A manager also works with new representatives to show them the best way to find sales prospects and how to use the sales tools.

In addition, Encyclopaedia Britannica features an innovative "Live Books" marketing plan. These are exhibits at thousands of high-traffic locations where prospects are introduced to the company. Another innovation is a special professional exhibit team (PET), a marketing group that travels throughout a region, working fairs and shows.

Representatives can move through the ranks to become district field trainers, branch managers, district managers, division managers, and ultimately, sales vice-presidents—with an earning potential in the six-figure range.

Patricia A. Wier, president of Encyclopaedia Britannica, USA (EBUSA), stresses the importance of direct selling in today's increasingly complex marketplace. "American consumers are finding their lives to be more complicated, especially as the multiple-income family becomes the norm," Wier says. "Under these circumstances, bringing together the product and the potential purchaser has reached a much higher level of importance. Britannica's long and distinguished history of direct selling positions it to function well in this ever-changing marketing atmosphere." She continues, "Direct selling has assumed strategic importance in today's economy, and at Britannica we are proud to be able to aid busy Americans in making the wisest use of their disposable income." Pat Wier is a member of DSA's Hall of Fame and has been a strong contributor to the industry's volunteer leadership for many years.

Peter Norton, president of Encyclopaedia Britannica, Inc., underscores Britannica's commitment to direct selling and to the printed word. "At Britannica, we are keeping pace with the changes that are taking place in the publishing world and believe that direct selling will continue to be the key element of our marketing efforts and that the printed word in book form will continue to be the mainstay of the publishing industry," Norton says. "While technology will impact on publishing, we are confident that technology—as it unfolds—will actually enhance book sales. Just as an educated consumer is of critical importance to a reference publisher, education will become even more important in our future publishing efforts. Our commitment to an educated and literate America goes hand in hand with our goal of providing a broader yet targeted marketplace for our leading sales force."

WORLD BOOK EDUCATIONAL PRODUCTS. Elk Grove, Illinois
   (708) 290-5300 or (800) 621-8202
Products: Educational Publications, Encyclopedias
Annual Retail Sales Estimate: Up to $500 million
Methods of Sale: person-to-person, direct mail, fairs, and exhibits
Amount of Initial Investment for Salesperson: $25

Year Founded: 1917
DSA Member since 1947

World Book bases its success on the principle of telling an honest story about an honest product. This means establishing and maintaining high standards of customer service, salespeople, and employees. The company believes that through quality, ethical marketing practices, and creative management, it can provide a fair return to ownership, value to customers, and an exciting direct-selling opportunity.

To create World Book in 1917, it took the knowledge of an eminent college professor, the bravado of a consummate promoter, and the common sense of a midwestern schoolteacher-turned-salesman to invest $150,000 for innovative revisions and a new name for a popular encyclopedia from Chicago. Today, World Book is the world's best-selling encyclopedia, with over 12 million sets estimated in use.

The company's founders—J. H. Hansen, owner and promoter of *The New Practical Reference Library* (the forerunner of World Book); Dr. Michael V. O'Shea, professor of education at the University of Wisconsin and World Book's first editor-in-chief; and Arno L. Roach, a former Kansas City teacher with big ideas about how to make an encyclopedia easier and more enjoyable to use—created World Book's mission statement: "To select out of the world's knowledge all that is more interesting, illuminating and useful, and to present it in an orderly manner so that it can be comprehended, enjoyed and utilized by young and old alike."

That goal—coupled with an overriding commitment to serve families—still motivates the company after more than seventy years. An estimated 112 million people have grown up reading *World Book*. In fact, four out of every ten homes in the United States currently own a set of *World Book* encyclopedia.

World Book has made numerous contributions to the encyclopedia field. It was the first encyclopedia written at the student level. It was the first to use photographs and color extensively. It was also the first to study classroom curricula and conduct student-use research to ensure the encyclopedia included most topics currently being taught.

The World Book mission is to demonstrate its products to one out of every six households with children each year. Area managers earn commissions and bonuses on their own sales plus overrides and bonuses on the sales of representatives. World Book has a very comprehensive sales lead generation program, including an innovative program called "Early World of Learning" (EWOL). This show is designed to be presented to young children in preschool and kindergartens and entertains children with a delightful "Early World of Learning" story. The children take a letter home asking parents if they are interested in receiving information on school reading skills and in previewing World Book products. Representatives can then contact interested parents in person.

The World Book advancement program encourages representatives to climb the ladder of success from area manager to district manager to division manager. District managers have the opportunity to develop several area managers, while continuing their own personal selling and recruiting. In addition, district managers are often able to serve local school systems. The school market offers great opportunities for business building. One program is the Partners in Excellence Program (PIE). This highly successful program builds relations with the community and provides a way for schools to acquire World Book products for the classroom at no cost to the school, which is very important in this era of tight educational funding. Since 1986, PIE has encouraged more than 6 million students in more than 200,000 classrooms throughout North America to read millions of books. Children read seven books in seven weeks and sign up seven sponsors. For every two dollars they raise, World Book matches it with one. There are also many other creative programs including the Look Again Club and the Look-It-Up Club that help create leads for representatives.

World Book also sponsors "Company with a Heart," through which thousands of encyclopedia sets are donated each year to needy families and organizations—more than 30,000 since 1983. In addition, the company conducts joint literacy programs for children and adults with organizations such as Reading is Fundamental, Capital Cities/ABC, and Literacy Volunteers of America. World Book sponsors the literature competition of the National PTA Reflections project to recognize creative student achievement and numerous scholarship programs for library science students through the American Library Association and the Catholic Library Association.

SOUTHWESTERN COMPANY. Nashville, Tennessee (615) 391-2500, (800) 843-6149 (parents and school officials), (800) 424-6205 (students)

Products: Books, Educational Publications

Annual Retail Sales Estimate: $25 million–$50 million

Method of Sale: person-to-person

Amount of Initial Investment for Salesperson: not available

Year Founded: 1855 (direct selling in 1868)

DSA Member since 1964

The Southwestern story really began before the Civil War, in 1855, when the Southwestern publishing house opened its doors in Nashville as a publisher and distributor of Bibles. The direct-selling division started in 1868, offering an opportunity to college students seeking a way to finance their educations by selling books door to door.

The company's growth really accelerated in 1960, and today thousands of students from more than 500 colleges and universities across the United States and Canada, as well as from Europe, participate in the program. The company continues to grow in both size and productivity; in fact, in recent years it has doubled its sales revenues. Southwestern's focus now is primarily on educational books, having shifted away from a predominantly religious product line in the 1960s and 1970s. The company is also considering product lines such as video training, electronic systems, and other educational materials.

Southwestern's management recognizes college students' needs not only for profitable work in the summer, but also for valuable work experience applicable to a variety of careers later in life. While company executives take pride in the quality of their editorial product, they really feel their most significant "product" is the young people who develop and grow through the program.

A legacy of the program's success lies in the success of thousands of men and women across the country who gained business training with Southwestern. The company's motto has always been, "Building character in young people." The company's president, Jerry Heffel, says, "Experience has shown that young people who can discipline themselves to be successful in this kind of business will develop qualities and characteristics that will help to make them successful, whatever they do, the rest of their lives." The statement is equally true of other DSA member companies but is especially meaningful to Southwestern.

Floyd Soeder, major accounts sales manager for Xerox Corporation, comments, "I have found that quite a few of the more impressive college graduates I interview every year have sold books for Southwestern as students. Now, when a position calls for real initiative and responsibility, I tend to look for a person with Southwestern experience."

Southwestern is known for its excellent sales training programs. Because people in the sales profession agree that door-to-door selling is the most difficult and challenging of all kinds of direct sales, appropriate training is critical to the success of each individual. Southwestern's training begins on the college or university campus, where experienced instructors hold weekly seminars relating to pre-summer preparation. Training continues in its most refined form after spring exams, with a week in Nashville for Sales School. This program, which is repeated twelve times between the end of April and the beginning of July, consists of eighteen hours of formal lectures and ten additional hours of small group discussion sessions, enhanced by additional time for individual study and practice.

During the summer, dealers are invited to attend weekly sales education meetings, in which an additional twenty to thirty hours of instruction are offered. At the end of the summer, students attend other seminars relating to college success and career planning. Finally, students are invited to a resort area at a later date for additional training in organizational development and management. It's like earning a college degree in sales and sales management while being handsomely rewarded at the same time. The quality of sales education given by Southwestern has been recognized by a number of universities, which offer internship and college credit to students who complete the Southwestern program.

Advancement comes through a promote-from-within policy. Sales managers and sales executives start in the summer sales program as college students and build organizations of their own while still in college. It's not unusual for a college student to graduate from college having built an organization with wholesale sales of up to $500,000 in a three-month summer selling season.

Southwestern executives emphasize that, "character and experience are valued commodities in the American business community." In Southwestern, these valuable "commodities" are learned early. A college degree today is no longer a guarantee of successful and satisfactory employment. In late 1991, a survey of employers showed they expected hiring of new college graduates to be down 10 percent in 1992—the third annual decline in a row. In the increasingly competitive job market, only the student who has worked to earn more than "just a degree" can be assured of getting the job he or she wants. Southwestern points out, "Recruiters of college graduates for business and industry consistently agree that while educational preparation is important, even more so are personal qualities which show character in a potential employee—maturity, initiative, enthusiasm, poise and the ability to work with other people." These are traits that may be learned in *The Direct Option*, and certainly in the summer program offered by Southwestern.

DISCOVERY TOYS, INC. Martinez, California (510)370-7575
Products: Books, Toys, Games
Annual Retail Sales Estimate: $100 million
Method of Sale: party plan
Amount of Initial Investment for Salesperson: $99
Year Founded: 1978

DSA Member since 1981

Discovery Toys, Inc., a California-based direct-sales toy company, was founded on the belief that play is a child's work—that children need to play to learn, grow, and experience the world around them. Since its inception in 1978, the company has used this philosophy as its guiding principle, according to founder and president Lane Nemeth.

Nemeth says, "Our children deserve the very best as they begin to explore their capabilities, meet fresh challenges, and discover new opportunities in their lives. The skills they learn as children are the skills they will need as adults—talents that will encourage them to build a more peaceful, loving world."

To help children achieve this ultimate goal, Discovery Toys equips them with what the company describes as "developmental toys, books, and games"—products like Marbleworks, a freeform construction toy with bridges, jump chutes, and racing marbles, or A B Seas, a junior fishing game that teaches the alphabet in both upper and lower case letters.

The company offers approximately 135 such items at any one time, with the majority priced at less than $15. More than two-thirds of the line is exclusive to Discovery Toys only, and the quality has been well received by educational associations and parent groups. In fact, selected DISCOVERY TOYS® products have been recognized four times with the prestigious Parents' Choice Foundation National Award for "likability . . . and positive impact on children's values."

Discovery Toys' origins are a classic rags-to-riches, American success story. Nemeth, a former director of a day-care center with a master's degree in education—and a talented performing artist, as well—founded the company in the garage of her home in Martinez, California. She began acquiring toys by searching toy fairs and browsing through instructional catalogs for products important to parents and children, but not normally available in stores.

Today, Discovery Toys' nationwide sales force of over 22,000 sells the product in essentially the same way, by contacting parents and asking them to host a demonstration. With a sophisticated network marketing structure, the company nurtures and develops each of its educational consultants, who sign on with the organization as entrepreneurs interested in creating their own independent businesses.

The career track within Discovery Toys rewards these individuals as they build their sales volume and recruit others to join the business. Salespeople may progress from educational consultant to manager, advanced manager, senior manager, sterling senior manager, and finally, sales director. Cash rewards increase with each promotion, as do the training and support the company provides.

As Nemeth's company continues its second decade of service to the American family—and to families in Canada and Japan—she reiterates the egalitarian nature of the Discovery Toys opportunity. "Knowing, loving parents are our best teachers," Nemeth says. "As parents around the world continue to share our toys with their own children and with families in their community, they'll discover in themselves skills and abilities they never knew they had. And at the same time, as the toys are played with and explored, their *kids* will develop a joy of learning that will last them into *their* adult years. My goal is simple, really—to allow both adults and children to open their minds and to dream big dreams. With our toys and a little childlike enthusiasm, all ages may be surprised at the joy they'll discover!"

Other Direct Option Products

Many other products are sold by DSOs, including computers and home technology, photo album plans, self-improvement and vocational training programs, buying and travel clubs, insurance, home improvements, durable medical equipment, candles and ceramic giftware, foliage plants and hydroculture, novelties, household furniture and furnishings, photographic enlargements and supplies, wicker, fuel treatment products, air filtration, socks and accessories, high fidelity stereo equipment, health and fitness equipment, and clothing lingerie.

There is a wide array of choices of product lines. As a sample of an intriguing DSO, Cameo Coutures offers an especially glamorous career.

CAMEO COUTURES, INC. Dallas, Texas (214) 631-4860 or (800) 767-2789 (800) 76 PARTY
Products: Lingerie and Loungewear
Annual Retail Sales Estimate: $50 million–$100 million
Method of Sale: party plan
Amount of Initial Investment for Salesperson: $20
Year Founded: 1970
DSA Member since 1974

Cameo Coutures creates and manufactures designer lingerie at affordable prices. The company was started by J. Stanley Fredrick (Stan) and John Fredrick in 1970 with, in John's words, "one bra and one girl." In fact, some of Cameo's products are actually designed by Stan, a former DSA chairman and a member of the DSA Hall of Fame. Today, over 1 million women have attended Cameo's unique home fashion shows where clients are given the opportunity to try before they buy.

The company's product line ranges from expensive designer loungewear and lingerie to fantasy collections for "The Total Woman." This includes sleepwear, loungewear, daywear, and a Liaisons Collection, which can be worn both in the home and out.

In addition, Cameo is the official loungewear/lingerie sponsor for most of the state pageants leading to the Miss America Pageant as well as the Mrs. U.S.A. Pageant.

According to Nicole Woolsey Biggart in her book, *Charismatic Capitalism,* Cameo's couturieres begin their presentations stating that women typically have four dominant moods—wife, mother, sweetheart, and personal self. According to Biggart, guests at the parties are "encouraged to buy a 'uniform' for each mood." In other words, Cameo suggests different lingerie to depict the different moods a woman has.

Cameo has developed a very profitable plan for its independent couturieres, who may earn their way to positions as directors and may even run independent regional directorships. Directors and regional directors are eligible for Cameo's "Task Force Bonuses," and there is a "Star Regional Car Program" for a specified amount of regional group sales. Mercedeses and Lincolns are currently offered through the program. The company has more than 28,000 couturieres, 1,500 directors, and 300 regional directors.

Regional Directors also participate in The Farm Experience, a week-long training course with recreational activities worked in. What is unique about the company's Farm Experience is the fact that Stan, John, and employee management totally cater to the regional directors. They cook for them, clean up after them, and even serve them coffee every morning in bed. Stan says, "If you want to be a leader, be a servant."

In addition to the training, the excellent food and the recreational activities (everyone must play volleyball, etc., to build camaraderie and team spirit), a lot of *listening* occurs. "The people who are successful are listeners," Stan said. "We listen to our sales force."

Like Cameo, other DSOs listen to the sales force. The sales force is the only link between the customer and the DSO, so feedback is of utmost importance.

DONCASTER, DIVISION OF TANNER COMPANIES, INC. Rutherfordton, North Carolina (704) 287-4205 or (800) 669-3662 ext. 731
    Products: Women's Apparel and Accessories, Men's Shirts and Ties, Gifts

Annual Retail Sales Estimate: $50 million–$100 million
Method of Sale: person-to-person
Amount of Initial Investment for Salesperson: $450
Year Founded: 1931
DSA Member since 1959

Doncaster prides itself not only on the way its high-quality clothes are made, but also on the high-quality way its clothes are sold. Each Doncaster fashion consultant offers her customer something she won't find anywhere else—personal attention and consultation in choosing and designing her wardrobe. It is this personalized method of selling, coupled with the line itself, that singles out the Doncaster line as unlike any other.

The company was founded by a husband-and-wife team, S. B. Tanner and Millie Tanner, and the business has been passed along to three sons, Bobo, Jimmy, and Mike. Today, Doncaster remains a family business.

Doncaster collections include sportswear, separates, dresses, suits, coats, and a variety of accessories designed to complement the clothing. The company has established a reputation for quality—using the finest fabrics available from all over the world. Most of the products are manufactured in North Carolina in company-owned facilities.

Fashion consultants hold four one-week trunk showings that coincide with the four seasons of the year. Clothes are displayed in the home or private studio of the consultant and are shown to clients by private appointment. According to Doncaster executives, if you keep up with the latest fashion styles and know women who would love wearing classic apparel, you would be an ideal prospect for Doncaster.

The initial investment of $450 for consultants covers an extensive training process that includes a manual, video, and audio cassettes as well as practice sessions conducted by a district sales manager. Training covers basic selling skills and information about color, style, body types, fabrics, and fitting customers.

Local sales meetings and a national sales meeting held each year provide ongoing training as well as an opportunity to meet other consultants and receive recognition. With generous commissions, bonus plans, and wardrobe discounts, many consultants find selling Doncaster very lucrative. Consultant Tracy Kirkland sums up, "We are in the business of reducing the frustration often associated with shopping for clothes."

Like many other fine DSOs, Doncaster appeals to women who are longing to fulfill their needs as individuals, who would love having others respect and value their opinions, and who want to feel a real sense of accomplishment by asserting their financial independence and being their own boss.

Note: The sales plans and business details presented in the selected companies profiled in this chapter are obviously subject to modification due to today's volatile economic conditions, new managements, and the many other variables of a world whose only constant is change. Readers are urged to contact the Direct Selling Association (202) 292-5760 for updated information before making career choices.

Chapter 12

Going Global:
The International Direct Option

There is no freedom without free enterprise. This is a concept I have believed in and espoused for more than three decades, as I helped introduce direct selling to international markets. Ever since then, direct sellers have been a volunteer, for-profit "Free Enterprise Corps," akin to the Peace Corps, only private and far more dynamic, spreading the concepts of economic freedom globally.

As chairman of the U.S. Direct Selling Association in 1991–93, I called for a volunteer, not-for-profit "Free Enterprise Corps" to be sponsored by our government and staffed by college students of marketing, sales, and distribution, as well as retirees from these key disciplines and others whose jobs had disappeared in the changing environment of U.S. employment opportunities. During his term, President Bill Clinton has called for a domestic "job corps," but what is really needed is a global understanding of the powerful, positive impacts of ethical marketing practices on the global society. Simply put, if the world is to feed 10 billion people sometime in the 2000s, let alone enhance their quality of life, it will have to be *market-driven*. No small group of control-and-command gurus can possibly cope with what will be required—history has already proven this with the failure of totalitarian governments.

Direct selling's role has not yet been fully realized in the decade of the 1990s. The U.S. Direct Selling Association acts as Secretariat for the World Federation of Direct Selling Associations (WFDSA), and the WFDSA will play a major role in linking our efforts with those of governments in championing international free enterprise precepts. There are thirty-six WFDSA associations, reporting sales in 1992 of more than $50 billion U.S. from more than 11 million independent salespeople. Ongoing goals of the WFDSA include development of more understanding at the United Nations Economic and Social Council (ECOSOC), through obtaining Non-Governmental Organization (NGO) status. Additionally, the WFDSA is seeking a better understanding and cooperation with private-sector inter-

national organizations such as the International Organization of Consumer Unions (IOCU) and International Chamber of Commerce (ICC).

In the Commonwealth of Independent States and Eastern Europe,
the end of massive subsidies, of Communism itself, has closed many inefficient state-controlled enterprises and factories, and tens of millions
have lost their so-called jobs. Polish President Lech Walesa said on the
eve of Mikhail Gorbachev's resignation as head of the Soviet Communist
Party, "The danger has just started and has not finished. They [the Soviets]
will face real problems when they start real reforms." Clearly, Walesa's
"real problems" reference was an understatement as the 1990s unfolded.
Gorbachev's successor, embattled Russian President Boris Yeltsin, faced
hyperinflation and great pressure from nationalists who wanted to see a
return to some form of authoritarian state. The fate of the Russian Federation is crucial to all humanity, not just those who reside within its vast
borders. The Russians are struggling to find their direction without much
of a compass, but they must seek their way within the dimensions of their
own culture and politics. I believe the Russians will continue to stumble
toward some form of democratic, free market system, but almost anything
can happen, from a new coup to a full-blown civil war.

In 1990, when I was invited by the Ministry of Economics in Moscow
to lecture on free enterprise and incentive-based compensation programs,
I found a gap of comprehension far wider than I could bridge—or even
conceive. We were like aliens attempting to understand one another. To
bridge that gap will take a full generation; plans to establish free enterprise zones and call for a "Free Enterprise Corps" to show the way are, in
my view, right on target. We must show the way—not preach democratic
principles from the safety of our nation's insular borders.

When I met with Harvard professor Jeffrey Sachs in 1992 and asked
if he would invest his own money in the former Soviet Union, he quietly
responded no. In 1993, Sachs was quoted in the *Wall Street Journal* (April
2) as having said, "There is no way Russia can succeed without a stable
currency."

Over the next twenty-five years, Russia and other former Soviet
Union nations will need billions of dollars to stabilize the ruble, to feed
their people, and provide new jobs. This before the Russian Republic can
even begin to close inefficient factories and state-controlled enterprises
and move toward a free market economy. It is estimated that it will take
fifteen years for most other Eastern European countries to "catch up" with
Western Europe.

When I watched the bronze statue of Lenin being hauled away in
1991 from the headquarters building in Tallinn, Estonia, I knew the icons
of Communism were finally toppling and the world I'd known for almost

sixty years had fundamentally changed for the better. The first Mary Kay consultants from East Germany—after the Berlin Wall came down but before unification—had tears in their eyes when they realized their earnings were theirs to keep and spend as they chose. Since then, countries such as Hungary, Poland, and the Czech Republic have embraced direct selling, with companies such as Amway and Avon leading the way by establishing sales forces composed of thousands of independent entrepreneurs.

You can even start a direct-selling operation in a Communist nation. In 1991, Avon launched its Chinese operations in Guangzhou, and in just a few weeks had more than 1,000 "Avon Ladies" selling cosmetics and toiletries much as they do elsewhere in the world. Avon's sales force had grown to more than 16,000 by 1993 in Guangzhou alone, and many of these women were earning more than $500 in monthly commissions. In China, Avon's sales managers recruit and train "dealers" who earn money not only through their own sales, but also through the appointment of "Avon Ladies." Some Avon dealers are earning over $3,000 a month—over 100 times greater than the national average per capita income of Chinese workers. This will continue to stimulate their capitalistic growth, even within a country whose Communist leadership still has Tiananmen Square on its mind and which continues to exercise strong central control.

When I toured China in 1990, I suggested a commission structure in the "Friendship Stores" for foreign tourists, after observing scores of do-nothing salesclerks. My PRC hosts pointed out that this was "incompatible with Communism." Karl Marx knew very little about human motivation and less about sales and marketing. Former Avon president Rick Goings, now president of Tupperware Home Parties, says the first question asked by Chinese women in focus-group interviews conducted before the company launch in Guangzhou was, "How much commission do you pay?"

But there is still much to be done. A whole new ground floor of opportunity is opening to those who can practice the art and science of direct selling. Speaking at an International Leadership Conference of the DSA in 1991, former U.S. Senator Charles H. Percy said, "The sales skills practiced by members of DSA organizations are in tremendous demand around the world as economies struggle to emerge from command economies." Proof of this is the accelerated success in the early 1990s of companies such as Amway and Avon in Eastern European countries, with Avon announcing they had established 23,000 new representatives in Eastern Europe, and Amway claiming 80,000 distributors in Hungary alone. (Amway's sales were to grow to almost $1 billion in 1990–91, with most of that growth in international market areas. Avon's international sales and profits were its major source of growth. This has also been true of Tupperware and other U.S.-based direct-selling companies.)

A list of multinational direct-selling organizations follows. It was compiled by the U.S. Direct Selling Association in 1992 and is subject to frequent change as new markets are constantly opened by DSOs. Readers interested in current information are advised to contact the company of choice directly.

Table 12-1

Selected List
Multinational DSOs

Company Name	No. of Countries (Excluding the United States)
Act II Jewelry, Inc.—Lady Remington	2
Alfa Metalcraft Corporation	23
American Horizons, Inc.	2
Amway Corporation	25
Avon Products, Inc.	60
Cameo Coutures, Inc.	7
Discovery Toys, Inc.	2
Ekco Home Products Company	24
Electrolux Corporation	2
Encyclopaedia Britannica	47
Finelle Cosmetics	11
Fuller Brush Company	3
Jafra, U.S.A.	13
Kirby Company	34
Mary Kay Cosmetics, Inc.	19
Nature's Sunshine Products, Inc.	3
Noevir, Inc.	4
Nutri-Metics International, Inc.	15
Oriflame Corporation	29
Princess House, Inc.	4
PRO-MA Systems (U.S.A., Inc.)	3

Regal Ware, Inc.	19
Rexair, Inc.	21
Saladmaster, Inc. (Regal Ware, Inc.)	9
Society Corporation	3
Stanley Home Products Division of Stanhome Inc.	15
Tiara Exclusives	9
Time-Life Books, Inc.	42
Tri-Chem, Inc.	21
Tupperware Home Parties	37
WeCare Distributors, Inc.	3
West Bend Company	24
World Book Educational Products	30

I can vicariously share the thrills of those who do go—and perhaps they'll be your thrills—because my pioneering efforts more than thirty years ago in free-world countries broke new ground for free enterprise. In 1960, Europe was still frozen in a post–World War II marketing posture, where the son of a shoemaker was pretty certain to be a shoemaker, supermarkets were a rarity, and class discrimination kept the majority of people locked into low-income status.

I can never forget being told, in 1960, by a high-level consultant in the United Kingdom: "Party plan sales may be acceptable in the United States and Canada, but not here. Young man, you need to take your Tupperware, put it on a pushcart and sell it on High Streets in towns throughout Great Britain each market day Thursday." And we paid this guy a handsome fee for his erroneous, egregious advice!

Looking back, it would have been very easy to give up and pull out. We had invested very little—not much more than my time and meager salary and a boatload of plastic housewares. The product itself was unknown and not at all accepted; the name "Tupperware" was not a name you'd select for international marketing—it resisted any translation; and the method of sale was alien. (The headline on one major article about me, in a "yellow" tabloid circulated throughout England, blared, "He's turning our homes into shops!" I was sure I'd be fired.)

But I wasn't. Tupperware spread rapidly to the continent, first to Belgium, then to France, Italy, Germany, the Scandinavian countries, and eventually to Greece and even the Middle East. Later Tupperware came to Spain. Simultaneously, another team was working on the Pacific rim and another in South America. By the mid-1960s, Tupperware's brand name, products, and plan were accepted in forty-three countries, with worldwide sales soon to top a billion. Avon was also enjoying great expansion at the same time, and just a few years later, Amway, Encyclopaedia Britannica, Stanhome, World Book, and a host of other globally oriented companies made their mark. (Later in this chapter, we will detail the size of direct selling in dozens of markets to give you an idea where you might establish your next business, with the help of an experienced "partner.")

It was marvelous to watch direct selling adapt to the customs and mores of each new country yet retain its essential free enterprise nature. In Japan in 1962, the Tupperware pioneers were told, "Only Japanese *men* conduct business, never women. Your plan will not work here." In just a few years, the company had achieved a multi-million–dollar sales level and was still growing rapidly—with an almost all-female sales organization. The Japanese overlooked the fact that there were many widowed, divorced, and single women, not to mention some married women, who didn't know or care that they were not supposed to conduct business, but did it anyway. In many cases, they've surpassed the income of their male peers. Surprisingly, the attitude of gender discrimination persists to this day in Japan, yet direct-selling companies continue to do well with predominantly female sales organizations.

In the early 1960s, outside Nairobi, traders would start with a large supply of lightweight, unbreakable Tupperware, trade their way towards Mombasa (sometimes carrying the Tupperware on their heads for demonstrations around campfires in the bush), and return with native goods to be sold for cash back in Nairobi. Talk about a party plan succeeding without an infrastructure!

No doubt some imaginative sales and service techniques will have to be mastered by those pioneering the newly opening markets of the future, for there are nearly fifty nations yet to be opened to such free enterprise. To my knowledge, direct selling is the only form of retailing that can adapt to virtually any condition, any circumstance. The only thing I've known to stop a successful DSO is government interference, never the marketplace.

The continuance of democracy, however, will require market reforms and more free market economies. These reforms will be difficult, will create great hardships in the early years, and will require the creation (virtually from scratch in many nations) of an infrastructure of marketing and distribution that simply doesn't exist today.

According to Senator Percy, the unavailability of skilled workers, especially with business, sales, and marketing skills, is a major problem in less developed countries. He points out that there is "growing recogni-

tion that women make up a vital part of a country's human resource base."
Senator Percy also points out that "microenterprise development is gaining converts among development specialists."

The world's premier microenterprise specialists in individual opportunities are DSOs. The WFDSA has already begun a dialogue with scores
of governments with respect to our industry's ability to help create jobs,
teach business skills, provide opportunity for younger people and
women, and, above all, help develop an understanding of the value
added by marketing and distribution in a free market economy.

The Challenges and Advantages
of Doing Business Overseas

The experiences of U.S. Ambassador to the United Nations Made-
leine Albright when she was president of the Center for National Policy
in Washington reveal what challenges free enterprise must surmount in
emerging democracies—and some of the advantages direct sellers will
enjoy. Born in Prague, Czechoslovakia, Albright earned her doctorate at
Columbia University and served on President Jimmy Carter's National Security Council. She was also Donner Professor of International Affairs and
director of the Women in Foreign Service Program at Georgetown University's School of Foreign Service.

In 1991, she had just returned to the United States from conducting
a Times Mirror survey throughout the former Soviet Union and several
Eastern European countries using focus groups and in-depth interviews.
Of course, that put her in direct contact with people, rather than relying
solely on statistical polls, government sources, or public relations material.

In her interviews, Albright gained insights into how people in these
countries react to democracy, to the prospect of a free market system, and
to private versus public ownership of key industries. She found almost all
the people interviewed were in favor of personal freedoms, but still
wanted public ownership of most sectors of the economy. In the former
Soviet Union, for example, she found the people favored private ownership in only one sector, farming. In other words, people in the former
Soviet Union and Eastern European countries were unprepared for a free
market economy.

In addition, a "Ladder of Life" scale was used to allow people to
forecast the next few years of their lives, and most felt their life-style
would be lower on the scale, an accurate reflection of what must—and
did—happen in the early years of freedom. Albright found people in the
former Soviet Union were "obsessed by economic problems . . . they
would talk endlessly about foraging for food." Albright also found a "mas-

sive gender gap," where women were 20 percent more conservative on any issue and were much less interested in a free market, since they were concerned with their families first. "They had been 'liberated' for 70 years to work twice as hard as men," Albright pointed out.

Although Albright's research showed that most people wanted private business, they had no understanding of the role of profit. Until now, they had used their entrepreneurial abilities to get around the system. There was a "dictatorship of jealousy," according to Albright, with respect to those individuals who seemed to be making a lot of money through sales and marketing activities.

Albright illustrated this point by describing the anger of a woman with whom she was shopping at a vegetable market. Complaining about the price, the woman said, "He did not add to the value of the tomatoes." Albright could not persuade her that it was difficult and expensive to find a truck, buy gas, get the tomatoes to market, and stay there all day "selling." The Russian woman saw no value added, which will be one of the great contributions of direct sellers as they begin to conduct business in these and other less developed countries (LDCs), because "value added" is what each one of the more than 12 million direct sellers around the world provides each day. In fact, Albright quoted the then Czechoslovakian ambassador to the United States, Rita Klimova, as saying, "Direct selling is an absolutely perfect mechanism to introduce products into Eastern Europe."

Klimova went on to say that people in these countries were used to part-time work and that normal mass-marketing techniques (including telephone usage) were handicapped by the lack of infrastructure. She also stated that knocking on doors was not welcome—understandably, in the wake of dictatorships and police-state controls. Fortunately, many forms of direct selling (especially party plans) rely on other networking techniques so that such a business can flourish. Klimova summed up by stating that direct sellers could help create societies in which people begin to rely on selling.

Another factor paving the way for DSOs is the fact that, as Albright noted, "People in Eastern Europe and Russia want Western goods . . . to have them is a sign of having arrived. They are very attuned to Western products, and America is very popular."

As the former chairman of the Senate Foreign Relations Committee and as a former special ambassador and personal representative of the president in Peru and Bolivia, Senator Percy also perceives great opportunity for direct sellers throughout the world. He is a consultant to one of the DSA's most outstanding member companies, World Book, and credits his basic education in the Great Depression to a set of *World Book Ency-*

clopedias purchased for him by his father, then a bankrupt banker. In fact, one of Percy's Depression jobs was selling the *Saturday Evening Post, Ladies Home Journal,* and *Country Gentleman* door to door. He learned about direct selling's use of incentives when he won a national selling championship at age nine. Percy points out, and most major company CEOs now agree, "The companies that are really growing fast in direct selling are the international companies."

Language Barriers

Although those planning to set up shop in an international market are best advised to be a national of that country, or at least have roots and speak the language fluently, it is possible to succeed with only English-language skills in many areas. Today almost a billion people speak English around the world, and our language is more widely spoken and written than any other language has been. It has become the first truly global language.

Retail Resistance

As direct sellers have amply demonstrated, U.S. retailers are in a remarkable position to capitalize on the rapid growth and favorable changes in retailing in Asia, Europe (even Eastern Europe), and South America. They are experienced in working with constant change, with experimentation, and with marketing fundamentals and should be able to translate these hard-won skills to any international venue. But they have held back, leaving the field open to the direct option.

Despite the favorable changes in the world, in-store retailers in the United States have resisted going global. U.S. retailers appear to suffer from a strange paralysis when considering international expansion. Unlike direct sellers, who have been competing with great success for three decades or more, many American retailers seem to fear they cannot compete internationally because they do not know the territory, the language, or the culture. In the mid-1990s, powerful retailers such as Toys R Us, Wal-Mart, and JC Penney were beginning to expand their international presence, especially in the Americas, but they were among the exceptions.

There has been relatively little movement by U.S. retailers to other countries. Instead, the large investment is *from* overseas, with approximately 10 percent of U.S. retail sales now under substantial control of foreign companies. This is in sharp contrast to direct sellers, who are net exporters from the United States, favorably affecting the balance of trade.

Even today, many in-store retailers tend to react as if they compete in an insulated, island economy. They are content with their own geographic and cultural ethnocentricity. And sadly, most retailers do not seem to exhibit the leadership to meet the challenges and opportunities of the international marketplace. Global marketing is not likely to cause displacement by foreign competitors in the United States, but will create new opportunities for growth and profits abroad. American retailers have greater opportunities of penetrating retail markets abroad than retailers from any other country, whether they realize it or not.

Distribution

The major problem facing U.S. companies trying to enter foreign markets is almost always the difficulty of breaking into long-established distribution systems. This is well illustrated by the structural impediments to in-store retailing faced in Japan. However, creativity can overcome such impediments. For example, by utilizing direct selling, traditional distribution systems, as we've seen earlier in this chapter, can be bypassed.

Researching the International Direct Option

If you are considering an international direct option, you have much homework to do. In many instances, some familiarity with international product lines can be gained by contacting—or better yet, by *becoming*—an independent contractor with a globally oriented U.S. company.

Of the DSA member companies profiled earlier, several operate internationally. In most cases, international expansion is growing rapidly, so we won't attempt to list the countries in which each company is represented. Some of the largest global companies with U.S. bases are Amway, Avon, Encyclopaedia Britannica, Jafra Cosmetics, Kirby, Mary Kay Cosmetics, Nutri-Metics International, Stanhome, Tupperware, West Bend Company, and World Book. Information on these and other DSA member companies can be found by consulting the U.S. Direct Selling Association. Obviously, not every company does business in every country, and there are hundreds more direct-selling companies throughout the world that can be reached through their respective national associations. One way to view the fascinating world of international direct selling is to focus first on major "economic blocs." Bill Archey of the U.S. Chamber of Commerce and management consultant Peter Drucker both believe the 1990s will be an era of economic blocs, whether organized (such as the European Community) or de facto (such as in the Far East because of the influence of Japan). I share this view, so the information I've prepared for *The Direct*

Option is organized by large, logically aligned "blocs" of countries, whether they are connected by treaties or not. We'll look at population information and recent gross domestic product (GDP). The only figures currently available for former Communist nations are expressed in net material product (NMP).

Obviously, such data change frequently. But the data provided will give you an insight into the relative size and wealth of nations, as well as the extent of direct-selling penetration where known. The information presented will be useful to anyone in initial planning stages during most of the 1990s. (Updated information can be obtained on a country-by-country basis from respective WFDSA member associations.)

Table 12-1

The North American Free Trade Bloc

Country	Population	GDP Per Capita	Est. Retail Sales of DSOs	No. of Salespeople
Canada	26.5 million	$21,908	$1 billion	500,000
Mexico	4.5 million	$ 2,376	$636 million	605,000
United States	250.0 million	$21,696	$12.96 billion	4,500,000

Source: U.S. Direct Selling Association, 1992.

A North American Free Trade Agreement (NAFTA) would create the largest single market in the world, estimated by the U.S. Chamber of Commerce to represent a combined GDP of $6 trillion, 25 percent larger than estimates for the European Community (about $4.8 trillion). The long-term benefits of such an agreement are clear, combining Canadian resources, U.S. manufacturing capacity, and Mexican labor, with an intra–North American trade of $237 billion in 1990. In the United States, pressure groups including those from labor, textile industries, glass industries, citrus and other agricultural interests, and eco-radicals remained steadfast in 1993 in opposing such an agreement. Nonetheless, an agreement should be reached in the Clinton presidency, following negotiation of "side agreements" with respect to employment and environmental issues.

Canada, as a result of current trade agreements with the United States and its own recession, became an expensive place to live in the early 1990s, with additional taxes further eroding disposable income. Direct selling in Canada continues to expand at a rate comparable to that of the United States. More than 700,000 direct salespeople were added to

U.S. organizations between 1988 and 1990, and retail sales jumped from $9.6 billion to almost $12 billion in the same period.

Meanwhile, Mexico has risen to the number-four position in the world in numbers of people in direct selling, and under President Carlos Salinas de Gortari the economy has been revitalized. One important fact is that 75 percent of the jobs created since 1988 have been outside the government: this would not have been possible in regimes preceding Salinas. And the middle class in Mexico is growing rapidly, a key to developing a successful direct-selling business. Many Mexican business interests are still concerned about their ability to compete with American organizations, however, despite the success of "Salinastroika."

The North American Free Trade Agreement will institutionalize the remarkable changes in Mexico, including allowances for 100 percent foreign ownership, the technology transfer law and the intellectual property law (which allows direct selling companies to protect trademarks and tradenames). As a conservationist, I believe NAFTA presents the only real solution to environmental degradation in Mexico, for several reasons. The most compelling argument is that to control industrial pollution is expensive and requires a growing economy. Additionally, a conservation ethic requires an educated populace, and education, too, comes from increased prosperity. Of great importance will be the positive influence of major U.S. companies establishing manufacturing in Mexico. The great majority of these companies have excellent environmental records and practices, and they are already showing the way, not only by technology transfer, but by training their Mexican work forces to be better conservationists. Finally, the Mexican government has now formed the equivalent of our Environmental Protection Agency. This agency is, for the first time, enforcing already existing laws as well as adopting new anti-pollution policies, shutting down heavily polluting plants, and even jailing flagrant offenders.

When a North American Free Trade Agreement is completed in the 1990s, the bloc will have tremendous leverage in future negotiations, and greater market access to other Western Hemisphere nations will result. According to Manuel Suarez-Mier, economics minister of the Embassy of Mexico, that country's 2.6 percent GDP growth rate in 1992 could easily swell to 4 or 5 percent with NAFTA in full swing. There are many positive implications for direct sellers in the expanding Mexican economy.

Table 12-2

South American Trading Bloc

Country	Population	GDP Per Capita	Est. Retail Sales of DSOs	No. of Salespeople
Argentina	31.9 million	$1,889	$336 million	215,000
Brazil	147.4 million	$3,031	$1.1 billion	400,000
Chile	12.8 million	$1,732	$40 million	37,000
Venezuela	19.7 million	$2,447	N/A	N/A

Source: U.S. Direct Selling Association, 1992.

South America, with 335 million people, has a combined GDP exceeding $600 billion. The 1985–89 growth in real GDP was a little over 2 percent, with external debt approaching $400 billion.

The three largest populations of South America have the largest per capita incomes. But all continue to have serious debt problems. Brazil's inflation and unstable currency present serious drawbacks. Argentina's raging inflation has abated significantly, and the country will continue to increase in prosperity throughout the decade.

The good news for direct-selling companies is that the area is showing signs of long-term recovery, and the middle class is growing in Argentina, Brazil, Chile, and Venezuela. WFDSA associations are already established in Argentina, Brazil, and Chile, and a new association was established in Venezuela in 1993. In addition, the middle class in these countries is already forming consumption patterns similar to the U.S. middle class.

Chile has a strong growth rate at over 5 percent and has become a model for other South American countries. Chile will be first in line to join NAFTA when negotiations are complete. There is a feeling that the United States' positive initiatives in South America, including the possibility of some debt forgiveness, has opened the door to more American business involvement, including direct selling. For the first time in decades, the United States is paying attention to issues other than Communism in this hemisphere.

Also good news for direct sellers is the fact that Latin America is democratizing almost universally. In 1980, only 35 percent of its governments could be described as democracies. In 1990, according to the Organization of American States (OAS), the majority of the thirty-three countries that comprise Latin America could now be described as democracies, with people living in freely elected government states.

However, privatization is the key in South America. If the countries involved are successful, much of the debt could be written off through debt-equity swaps, the infrastructure could be modernized (which any traveler can tell you is sorely needed), and the size and cost of the traditionally huge bureaucracies could be reduced.

Table 12-3

Africa And Middle East Trade Blocs

Country	Population	GDP Per Capita	Est. Retail Sales of DSOs	No. of Salespeople
Algeria	23.7 million	$2,288	N/A	N/A
Egypt	51.7 million	$497	N/A	N/A
Israel	4.7 million	$10,991	N/A	N/A
Kenya	24.9 million	$333	N/A	N/A
Nigeria	105.0 million	$254	N/A	N/A
Saudi Arabia	14.4 million	$5,752	N/A	N/A
South Africa	35.3 million	$2,879	$200 million	60,000
Zimbabwe	8.6 million	$622	N/A	N/A

Source: U.S. Direct Selling Association, 1992.

With few exceptions, Africa does not offer much immediate promise for direct selling, although South Africa has long been an excellent market and there is some direct selling in both Algeria and Nigeria. Egypt, too, offers long-term promise, as could Israel and even Saudi Arabia.

Although state socialism has ruled Algeria since its independence, there are positive pressures for market reform and privatization. New laws are in place liberalizing foreign investment. But the hard-liners remained in control after attempts early in the 1990s at free elections. Unemployment is over 20 percent, with foreign debt at high levels. This presents a "wait and see" situation for DSOs.

The U.S. government's lifting of economic sanctions in South Africa may well signal an opportunity for renewed growth of direct selling there. WFDSA Chairman Jim Threlfall reported "much optimism" following a late 1991 visit. I trained the Tupperware team that opened South Africa to direct selling some thirty years ago and also developed a direct-selling cosmetics business there. All this occurred before the world rightly recognized the tragedy of apartheid and reacted to it with strong trade sanctions. As political problems are resolved, South Africa presents an excellent opportunity for the direct option since its economy and quality of life are excellent. The De Klerk government's actions to repeal the Land Acts of 1913 and 1936 and to abolish the Population Registration Act of 1950 the bedrock apartheid law removed the statutory basis for apartheid and moved South Africa closer to the international community. As the 1990s have unfolded, De Klerk's position and that of Nelson Mandella have moved closer, and the prospects for a democratically based government continued to brighten; but there are still serious issues to be resolved and much tension between the major political forces. When the political situation is resolved, this will again be a very attractive market for DSOs, and the lessons of free enterprise learned by participating in a direct-selling environment will benefit many.

This is not at all true of most of the rest of Africa, particularly sub-Saharan Africa, where many countries and millions of people started the 1990s in crisis conditions such as found in Somalia. The economic structure is in disarray, and already low per capita incomes are falling even lower. For example, the per capita gross national product (GNP) in Ethiopia is $130; in Chad and Zaire it's $150; and in Tanzania it's $180. To bring this into focus, China has more than doubled these per capita incomes at $350. Most countries in Africa's heartland are a great deal poorer than they were when I first visited this continent three decades ago. Television news coverage from Somalia and other countries has made it clear that human deprivation is the norm, that millions are suffering from malnutrition and hundreds of thousands are starving.

A free market approach has seldom been taken in most of Africa, and governmental bureaucracies dominate. Perhaps the most significant failure of African governments is the neglect of human rights. But direct selling can work in Africa, and in fact has worked in the past until driven out or discriminated against. The solution for sub-Saharan Africa is the same as what will ultimately work in Eastern Europe and the former Soviet Union a shift to democratic and market-driven economies and a shift away from state-controlled ones.

According to Senator Percy, Egypt (the largest country in the Middle East) is the best opportunity for direct selling in the long run. Although Avon currently operates in Saudi Arabia and World Book is in Kuwait, Muslim mores, restricting women from commerce, have had a dampening effect on these markets as well as those of Jordan and United Arab Emirates. A major breakthrough in which the Arab nations lift their boycott of Israel could open up a "free trade zone" in the Middle East, but this is not a likely prospect. A hopeful sign for direct selling is the establishment in 1993 of a WFDSA association in Israel. My own travels in this country, with its indomitable people, lead me to believe that direct selling could flourish here.

For now, except for the markets noted, international direct option aspirants are well advised to select other markets.

By the end of 1993, a "new" market of 350 million consumers, not including Eastern Europe and the former Soviet Union (in whatever form of independent republics it might assume), will effectively trilateralize world trade. Although the economy of Europe will flounder in the 1990s, this could still be the "European Decade" in many ways. Goods, services, and exports now flow freely between twelve EC (European Community) nations, with some restrictions on the flow of people. In many countries, including the most affluent, mid-1990s unemployment was high, reaching double-digit proportions in many Western European countries. Political unrest was evident almost everywhere.

Table 12-4

The European Community And Neighbors

Country	Population	GDP Per Capita	Est. Retail Sales of Dsos	No. of Salespeople
Austria	7.7 million	$20,646	$139 million	4,000
Belgium	9.9 million	$15,923	$111 million	8,566
Denmark	5.1 million	$20,693	$14 million	1,500
Finland	5.0 million	$27,626	$53 million	6,400
France	56.4 million	$20,804	$1.06 billion	260,000
Germany	63.2 million	$23,555	$1.95 billion	175,000
Greece	10.0 million	$5,429	$30 million	21,560
Ireland	3.5 million	$9,670	$13 million	3,000
Italy	57.7 million	$18,917	$1.11 billion	167,866
Netherlands	14.8 million	$15,084	$105 million	11,000
Norway	4.2 million	$24,959	$100 million	10,000
Portugal	10.3 million	$3,962	$114 million	50,000
Spain	39.0 million	$12,613	$720 million	92,300
Sweden	8.6 million	$26,448	$41 million	23,000
Switzerland	6.7 million	$27,941	$161 million	6,000
Turkey	54.2 million	$1,303	N/A	N/A
United Kingdom	(est.) 57.4 million	$16,918	$1.4 billion	580,000
Yugoslavia	23.7 million	$4,143	N/A	N/A

Source: U.S. Direct Selling Association, 1992.

Table 12-5

Eastern Europe & Soviet Union

Country	Population	GDP Per capita	Est. Retail Sales of DSOs	No. of Salespeople
Czech Republic	10.7 million	$2,800	Unknown	Unknown
Slovak Republic	5.0 million	$2,800	Unknown	Unknown
Hungary	10.4 million	$2,777	Unknown	Unknown
Poland	37.9 million	$2,172	Unknown	Unknown
Common-wealth of Independent States	291.0 million	GNP per capita $9,142	N/A	N/A

Source: U.S. Direct Selling Association, 1992.

In late 1991 at Maastricht, Netherlands, European Community leaders agreed on a single currency to go along with their single, barrier-free market. But by 1993, hopes had dwindled for this to be completed in full by the target date of 1999 because Great Britain backed away and other European countries failed to meet the treaty's financial "tests." In 1993, Ambassador Andreas van Agt, European Community Ambassador to the United States, told me at a DSA meeting that he believed that there would first be a "single EC currency for a smaller group of countries" to include France, Germany, and the Benelux countries of Belgium, Luxembourg, and The Netherlands.

But many of the EC rules and agreements are undecided. The current European Community consists of twelve countries: Belgium, Denmark, France, Greece, Ireland, Italy, Luxembourg, The Netherlands, Portugal, Spain, United Kingdom, and unified Germany. Of these, the best direct option markets are France, Germany, Italy, Spain, and United Kingdom. In 1992, Denmark reopened to direct selling, but Sweden, despite the presence of the giant Electrolux company, was considering restrictive legislation on direct selling in 1993. Before deciding on the country or countries of your choice, checking with the WFDSA's Secretariat in Washington, D.C., would be wise, as ever-changing laws can affect your business plan.

There are more than three hundred direct-selling companies in Europe, two hundred of which are of European background and origin. The European Federation of Direct Selling Associations (FEDSA) proposed to the EC Commission adoption of a universal direct-selling code, based on that developed by the U.S. DSA. When adopted, this would protect the consumers of both products and opportunity in these nations.

An "exclusive EC club" may no longer be feasible. Austria, Finland, Norway, and Sweden are knocking on the door. These countries are members of the European Free Trade Association (EFTA), along with Iceland and Switzerland. It is likely these EFTA countries, except Switzerland, will be joining the EC in the mid-1990s. In a shocking 1993 vote, the Swiss decided not to apply for membership in the European economic area, a prerequisite for admission to the EC. The 700-year-old Swiss Federation proved too conservative to contemplate eventual EC membership, much to the chagrin of its business and political leaders. To remain isolated, eventually surrounded by a vibrant free market, may prove economically unfeasible for this beautiful and proud country, and most predict another vote sometime in the future. Even without Switzerland, the combined EC/EFTA GNP would still be more than $6 trillion, and the population 374 million.

Eastern European countries will also soon clamor for EC membership. But the current twelve members of the EC are very concerned about immigration from Eastern Europe and the former Soviet Union. Some estimate that up to 8 million immigrants from Eastern Europe alone will arrive. On the EC's eastern border, Turkey, which has been moving towards a free market economy and achieving a solid growth rate, is also knocking on the EC door. Turkish businesses have been actively seeking Western investment, and this country should now be viewed as having excellent potential for direct selling. In 1993, a new direct-selling association was formed in Turkey, with membership in the World Federation. Experts doubt that Turkey will be considered in this century for EC membership, but this will not impede the country's march toward economic stability.

Heating up the concern is the difficulty unified Germany is having overcoming the social, economic, and psychological differences between the two Germanies. Although the language is common, the work ethic and cultural mores are not. In overcoming forty years of Communist control, the Germans are showing the way for what must come in Eastern Europe. According to Ambassador Agt, German unification has cost Germany dearly, thus "seriously slowing down not only that country's economic development, but that of all Western Europe." A major obstacle is property ownership, a complex legal mess. The disparity in wages between east and west is putting stress on the country's social stability. However, this actually provides an opportunity for someone taking advantage of the direct option, because new sales organization members can be expected to earn comparable profits in any area of unified Germany, especially with a booming market for all consumer goods. In the long run, Germany will emerge with an even stronger economy, with West Germany supplying capital and technology, East Germany labor and land.

Hungary, Poland, and the Czech Republic are making excellent economic progress, although struggling with the massive transition from Communism and a controlled state towards free market economies. In 1993, there were at least fourteen direct-selling companies operating in Hungary alone. Direct sellers in these three nations have applied for membership in the European Federation of Direct Selling Associations, and full membership will be granted in 1993–94. Of course, with the establishment of the Czech Republic, the FEDSA now contemplates a separate association for the new Slovak Republic. This will bring DSOs in these countries under the strict codes of FEDSA.

The newly independent Baltic countries of Lithuania, Latvia, and Estonia will be quick to move toward a free market. In 1993, I met with the prime minister of Latvia, Ivars Godmanis, a physicist by education and vocation, but a superb leader who welcomed free trade to his tiny nation. Latvia, once artificially attached to the Soviet Union, is attuned to Western mores and culture and may represent a direct option opportunity for the 1990s; Lithuania and especially Estonia will take longer to develop free markets. Other former Soviet Union countries are not as fortunate, as ethnic confrontations and even wars continue. And, of course, the world is focused on the terrible events in former Yugoslavia, where Serbs created the terrible phrase "ethnic cleansing" (of Muslims), and thousands have died in Bosnia and Croatia. Despite the ongoing war, forward-looking DSOs in FEDSA are planning the creation of DSAs in Slovenia, Croatia, and Serbia.

Archey warns that people in the United States have greatly romanticized what is going on in Eastern Europe. "Eastern Europeans do want democracy, but it is much less clear how much free enterprise they want. They really challenge most people who succeed at free enterprise activities, in many cases think they have somehow cheated and been unfairly compensated, and you can be suspect in these countries as a result of your free enterprise activities."

There is obviously a problem convincing some Eastern Europeans about the desirability of the direct option, a problem that will diminish over time as these countries move inexorably toward free market conditions. This is precisely why a formal "Free Enterprise Corps" is desirable.

U.S. direct-selling companies that are not already established in the European Community may have a difficult time competing because rules of origin, local content rules, local packaging requirements, and special rules governing beauty and health care products may prove too expensive and cumbersome.

There are many mandated benefits for independent contractors in Europe that do not exist in the United States. But because of prior abuses by U.S. pyramid companies, now declared illegal throughout the world, other restrictions exist.

Samuel Berger, former senior partner in the International Trade and Government Relations Group of the Washington law firm Hogan & Hartson (which counsels the USDSA) and currently deputy assistant to the president for national security affairs in the Clinton administration, has insights from his experience as deputy director of the Policy Planning Staff at the U.S. Department of State. "The regulatory issues involved in the EC are both national and community-wide," he says. "France has the lowest threshold for considering salespeople as independent contractors, making it difficult for new direct selling companies to become established." By 1993, a new APB Code in national statistics will allow companies wishing to appear under the heading "direct selling" to do so.

Berger has predicted that Spain will follow the direction of France. A law on unfair trading was approved in Spain in 1991 with a provision that limits "gifts and prizes" to 15 percent of the value of products offered. Obviously, that affects direct sellers, as does multilevel marketing (MLM) legislation proposed in 1993.

Belgium, where I participated in the first Tupperware party with then-president Hamer Wilson in 1960, is now highly restrictive of party plan sales.

In Germany, the law on consumer credit was in place in 1991, with provisions for the law on installment sales. This provides consumers with a right of cancellation within one week. Months before German federal consumer laws applied in the former DDR, the German association Arbeitskreis supplied information to East Germans concerning the risks of a free market. This campaign informed them about direct selling as a marketing system, about the various forms of direct selling, and about the rights of customers as guaranteed by the WFDSA. The importance of direct selling in Germany was highlighted by a study by the University of Bochum revealing that 23 percent of all commercial transactions with consumers are conducted in their homes.

Italy requires much training to become a direct seller. And after this training is completed and approved, a license is required. Due to its training and license requirements, Italy continues to provide an excellent opportunity for ethical direct selling.

For the truly enterprising direct seller, Europe presents a fantastic opportunity for the 1990s into the twenty-first century. Despite the cautions I've presented, individuals establishing direct-selling businesses in Europe (especially in concert with established companies) can look forward not only to an interesting, challenging life-style, but also to great financial rewards.

Senator Percy summed up what's required: "We have to make an investment in human resources. Trying to teach business skills is extremely difficult. You cannot have the mind-set of sitting back and waiting for business to come to you . . . you must go out and dig for it. This is exactly what direct selling does!"

Table 12-6

India

Country	Population	GDP Per Capita	Est. Retail Sales of DSOs	No. of Salespeople
India	811.8 million	$336	N/A	N/A

Source: U.S. Direct Selling Association, 1992.

It appears that India will be one of the boom markets for direct selling in the next two decades. By the year 2020, India may well be the most populous nation on earth, perhaps surpassing China as the latter's government-mandated birth control takes statistical effect. India now has the largest middle class, estimated at 250 million, and is the largest democracy on earth. Proof of its potential for the direct option lies in the fact that India is World Book's second largest market. The Indian DSA was founded by World Book's Srinivasan and Mina Krishnan in 1991.

However, statistics can be misleading. Direct-selling companies will also confront obstacles to expansion. During his fifty-eighth visit to India in 1991, Charles Percy said he encountered great difficulties just getting from place to place. There are large disparities of income and, to quote economist John Beyer of Nathan Associates (a market research firm and economic advisor to the U.S. DSA), "Within the many layers of the Indian market, two centuries live side by side . . . a ready market for Mercedes and Toyotas, a *vast* market for bullock carts and bicycles."

Demographics support the view of India as an attractive potential market. According to Beyer, there are about 150 million moderate-income Indians who consider quality before price and who tend to buy brand-packaged goods, such as those offered by many direct-selling companies. These Indians live in modestly furnished homes and consume a range of toiletries, clothing, and footwear. They own a variety of convenience items in the kitchen and status symbols in the living room. They are thus an ideal market for many DSOs.

But the best target for direct selling would be the upscale, affluent market, 50 million strong, which tends to follow Western trends, a lifestyle originally created by the British. These are individuals willing to adopt new habits and change to new products. In addition, status is very important to them. Most live in urban areas and are accessible to traditional direct-selling approaches. As urbanization increases, it will bring about 25 percent of the population within easy reach.

Literacy in India has climbed dramatically, with 50 percent of the population literate. As in the United States, Europe, and Japan, working women insist on convenience in both the purchase and use of products. Many women work outside the home, but they also continue to play the role of final decision maker for the purchase of products concerning the home.

With the assassination of Rajiv Ghandi in 1992, India experienced a severe setback. The horrible Bombay stock market bombing in 1993 underscored the dangers embedded in the ethnic strife of the nation. But their future economic plan (1990–95) is targeted on improving the distribution infrastructure, reducing unemployment and poverty, decreasing industry cost and increasing capacity utilization, emphasizing modernization, furthering private enterprise, and underscoring international competitiveness. In addition, the country's GDP has been growing at an average of 5.5 percent over the last decade. The pace of economic reform will continue to accelerate. The government has acknowledged it needs to make its public sector leaner and more efficient and that economic growth cannot be stifled because of the government's lack of growth capital.

Asia-Pacific

There are 1.7 billion people in this area, counting mainland China-close to 900 million, without the Chinese and major cities—the target markets—in these countries are expected to increase in size at an average of 50 percent by the year 2000.

The combined GDP is in excess of $4 trillion. Nearly $2.8 trillion of that is Japanese. Japan's direct investment in the Asia-Pacific region totaled $70 billion in 1989, whereas the U.S. direct investment in this same market (excluding Japan) was only $36 billion. Although Japan's sun is now setting, its economy in decline, it is still winning in the region through its willingness to make direct investments, and its dominance will continue to grow.

The economy of most of this area was on fire throughout the 1980s. The growth rate for the 1990s is more moderate, however. The collective annual growth rate in the 1980s was 7 percent. The range between 1985 and 1990 went from .8 percent in New Zealand to 11.6 percent in China. China had the highest inflation rate in this period, at 17.8 percent, while Singapore had the lowest at 2.4 percent.

Table 12-7

Asia-Pacific

Country	Population	GDP Per Capita	Est. Retail Sales of DSOs	No. Of Salespeople
Australia	17.1 million	$17,303	$720 million	350,000
China	1,122.0 million	$376	N/A	N/A
Hong Kong	5.8 million	$10,097	$50 million	80,000
Indonesia	179.1 million	$525	N/A	N/A
Japan	123.1 million	$23,276	$22 billion	1,500,000
Malaysia	17.4 million	$2,160	$416 million	300,000
New Zealand	3.3 million	$12,618	$80 million	60,000
Philippines	61.5 million	$713	$66 million	360,000
Singapore	2.7 million	$10,582	$100 million	40,000
South Korea	42.8 million	$5,603	N/A	N/A
		GNP per capita		
Taiwan	20.5 million	$5,922	$900 million	650,000
Thailand	57.2 million	$1,402	$400 million	220,000

Source: U.S. Direct Selling Association, 1992.

The forecast, according to the International Division of the U.S. Chamber of Commerce, is for continued strong growth led by domestic demand. There will be increasing intra-Asian trade and investment and regional cooperation, but the formation of a trade bloc is not predicted.

Japan. Japan is the largest direct-selling market on earth. The party plan (Tupperware) sales method was pioneered in Japan thirty years ago. The total market is now almost double that of the United States. As of 1990, Avon (established in 1969) had 370,000 sales representatives in Japan. Other companies include Pola Cosmetics (established in 1929), which had more than 150,000 sales representatives in the early 1990s, and Noevir, which had an estimated 100,000. Amway, with approximately 900,000 distributors in Japan, is one of the largest direct-selling companies and is said to be one of the largest exporters to Japan from the United

States. Shaklee is another market company of U.S. origin in Japan, although the company now has Japanese ownership.

The Japan Direct Selling Association (JDSA) is very proactive on consumer protection. The JDSA direct-selling hotline provides consumers with information and assistance. However, many of the claims relate to non-JDSA member company activities. The JDSA's program includes a consumer monitor system, distribution to nationwide consumer centers of leaflets explaining JDSA's telephone consultation system, and distribution of educational tools, leaflets, and videos.

Japan's GDP growth during 1985–90 averaged 4.1 percent, but during the 1990s it is expected to cool off. Inflation and unemployment remain at very low rates less than 3 percent. Most economic forecasters believe Japan will continue above-average growth and that Japanese industry will continue to strengthen its competitive position.

Of particular interest to DSOs is the size of the middle class, which encompasses most of the population. The Japanese are very quality conscious and demand satisfaction in every detail with respect to all products, especially consumer goods and packaging. In many ways, the Japanese are becoming more like Westerners, with an aging population and a demand for more consumer goods and services. Much more of the nation's financial resources will be consumed internally to meet these demands.

In the years following the introduction of Tupperware and Avon to the market (utilizing primarily single, widowed, and divorced women), there has been a major shift to a majority of married women entering the work force. Most of the female work force falls between thirty-five and fifty-four years of age, and there is still a large non-working female component. Significantly, although research shows that younger Japanese women "look down on" careers in favor of nurturing families, after their children are safely in school, many seek to re-enter the work force. At this point, the high value put on tenure in the Japanese system works against these women; and so in their mid- to late thirties they have a difficult time finding high-paying employment. These trends favor the direct option.

China. Avon has proven that a market can be developed in this nation, at least in southern China. During my 1990 visit I observed that American and European fashion concepts and other consumer goods were being adopted, especially by the urban Chinese, and at least tolerated by the Communists. In Shanghai, modern fashion magazines are very much in evidence, and stores feature fashion merchandise. Research done in 1993 revealed a pent-up desire to follow world fashion and other consumer goods trends, and savings were being used to satisfy the demand. China does have a tremendous consumer goods production capacity, greatly underutilized because of a lack of modern marketing skills; their capacity is well advanced over the former Soviet Union's.

However, what I noticed most during my many visits to China, especially Hong Kong (which officially reverts to Chinese ownership in 1997), was the entrepreneurial spirit, bordering on passion, possessed by many Chinese. In many provinces of China, *everybody wants to be an entrepreneur*. This is the principle reason for Avon's initial successes in Guangdong. It can serve as fuel for other direct-selling companies' successes as well.

Because of the vastness of China and the great disparities between provinces, DSOs will tend to concentrate on those with the most potential. The following table shows the ten provinces and municipalities with the highest GDP and growth rates:

Table 12-8

China

Province/Municipality (Capital)	Population (Million)	GNP ($Billion)	Growth (%)	GNP/ capita
Beijing	10.8	12.3	12.0	$1138
Shanghai	13.3	30.2	14.9	$2271
Shenzhen SEZ	0.6	N/A	N/A	N/A
Tianjin	8.8	9.9	12.7	$1125
Fujian (Fuzhou)	30.0	9.0	20.5	$300
Guangdong (Guangzhou)	62.8	38.3	26.6	$610
Jiangsu (Nanjing)	68.1	51.5	22.5	$756
Liaoning (Shenyang)	39.5	24.2	11.3	$613
Shandong (Jinan)	84.4	32.1	18.5	$380
Zhejiang (Hangzhou)	41.4	25.6	21.6	$618

Source: EEI, Inc., 1993.

According to Richard Johnston, Jr., president of EEI, Inc. and former principal deputy assistant secretary of international economic policy, U.S. Department of Commerce, as well as former commercial counsel, U.S. Embassy in Beijing, China's published growth rate of 9–12 percent of GDP is much lower than actual. This is especially true in the south and on the coasts, where growth rates range from 20 percent to 30 percent. High growth rates such as these do raise the concern of inflation, but it would appear the central Chinese government has, according to Johnston, "a strong inclination to keep going in the same direction."

China "specialists" (I agree with John King Fairbank who allowed that there are no China experts, only China specialists) rightly warn us of the "downside." China is still a Communist nation, as I was reminded personally by Premier Li Peng at the World Economic Forum. There is no freedom of press, a lot of Chinese are still in jail because of their protests at Tianenmen Square, there is no due process as we know it, and ethnic minorities and political dissenters are squashed immediately. According to Congressman Lee H. Hamilton, chairman of the Committee on Foreign Affairs, U.S. House of Representatives, speaking in April, 1993, to the Business Coalition for U.S. China Trade: "At this stage in its historical development, China still lacks a civic society the foundation for a pluralistic democracy. The political scene is polarized and confrontational with little or no mutual tolerance between the Chinese regime and its articulate and skillful opponents."

Congressman Hamilton, in urging Congress to continue to grant Most Favored Nation (MFN) status to China, listed a number of reasons why U.S.-China relations should remain healthy, including the following:

♦ Peace and stability in East and South Asia
♦ Global efforts to control the spread of weapons of mass destruction
♦ The economic and political welfare of the Chinese people
♦ The future of Taiwan and Hong Kong
♦ *The competitive vitality of American companies seeking access to the world's fastest growing market* (my emphasis).

South Korea. South Korea has proven to be somewhat difficult to establish for direct selling, but Encyclopaedia Britannica, Amway, CUTCO/Vector, and The West Bend Company have been very successful there. Tupperware and Amway have established a manufacturing presence. Although this market has been the focus of anti-MLM government activities, it will continue to open up to direct selling in the 1990s.

Taiwan. Taiwan is a booming direct-selling market, with $1 billion easily forecast in the early 1990s. The Taiwanese are very receptive to DSOs, and the DSA member companies doing business in this country all seem to be enjoying exceptional growth patterns. By 1992, Taiwan had grown to the number-three position in the world in numbers of direct sellers. A strong presence here could also be a launch point for establishing a beachhead in mainland China, especially as many Taiwanese have family or other connections there. But in its own right, this is a marvelous market, with great potential for the independent entrepreneur who is aligned with a progressive DSO.

Australia and New Zealand. Well into the early 1990s, both Australia and New Zealand were in a deep recession, with no end in sight. These have traditionally been excellent markets for direct sellers, with the industry itself being welcomed and absorbed into the culture, and both countries have high per capita purchases from DSOs. But due in part to isolation from other world markets and competitive trends, these two countries do not appear to have great GDP growth potential through the mid-1990s. This does not mean that individual DSOs cannot thrive in Australia many are furnishing much-needed opportunity to families requiring second incomes and entrepreneurs seeking to build profitable new businesses.

Australia's "workcare levies" are unfavorable to direct-selling independent contractors and are enforced by the Accident Compensation Commission (ACC). The WFDSA Australia is challenging a ten-day cooling off period for cash sales over $50, under the country's Door-to-Door Trading Act. There are continuing efforts by the government in Canberra to impose a withholding tax on independent contractors; if these efforts are successful, they will have an adverse effect on DSOs in this country.

Malaysia, Indonesia, Thailand, and Singapore. Malaysia and Thailand are the strongest economic performers in Southeast Asia. The forecast for Malaysia in 1991 is a GDP growth of 8.5 percent. This is one of the most open and supportive environments for private sector investment and growth in the region. It is at one of the major trading crossroads of the world, strategically well-placed for growth in the 1990s. Thailand continues to be an excellent direct-selling market for many companies, very receptive to new businesses, as is Indonesia. On the other hand, Singapore would appear to be moving toward more restrictive laws regarding direct selling, especially with respect to MLM plans.

Philippines. Despite a politically unstable situation, direct selling continued to do well in the Philippines in the early 1990s. The sales leader was Avon, with Tupperware and educational product DSOs also doing well in this market, which is receptive to DSOs.

Looking Forward

On the whole, the prospects for international direct selling are extremely exciting. At the 1991 World Economic Forum in Davos, Switzerland, I presented a briefing on how direct selling can jump-start consumer retailing in LDCs and in the new market economies of Eastern Europe. I referred to the low capital requirements of direct selling, which virtually eliminate the often substantial investment barriers other retailing and business formats require. "Direct selling can satisfy the worldwide consumer demand now unleashed by global media and other forces," I pointed out. "People in emerging economies are acutely aware of the candy on the other side of the window."

The sophistication of present-day global selling stems in large measure from the highly detailed, low-cost computer data available today. Today's best DSOs are virtual webs of information, stretching right around the world; but they succeed because these businesses operate through real people, not a faceless system of distribution.

At Davos, I foresaw an explosion of direct selling worldwide, and especially of women in direct selling. Women will be seeking more leadership responsibility and a greater role in the world economy through direct selling. Approximately 90 percent of the customer purchasing decisions around the world are made by women. Women have the best grasp of consumer distribution because of their experience. And women are natural at the one-on-one leadership contact required by modern retail management.

The leaders of these organizations and especially the leaders in the field sales organizations involved must not remain content to sit in their offices and supervise. Instead, they must support the people on the front lines of marketing, people who should now have the data and motivation to build long-term customer relationships effectively all over the world.

Appendix A

Direct Selling Association

The Direct Selling Association (DSA) is a national trade association representing more than 100 companies that manufacture and distribute goods and services sold directly to consumers. As a trade association, the DSA's services are geared to helping member companies and their salespeople succeed.

The **Government Relations** department tracks legislative developments on the federal, state, and local levels, lobbies appropriate officials on issues of concern to the direct selling industry, and keeps the members informed of important developments. In a typical year, the Government Relations staff will review approximately 15,000–20,000 federal legislative proposals and 150,000 state bills and make between 35 and 50 personal visits to state legislatures to explain the DSA's position on the issues.

Critical issues for the 1990s are: tax proposals that threaten the independent contractor status of direct sellers, extended cooling-off periods for purchases made from direct sellers, changes in the business opportunity thresholds, amendments to franchise laws, licensing and registration, and telemarketing legislation that can affect the way some direct sellers operate.

Educational Opportunities for member company executives abound. In addition to the Annual Meeting, the DSA offers a variety of meetings on special topics, such as recruiting, multilevel marketing, international issues, leadership summits for CEOs, and integration of telemarketing and direct mail with direct selling.

Sales Force Benefits are also provided to companies by the DSA. Scores of member companies participate in the DSA's major medical health insurance and term life insurance programs. Since 98 percent of direct salespeople are independent contractors rather than employees, the DSA administers an insurance program to provide them with benefits at the more favorable group rate. Salespeople from participating companies can also receive a gold "identity" card which tells potential customers that they are part of an association committed to the highest level of consumer ethics.

Information on the latest industry trends, sales and marketing aids, consumer tips, detailed profiles of other members, and guides to the laws affecting direct selling can all be found at the DSA. Providing a network to help members learn from one another is consistently rated as one of the DSA's most valuable services.

Consumer Services begin with the DSA's Code of Ethics, which spells out ethical guidelines for companies and salespeople to follow. Each company must pledge annually to follow the Code. An independent Code Administrator handles any consumer complaints against member companies and is empowered to decide on appropriate remedies. DSA publishes and distributes consumer education brochures that explain the Code of Ethics, offer tips on choosing the right selling opportunity, and outline guidelines for buying from direct sellers.

Direct Selling Association (DSA)
1776 K Street, N.W.
Suite 600
Washington, DC 20006
(202) 293-5760
FAX (202) 463-4569

Direct Selling Education Foundation (DSEF)
1776 K Street, N.W.
Suite 600
Washington, DC 20006
(202) 293-5760
FAX (202) 463-4569

DIRECT SELLING ASSOCIATION
FAST FACTS

♦ The Association was founded in 1910 in Binghamton, New York, by ten companies.

♦ The DSA moved to Winona, Minnesota, in 1924, where it was known as the National Association of Direct Selling Companies.

♦ Two of the founding members, the California Perfume Company (now known as Avon Products, Inc.) and Watkins Incorporated, are members of the Association today.

♦ In 1969, the DSA moved to Washington, D.C. and adopted its present name.

♦ The Direct Selling Education Foundation was founded in 1973 as a not-for-profit public educational organization to conduct educational outreach programs to academic and consumer protection audiences. To date, the DSEF has sponsored more than thirty consumer conferences, and its academic seminars and programs have reached 125 universities and 350 professors. Through the DSEF, dozens of direct-selling executives have spoken to marketing students on college campuses, and more than 50 professors have visited direct-selling companies. The DSEF also publishes a journal on consumer and citizen issues, which is mailed free to more than 21,000 consumer leaders, educators, and advocates.

♦ The World Federation of Direct Selling Associations was founded in 1978. It now has 36 member-nation direct-selling associations.

♦ In 1982, the DSA won an important legislative victory when the U.S. Congress declared direct sellers to be statutory non employees for federal tax purposes. This step reinforced the long-standing independent contractor relationship most sellers have with their companies. The action also ensured that direct-selling companies would not have to withhold income, social security, and unemployment compensation taxes from the commissions they pay to their salespeople.

AMENDED CODE OF ETHICS
1992

The DSA has always taken an active role in promoting the highest
levels of ethics among member companies. In 1991, the DSA formed an
Ethics Task Force to study recruiting issues and develop amendments to
the existing Code of Ethics. The original Code of Ethics, adopted in 1970,
was designed to establish industry standards of customer service. The
Ethics Task Force's assignment is to apply the same principles of fairness
and full disclosure to consumers of the direct-selling opportunity—the
potential salespeople.

In March, 1992, the DSA Board of Directors unanimously adopted
formal Code amendments requiring that:

(1) earnings and sales claims made by companies be based on documented facts;

(2) companies refrain from any deceptive, unlawful, or unethical
consumer or recruiting practices;

(3) the Code Administrator may recommend expulsion of companies that violate the Code or state or federal law and refuse to change
their practices.

These amendments strengthen the existing Code of Ethics and give
both the Board of Directors and the Code Administrator more options in
dealing with violators. Specifically, the expulsion provisions allow for
suspensions of membership and outright termination of membership.
Companies will have the opportunity to appear before the Board of Directors before such actions take effect but cannot be reinstated once suspension or termination has occurred until a ninety-day waiting period (in
the case of suspensions) or a one-year waiting period (in the case of
terminations) has expired. These procedures offer a counterpoint to the
existing requirement of a one-year waiting period for new members.

DIRECT SELLING ASSOCIATION
CODE OF ETHICS

Preamble

The Direct Selling Association, recognizing that companies engaged in direct selling assume certain responsibilities toward consumers arising out of the personal-contact method of distribution of their products and services, hereby sets forth the basic fair and ethical principles and practices to which member companies of the association will continue to adhere in the conduct of their business.

Introduction

The Direct Selling Association is the national trade association of the leading firms that manufacture and distribute goods and services sold directly to consumers. The Association's mission is "to protect, serve and promote the effectiveness of member companies and the independent businesspeople marketing their products and to assure the highest level of business ethics and service to consumers." The cornerstone of the Association's commitment to ethical business practices and consumer service is its Code of Ethics. Every member company pledges to abide by the Code's standards and procedures as a condition of admission and continuing membership in the Association. Consumers can rely on the extra protection provided by the Code when they purchase products or services from a salesperson associated with a member company of the Direct Selling Association. For a current list of Association members, contact DSA, 1776 K St., N.W., Washington, DC 20006, (202) 293-5760.

A. Code of Conduct
1. Deceptive or Unlawful Consumer Practices

No member company of the Association shall engage in any deceptive or unlawful consumer practice.

2. Products or Services

The offer of products or services for sale by member companies of the Association shall be accurate and truthful as to price, grade, quality, make, value, performance, quantity, currency of model, and availability.

3. Terms of Sale

A written order or receipt shall be delivered to the customer at the time of sale, which sets forth in language that is clear and free of ambiguity:

A. All the terms and conditions of sale, with specification of the total amount the customer will be required to pay, including all interest, service charges and fees, and other costs and expenses as required by federal and state law;

B. The name and address of the salesperson or the member firm represented.

4. Warranties and Guarantees

The terms of any warranty or guarantee offered by the seller in connection with the sale shall be furnished to the buyer in a manner that fully conforms to federal and state warranty and guarantee laws and regulations. The manufacturer, distributor and/or seller shall fully and promptly perform in accordance with the terms of all warranties and guarantees offered to consumers.

5. Pyramid Schemes

For the purpose of this Code, pyramid or endless chain schemes shall be considered consumer transactions actionable under this Code. The Code Administrator shall determine whether such pyramid or endless chain schemes constitute a violation of this Code in accordance with applicable federal, state and/or local law or regulation

B. Responsibilities and Duties

In the event any consumer shall complain that the salesperson or representative offering for sale the products or services of a member company has engaged in any improper course or conduct pertaining to the sales presentation of its goods or services, the member company shall promptly investigate the complaint and shall take such steps as it may find appropriate and necessary under the circumstances to cause the redress of any wrongs which its investigation discloses to have been committed.

Member companies will be considered responsible for Code violations by their solicitors and representatives where the Administrator finds, after considering all the facts, that a violation of the Code has occurred and the member has either authorized such practice found to be violative, condoned it, or in any other way supported it. A member shall be considered responsible for a Code violation by its solicitors or representatives, although it had no knowledge of such violation, if the Administrator finds that the member was culpably negligent by failing to establish procedures whereby the member would be kept informed of the activity of its solicitors and representatives. For the purposes of this Code, in the interest of fostering consumer protection, companies shall voluntarily not raise the independent contractor status of salespersons distributing their products or services under its trademark or trade name as a defense against Code violation allegations and such action shall not be construed to be a waiver of the companies' right to raise such defense under any other circumstance.

The members subscribing to this Code recognize that its success will require diligence in creating an awareness among their employees and/or the independent wholesalers and retailers marketing under the Code. No subscribing party shall in any way attempt to persuade, induce or coerce another party to breach this Code, and the subscribers hereto agree that the inducing of the breach of this Code is considered a violation of the Code.

C. Administration

1. Interpretation and Execution

The Board of Directors of the Direct Selling Association shall appoint a Code Administrator to serve for a fixed term to be set by the Board prior to appointment. The Board shall have the authority to discharge the Administrator for cause only. The Board shall provide sufficient authority to enable the Administrator to properly discharge the responsibilities entrusted to the Administrator under this Code. The Administrator will be responsible directly and solely to the Board.

The Board of Directors will establish all regulations necessary to administer the provisions of this Code.

2. Code Administrator

The Administrator shall be a person of recognized integrity, knowledgeable in the industry, and of a stature that will command respect by the industry and from the public. He shall appoint a staff adequate and competent to assist him in the discharge of his duties. During his term of office, neither the Administrator nor any member of his staff shall be an officer, director, employee, or substantial stockholder in any member or affiliate of the DSA. The Administrator shall disclose all holdings of stock in any member company prior to appointment and shall also disclose any subsequent purchases of such stock to the Board of Directors. The Administrator shall also have the same rights of indemnification as the Directors and Officers have under the bylaws of the Direct Selling Association.

The Administrator, in accordance with the regulations established by the Board of Directors as provided herein, shall hear and determine all charges against members subscribing hereto, affording such members or persons an opportunity to be heard fully. The Administrator shall have the power to originate any proceedings, and shall at all times have the full cooperation of all members.

3. Procedure

The Administrator shall determine whether a violation of the Code has occurred in accordance with the regulations promulgated hereunder.

The Administrator shall answer as promptly as possible all queries posed by members relating to the Code and its application, and, when appropriate, may suggest, for consideration by the Board of Directors, new regulations, definitions, or other implementations to make the Code more effective.

The Administrator shall undertake through his office to maintain and improve all relations with better business bureaus and other organizations, both private and public, with a view toward improving the industry's relations with the public and receiving information from such organizations relating to the industry's sales activities.

D. Regulations for Enforcement of DSA
Code of Ethics

1. Receipt of Complaint

Under receipt of a complaint from a bona fide consumer or where the Administrator has reason to believe that a member has violated the Code of Ethics, the Administrator shall forward a copy of the complaint, if any, to the accused member together with a letter notifying the member that a preliminary investigation of a specified possible violation pursuant to Section 3 is being conducted and requesting the member's cooperation in supplying necessary information, documentation and explanatory comment. If a written complaint is not the basis of the Administrator's investigation, then the Administrator shall provide written notice as to the basis of this reason to believe that a violation has occurred. Further, the Code Administrator shall honor any requests for confidential treatment of the identity of the complaining party made by that party.

2. Cooperation with the Code Administrator

In the event a member refuses to cooperate with the Administrator and refuses to supply necessary information, documentation and explanatory comment, the Administrator shall serve upon the member, by registered mail, a notice affording the member an opportunity to appear before the Board of Directors on a date certain to show cause why its membership in the Direct Selling Association should not be terminated. In the event the member refuses to appear before the Board or refuses to comply with the Board's decision, the Board may terminate the offender's membership without further notice or proceedings.

3. Informal Investigation and Disposition Procedure

The Administrator shall conduct a preliminary investigation, making such investigative contacts as are necessary to reach an informed decision as to the alleged Code violation.

If the Administrator determines, after the informal investigation that there is no need for further action or that the Code violation allegation lacks merit, further investigation and administrative action on the matter shall terminate and the complaining party shall be so notified.

The Administrator may, in his discretion, remedy an alleged Code violation through informal, oral and written communication with the accused member company.

If the Administrator determines that the allegation has sufficient merit, in that the apparent violations are of such a nature, scope or frequency so as to require remedial action pursuant to Part E and that the best interests of consumers, the Association and the direct selling industry require remedial action, he shall notify the member of his decision, the reasoning and facts which produced it, and the nature of the remedy he believes should be effected. The Administrator's notice shall offer the member an opportunity to voluntarily consent to accept the suggested remedies without the necessity of a Section 4 hearing. If the member desires to dispose of the matter in this informal matter it will, within 20 days, advise the Administrator, in writing, of its willingness to consent. The letter to the Administrator may state that the member's willingness to consent does not constitute an admission or belief that the Code has been violated.

4. Formal Hearing Procedure

If a hearing is requested by an accused member or, if in the opinion of the Administrator, the informal procedure provided for in Part D 3 above does not provide adequate remedy for the consumer, or, if in his opinion, the alleged violations of the Code are of such a nature, scope or frequency so as to support a reasonable belief by the Administrator that an evidentiary hearing is necessary to determine whether or not the allegations of Code misconduct warrant the implementation of the remedial sanctions of Part E, the Administrator may call for a formal hearing. The purpose of such a hearing is to gather evidence and take testimony surrounding the Code of Ethics complaint.

The Administrator shall notify, in writing, the accused member of his intent to hold a hearing, and shall specify in such notification the nature and substance of the consumer complaint to be heard at the hearing. The Administrator shall make reasonable attempts to arrange a mutually convenient place and time for the hearing to occur. Such notification shall precede by at least twenty days any proposed date for an evidentiary hearing concerning the allegations of the Code of Ethics misconduct. Hearings may be rescheduled for good cause shown.

The accused member shall have the right to submit any data deemed relevant to the proceeding, to appear in person or through counsel, and rebut the charges against it. Both parties shall have the right to call witnesses, and the accused party shall have the right to call and confront the complaining party, providing the calling party shall bear any costs involved in calling the complaining party or any witness. Both parties shall also have the right to cross-examine any witnesses who are called. The Administrator shall determine, based on evidence presented by the company and evidence submitted by the complainant, whether a Code violation has occurred. The decision by the Administrator shall be issued no later than ten days from the date of the hearing and shall be forthwith sent to the accused member, the President and the Chairman of the Board of DSA, and the complainant. The decision will include the remedial measures, if any, that the Administrator has invoked pursuant to Part E. The member shall then have ten days from date of receipt to comment to the Administrator, in writing, on the findings contained in the decision, or to request a special arbitration procedure as described in Part F.

E. Powers of the Administrator

If, pursuant to the hearing provided for in Part D 4, the Administrator determines that the accused member has committed a Code of Ethics violation or violations, the Administrator is hereby empowered to impose the following remedies, either individually or concurrently, upon the accused member:

(1) request complete restitution to the consumer of monies paid for the accused member's products which were the subject of the Code complaint;

(2) request the replacement or repair of any accused member's product, the sale of which was the source of the Code complaint;

(3) request the payment of a voluntary contribution to a special assessment fund which shall be used for purposes of publicizing and disseminating the Code and related information. The contribution may range up to $500 per violation of the Code.

(4) request the accused member to submit to the Administrator a written commitment to abide by the DSA Code of Ethics in future transactions and to exercise due diligence to assure there will be no recurrence of the practice leading to the subject Code complaint.

If the Administrator determines that there has been compliance with all imposed remedies in a particular case, he shall terminate the matter.

In the event that a member refuses to voluntarily comply with any remedy imposed by the Administrator within thirty days, the Administrator may then consult with independent legal counsel to determine whether the facts that have been ascertained amount to a violation of state or federal law. If the Administrator believes that a violation of state or federal law has occurred, he shall so notify the accused member by certified or registered mail, return receipt requested, and after ten days following such notice the Administrator shall submit the relevant data concerning the complaint to the appropriate federal or local agency.

F. Appeal to Outside Arbitrator

Following a final decision by the Administrator that a Code violation has occurred, the accused member may appeal the decision by the Administrator to an independent arbitrator. The request by the accused member must be in a written statement to the Administrator no later than ten days after receipt of the Administrator's final decision. Upon receipt of such request, the Administrator shall set a date for an arbitration hearing within a reasonable period of time not to exceed 60 days from the date of the request. If such an appeal is filed, any sanctions imposed under Section E shall be stayed until the conclusion of arbitration. The choice of said arbitrator shall be made by the accused company from a list provided by an existing arbitration organization such as the American Association of Arbitrators. All attendant costs of such an arbitration, including witness fees and travel expenses, but not including any expenses related to the time or travel of the Administrator and DSA staff, shall be borne by the requesting member.

The arbitrator shall receive, at least five days prior to the hearing date, submissions from the Administrator and the accused member outlining their respective positions concerning the allegations of Code violations. The accused member shall be given fifteen days' notice of the date of the hearing. At the hearing, the accused member shall have an opportunity to be represented by counsel, to refute the charges against it, and to hear the evidence and confront and cross-examine witnesses against it. The member will further have the opportunity to present witnesses for its position, which witnesses also shall be subject to confrontation and cross-examination by the Administrator. All witnesses and the Administrator shall be subject to questioning by the arbitrator. The Administrator also may be represented by counsel.

A transcript will be made of the hearing at the request and expense of the accused member, or at the expense of the Association if the Administrator determines that a transcript is necessary to protect the integrity of the Association and/or the rights of the complaining witnesses. If a transcript is so requested, or if the Administrator determines that a record of the hearing is necessary, a tape recording of the hearing may be made in lieu of a transcript if all parties agree.

The decision of the arbitrator is final and is binding upon both the Administrator and the member. The arbitrator may, upon completion of the hearing, affirm, modify, or reverse the original finding of the Administrator. The arbitrator shall, within ten days of the hearing, issue his decision in writing to the Administrator, the accused company and the President and Chairman of the Board of DSA.

G. Restrictions

(1) At no time during an investigation or the hearing of charges against a member shall the Administrator or outside arbitrator confer with anyone at any time concerning any alleged violation of the Code, except as provided herein and as may be necessary to conduct the investigation and hold a hearing. Any information ascertained during an investigation or hearing shall be treated as confidential, except in cases where the accused member has been determined to have violated federal, state or local statutes. At no time during the investigation or the hearing of charges shall the Administrator or outside arbitrator confer with a competitor of the member alleged to be in violation of the Code, except when it may be necessary to call a competitor as a witness to the facts, in which case the competitor shall be used only for the purpose of testifying as to the facts. At no time shall a competitor participate in the Administrator's or in the outside arbitrator's disposition of a complaint.

(2) Upon request by the Administrator to any member, all documents directly relating to an alleged violation shall be delivered to the Administrator. Any such information obtained by the Administrator shall be held in confidence in accord with the terms of these regulations and the Code. Whenever the Administrator, either by his own determination or pursuant to a decision by an outside arbitrator, terminates an action which was begun under the Code, a record of the member accused shall be wiped clean and all documents, memoranda or other written material shall either be destroyed or returned, as may be deemed appropriate by the Administrator, except to the extent necessary for submitting relevant data concerning a complaint to a local, state, or federal agency. At no time during proceedings under this Code regulation or under the Code shall the Administrator or outside arbitrator either unilaterally or through the DSA issue a press release concerning allegations or findings of a violation of the Code unless specifically authorized to do so by the Board of Directors.

H. Resignation

Resignation from the Association by an accused company prior to completion of any proceedings constituted under this Code shall not be grounds for termination of said proceedings, and a determination as to the Code violation shall be rendered by the Administrator and/or arbitrator, irrespective of the accused company's continued membership in the Association or participation in the complaint resolution proceedings.

I. Amendments

This Code may be amended by vote of two-thirds of the Board of Directors.

As Adopted June 15, 1970
As Amended by Board of Directors through December 5, 1988

The DSA Code Administrator is appointed by the Board of Directors to receive complaints against member companies from consumers, conduct investigations and determine in each case whether a violation has occurred and what remedy, if any, is appropriate. The Administrator is chosen on the basis of his knowledge of the industry, stature in the consumer affairs and business communities and reputation for competence and integrity. All investigations by the Code Administrator are completely confidential.

DSA Code Administrator
1776 K Street, N.W.
Suite 600
Washington, DC 20006
(202) 293-5760

SELECTED LIST OF DIRECT SELLING ASSOCIATION
MEMBER COMPANIES

An asterisk (*) denotes a company that is profiled in Chapter 11 of this book.

Act II Jewelry, Inc. - Lady Remington
818 Thorndale Avenue
Bensenville, Ill. 60106
(708) 860-3323
FAX (708) 860-5634

Alfa Metalcraft Corporation of America
GOS Int'l Distributors
6593 Powers Ave.
Suite 17
Jacksonville, Fla. 32217
(904) 731-8200
FAX (904) 737-4162

* Amway Corporation
7575 Fulton East
Ada, Mich. 49355-0001
(616) 676-6000
FAX (616) 676-4617

* Art Finds International, Inc.
10214 USA Today Way
Miramar, Fla. 33025
(305) 431-2277 FAX (305) 431-9885

Artistic Impressions, Inc.
240 Cortland Avenue
Lombard, Ill. 60148
(708) 916-0050
FAX (708) 916-1478

Avon Products, Inc.
Nine West 57 Street
New York, N.Y. 10019
(212) 546-6015
FAX (212) 546-6136

* Cameo Coutures, Inc.
9004 Ambassador Row
Dallas, Texas 75247
(214) 631-4860

FAX (214) 905-6011

Contempo Fashions (The Gerson Company)

6100 Broadmoor

Shawnee Mission, Kan. 66202

(913) 262-7407

FAX (913) 262-3568

Country Home Collection

1719 Hallock-Young Road

Warren, Ohio 44481

(216) 824-2575

FAX (216) 824-2577

Creative Memories

2815 Clearwater Road

P.O. Box 767

St. Cloud, Minn. 56302

(612) 251-3822

FAX (612) 251-6997

* CUTCO/Vector Corporation

1116 East State Street

P.O. Box 810

Olean, N.Y. 14760-0810

(716) 372-3111

FAX (716) 373-6155

* Diamite Corporation

1625 McCandless Drive

Milpitas, Calif. 95035

(408) 945-1000

FAX (408) 945-0157

* Discovery Toys, Inc.

2530 Arnold Drive

Suite 400

Martinez, Calif. 94553

(510) 370-3400

FAX (510) 370-0289

* Doncaster

Oak Springs Road

Box 1159

Rutherfordton, N.C. 28139

(704) 287-4205

FAX (704) 287-7771

* Dudley Products, Inc.
7856 McCloud Road
Greensboro, N.C. 27409
(919) 668-3000
FAX (919) 665-3160

Ekco Home Products Company
2382 Townsgate Road
Westlake Village, Calif. 91361
(805) 494-1711
FAX (805) 494-1810

Electrolux Corporation
2300 Windy Ridge Parkway
Suite 900 South
Marietta, Ga. 30067
(404) 933-1000
FAX (404) 933-1097

* Encyclopaedia Britannica North America
Britannica Centre
310 South Michigan Avenue
Chicago, Ill. 60604
(312) 347-7000
FAX (312) 347-7399

* Fuller Brush Company
3065 Center Green Drive
Boulder, Colo. 80301
(303) 440-9448
FAX (303) 440-8727

* Golden Pride/Rawleigh, Inc.
1501 Northpoint Parkway
Suite 100
West Palm Beach, Fla. 33407
(407) 640-5700
FAX (407) 640-5539

Highlights for Children, Inc.
2300 West Fifth Avenue
P.O. Box 269
Columbus, Ohio 43216
(614) 486-0631
FAX (614) 487-2700

* Home Interiors & Gifts, Inc.
4550 Spring Valley Road
Dallas, Texas 75244-3706
(214) 386-1000
FAX (214) 233-8825

House of Lloyd, Inc.
11901 Grandview Road
Grandview, Mo. 64030
(816) 966-2222
FAX (816) 763-4956

Jafra Cosmetics International
2451 Townsgate Road
Westlake Village, Calif. 91361
(805) 496-1911
FAX (805) 497-6604

Just America (Tanner Companies, Inc.)
Oak Springs Road
Rutherfordton, N.C. 28139
(704) 287-4205

* Kirby Company
1920 West 114 Street
Cleveland, Ohio 44102-2391
(216) 228-2400
FAX (216) 221-3162

* Kitchen Fair (Regal Ware, Inc.)
1090 Redmond Road
P.O. Box 100
Jacksonville, Ark. 72076
(501) 982-7446
FAX (501) 982-0563

Lady Love Skin Care
P.O. Box 867687
Plano, Texas 75086-7687
(214) 596-5239
FAX (214) 596-4080

* Longaberger Company
95 North Chestnut Street
Dresden, Ohio 43821-9600
(614) 754-6300
FAX (614) 754-2004

* Mary Kay Cosmetics, Inc.
>8787 Stemmons Freeway
>Dallas, Texas 75247
>(214) 630-8787
>FAX (214) 905-5999

Nature's Sunshine Products, Inc.
>75 East 1700 South
>P.O. Box 19005
>Provo, Utah 84605-9005
>(801) 342-4300
>FAX (801) 342-4305

Noevir, Inc.
>1095 S.E. Main Street
>Irvine, Calif. 92714
>(714) 660-1111
>FAX (714) 660-9562

Oriflame U.S.A.
>76 Treble Cove Road
>North Billerica, Mass. 01862
>(508) 663-2700
>FAX (508) 663-0254

The Pampered Chef, Ltd.
>205 Fencl Lane
>Hillside, Ill. 60162
>(708) 449-3906
>FAX (708) 449-2941

Primerica Financial Services
>3120 Breckenridge Blvd.
>Duluth, Ga. 30199-0001
>(404) 381-1000
>FAX (404) 564-6213

* Princess House, Inc.
>455 Somerset Avenue
>North Dighton, Mass. 02754
>(508) 823-0713
>FAX (508) 823-5182

RACHAeL Cosmetics, Inc.
>155 W. Highway 434
>Winter Springs, Fla. 32708
>(407) 327-5032

FAX (407) 327-5034

Regal Ware, Inc.
    1675 Reigle Drive
    Kewaskum, Wis. 53040
    (414) 626-2121
    FAX (414) 626-8565

Rexair, Inc.
    3221 W. Big Beaver Road
    Suite 200
    Troy, Mich. 48084
    (313) 643-7222
    FAX (313) 643-7676

Rich Plan Corporation
    4981 Commercial Drive
    Yorkville, N.Y. 13495
    (800) 243-1358
    FAX (315) 736-7597

Saladmaster, Inc. (Regal Ware, Inc.)
    131 Howell Street
    Dallas, Texas 75207
    (817) 633-3555
    FAX (817) 633-5544

* Shaklee Corporation
    Shaklee Terraces
    444 Market Street
    San Francisco, Calif. 94111
    (415) 954-3000
    FAX (415) 986-0808

The Southwestern Company
    P.O. Box 305140
    Nashville, Tenn. 37230-5140
    (615) 391-2500
    FAX (615) 391-2846

* Stanhome Inc. (Stanley Home Products Division)
    333 Western Avenue
    Westfield, Mass. 01085
    (413) 562-3631
    FAX (413) 568-2820

Time-Life Books, Inc.
    777 Duke Street

Alexandria, Va. 22314
(703) 838-7000
FAX (703) 838-7474

Tri-Chem, Inc.
One Cape May Street
Harrison, N.J. 07029
(201) 482-5500
FAX (201) 482-0002

* Tupperware
P.O. Box 2353
Orlando, Fla. 32802
(407) 847-3111
FAX (407) 826-8872

Vita Craft Corporation
11100 West 58 Street
P.O. Box 3129
Shawnee, Kan. 66203
(913) 631-6265
FAX (913) 631-1143

* Watkins Incorporated
150 Liberty Street
Winona, Minn. 55987-0570
(507) 457-3300
FAX (507) 452-6723

The West Bend Company
400 Washington Street
West Bend, Wis. 53095
(414) 334-2311
FAX (414) 334-6800

* Winning Edge (The Southwestern Co.)
P.O. Box 305140
Nashville, Tenn. 37230
(615) 391-2500
FAX (615) 391-2815

* World Book, Inc.
101 Northwest Point Blvd.
Elk Grove, Ill. 60007
(708) 290-5300
FAX (708) 290-5301

DIRECT SELLING ASSOCIATION
DIRECT SELLING HALL OF FAME
Members

1993
Spencer Hayes
The Southwestern Company

1992
Gerald E. Gibert
Hogan & Hartson

1991
Patricia A. Wier
Encyclopaedia
Britannica, USA

1989
Stan Fredrick
Cameo Coutures

1988
Monty Barber
Mary Kay Cosmetics

1987
Jay Van Andel
Amway Corporation

1986
Charles E. Swanson
Encyclopaedia
Britannica, Inc.

1985
Richard H. Bell
Highlights for
Children

1984
James E. Preston
Avon Products

1983
Neil H. Offen
Direct Selling
Association

1982
David W. Mitchell
Avon Products

1981
Charles A. Collis
Princess House

1980
Robert H. King
World Book

1979
Richard M. DeVos
Amway Corporation

1978
John S. Hamilton
Wear-Ever Aluminum

1977
Homer G. Perkins
Stanley Home Products

1976
Mary Kay Ash
Mary Kay Cosmetics

1975
Mary C. Crowley
Home Interiors &
Gifts

Richard Polinsky
Minnesota Woolen Co.

1974
H. Thomas McGrath
Avon Products

1973
E. Cabell Brand
The Stuart McGuire
Company

1971
Alfred C. Fuller
The Fuller Brush
Company

E.J. "Pete" Sievers
Watkins Products

1970
H. Edison Briginal
Beeline Fashions

Harry F. Taylor
Studio Girl
Cosmetics

1969
Gary J. McDonald
The Management Team

Alfred G. Winfrey
Sarah Coventry

1968
John A. Ewald
Avon Products

C. Clair Knox
Knox Associates

1967
L.J. "Les" Engleson
C.W. Stuart & Co.

1966
Charles C. McPherson
Stanley Home Products

Alvin L. Saeks
The Puro Company

1965
Harold A. Schatz
The West Bend
Company

Lyman K. Stuart
C. H. Stuart

1964
James M. George
National
Association of
Direct Selling
Companies

1963
Wallace E. Campbell
The Fuller Brush
Company

John C. Luhn
The Easterling Co.

Stephen Sheridan
Electrolux

**Gov. Lloyd Crow
Stark**
Stark Bros'
Nurseries

Appendix B

A Profile of Direct Salespeople:
Survey for the Direct Selling Association

By Nathan Associates
1992

1. Introduction

A Profile of Direct Salespeople presents information on the demographic characteristics and direct-selling experience of direct salespeople. More specifically, the report covers the following areas:

- Personal characteristics of direct salespeople, including gender, age, ethnicity, education, marital status, and household income.
- Reasons for entering direct selling.
- Direct-selling employment experience as measured by average weekly hours in direct selling, direct-selling income and expenses, and other items.
- Key salespeople characteristics by type of salesperson.

In addition, the report provides recommendations for future research.

The information in this report is based on data collected in interviews with 1,382 direct salespeople during a nationwide telephone survey conducted in March and April of 1992. In addition, the survey also completed interviews with 218 persons who had dropped out of direct selling with no plans for re-entering direct selling within twelve months. The names for the 1,600 interviews completed during the survey were drawn from the sales force rosters of twenty member companies of the DSA that account for a statistically significant percentage of the salespeople in the direct-selling industry.

This survey of direct salespeople is the most comprehensive conducted since Louis Harris and Associates, Inc., fielded a survey of direct salespeople on behalf of the DSA in August of 1976. Comparisons between the two surveys are made throughout this report when appropriate.

In summary, the "average" person working in direct selling is a white, married woman aged 35–44, with some college education, a household income of $25,000–$30,000, a working husband, and children. The typical direct salesperson became involved in direct selling for the first time less than two years ago and worked at another paid job before first entering direct selling. Some important reasons for starting direct-selling careers are a liking for and belief in the product, a desire to earn extra income, and a desire to work independently. The average direct salesperson works alone and spends 5–10 hours per week on direct-selling activities. The average salesperson earns $50–$75 dollars per week from direct selling, accounting for 6–10 percent of their household income.

2. Demographic Characteristics

Gender

A total of 90 percent of the salespeople are women. This compares with 80 percent in 1976 and 88 percent in 1990. The percentage of women, however, varies among subgroups of salespeople. The percentage of women decreases with increases in hours spent per week in direct selling, declining from 95 percent among those working in direct selling less than five hours per week to 79 percent among those working over twenty hours per week.

The percentage of women decreases with increases in education level, declining from 97 percent among those with less than a high school diploma to 80 percent among those with a college degree. A notable exception to this pattern is the percentage of women among those with post-graduate degrees, where the percentage is 96 percent. The percentage of women is larger among whites than blacks (91 percent vs. 84 percent) and larger among the married than the never married (91 percent vs. 83 percent)

Age

A total of 63 percent of direct salespeople over 17 years of age are between the ages of 25 and 44. This is significantly greater than the 44 percent of the American people over 17 years of age that are between the ages of 25 and 44. Direct salespeople have about the same percentage as the American people as a whole in the 45–64 age group (24 percent vs.

25 percent) and have a lower percentage in the 18–25 age group (8 percent vs. 15 percent) and in the over 64 age group (4 percent vs. 17 percent).

From 1976 to 1992 the percentages of salespeople under age 25 (11 percent vs. 8 percent) and over age 64 (7 percent vs. 5 percent) have declined slightly. The age distribution varies somewhat with the hours spent per week in direct selling. The percentage for the 25–34 age group decreases from 37 percent among those working under five hours per week to 23 percent for those working over twenty hours per week. The percentage for the 35–64 age group increases from 49 percent among those working under five hours per week to 66 percent for those working over twenty hours per week.

Ethnicity

The percentage of white people among salespeople has declined from 86 percent in 1976 to 80 percent in 1992. The percentages of ethnic minorities increased from 1976 to 1992: blacks (10 percent vs. 13 percent), Hispanic/Spanish (3 percent vs. 5 percent), Asian/Pacific islander (less than 1 percent vs. 1 percent), and other ethnicities (1 percent vs. 2 percent).

While the percentage of whites among salespeople is above that for the American public (80 percent vs. 76 percent), the percentage for Asians/Pacific islanders is lower (1 percent vs. 3 percent). The percentages of blacks, Hispanics, and American natives among salespeople closely matches those for the American public.

The percentage of whites tends to increase with hours spent per week in direct selling, increasing from 75 percent among those working under five hours per week to 86 percent among those working over thirty hours per week. The percentage of whites is lower among those who recruit than those who do not (78 percent vs. 84 percent) and lower among those who have other paid jobs than those who do not (75 percent vs. 85 percent).

Education

Based on persons 25 years of age or older, salespeople have a larger percentage than the American public in the middle education categories: high school graduate; some college, no degree; associate degree; and bachelor's degree. Salespeople have a lower percentage of people without high school diplomas and of people with graduate degrees than the American public.

Based on salespeople of all ages, the direct sales force has become better educated since 1976. The percentage of salespeople without a high school diploma declined sharply from 18 percent in 1976 to 6 percent in 1992. The percentage with a high school diploma, some college (no degree), or an associate degree increased slightly from 69 percent in 1976 to 73 percent in 1992. The percentage with a bachelor's or post-graduate degree increased from 13 percent in 1976 to 21 percent in 1992.

The percentage of salespeople with a high school diploma decreases with increases in direct-selling income, declining from 35 percent among those earning $25 or less per week to 28 percent among those earning $100 or more per week. The opposite trend exists for salespeople with some college or an associate degree; their percentage increases from 34 percent among those earning $25 or less per week to 44 percent among those earning $100 or more per week.

Marital Status

From 1976 to 1992, the percentages of the married (77 percent vs. 72 percent), the widowed (5 percent vs. 3 percent), and the separated (3 percent vs. 2 percent) declined. During the same period, the percentage of the divorced (6 percent vs. 10 percent) and the never married (1 percent vs. 9 percent) increased.

Among people 25 years or older, the percentage of married people is higher for salespeople than for the American public in general (74 percent vs. 66 percent). The percentage of married people is higher among women than men (73 percent vs. 67 percent), among whites than blacks (77 percent vs. 51 percent), and among those without an additional paid job than those with an additional paid job (80 percent vs. 67 percent).

Dependents

A total of 37 percent of direct salespeople have no dependents, besides themselves and their spouse, and a slightly higher percentage (41 percent) have no dependent children under 18 years of age. Among salespeople with dependent children, 33 percent have one child, 44 percent have two children, and 23 percent have three or more children.

Paid Employment besides Direct Selling

In 1976, 43 percent of the salespeople held another paying job in addition to direct selling. This percentage has increased to 56 percent in 1992, and a significant percentage of salespeople (8 percent) have two or more jobs in addition to direct selling.

The probability of having other paid employment is higher among blacks than whites (68 percent vs. 53 percent), among college graduates than high school graduates (66 percent vs. 51 percent), and among the never married than the married (73 percent vs. 51 percent). The percentage of salespeople with other paid jobs decreases with increases in the number of hours spent per week in direct selling. Among those working under five hours per week, 69 percent have other paid jobs, compared with 37 percent among those working over thirty hours per week.

Spouse Employment

The percentage of married salespeople with employed spouses is 86 percent. The percentage tends to decrease with increases in hours spent per week in direct selling: the percentage is 91 percent among those spending under five hours per week and 81 percent among those spending over thirty hours per week. Decreases in the percentage also occur with increases in respondents' age. The percentage is higher among women than men (88 percent vs. 71 percent), among college graduates than high school graduates (92 percent vs. 82 percent), among whites than blacks (87 percent vs. 79 percent), and among those with other paid employment than those without other paid employment (91 percent vs. 82 percent).

Household Income

The median household income of salespeople was $28,635 in 1992, up from $13,840 in 1976. The household income of salespeople increases significantly with time spent in direct selling. The median household income for salespeople is $26,760 among those working less than five hours per week, $29,445 among those working five to twenty hours per week, and $33,540 among those working over twenty hours per week.

Disabilities and Military Status

Among salespeople, 8 percent have a physical or medical impairment or disability. Of these salespeople with a disability, 71 percent have a permanent disability and 59 percent have a disability which makes working in direct selling particularly attractive or convenient. Among salespeople, a total of 3 percent reported that they or their spouses were on active military duty.

3. Entering Direct Selling

When First Entered Direct Selling

The direct-selling sales force is usually characterized as having a high percentage of new salespeople. This characterization is confirmed by the 30 percent of the salespeople first entering direct selling within one year. The newness of the sales force was greater in 1992 than in 1976 when the Harris survey was conducted: the percentage of salespeople first entering direct selling within one year was 30 percent in 1976 and 39 percent in 1992. The percentage of salespeople first entering direct selling six or more years ago was 31 percent in 1976 and 11 percent in 1992.

Exiting and Re-entering Direct Selling[1]

A substantial majority of salespeople (74 percent) have never left and re-entered direct selling. A total of 27 percent of salespeople have exited and re-entered direct selling. Of salespeople, 13 percent have left and re-entered once, 6 percent twice, 3 percent three times, and 5 percent four or more times. The percentage of salespeople who have left and re-entered direct selling increases significantly with length of time in direct selling. The percentage is 18 percent among salespeople who first entered direct selling within one year, compared with 43 percent among those who first entered direct selling over five years ago.

Activity before First Entering Direct Selling

An absolute majority of salespeople (57 percent) have some form of paid employment before first entering direct selling. The second largest percentage of salespeople (28 percent) are unpaid family workers or housewives when they first enter direct selling. The remaining sales-people are either in school (7 percent), unemployed (6 percent), or in some other activity (2 percent).

The percentages of salespeople who are in school, unemployed, or in some other activity when first entering direct selling have remained the same or changed only slightly since 1976. There has been, however, an increase in the percentage of salespeople who are working in paid em-ployment before first entering direct selling (increasing from 47 percent in 1976 to 57 percent in 1992), and a decrease in the percentage working as an unpaid family worker or housewife (decreasing from 41 percent in 1976 to 28 percent in 1992).[2]

Reasons For Entering Direct Selling

Ranking of Reasons

The 1992 survey asked respondents to rate the importance of eleven reasons for entering direct selling on a scale of "very important" to "not at all important." Among the eleven reasons, four were considered very important by a majority of the salespeople responding to the survey: "liked and believed in the product" (90 percent), "having my own business and working when I wanted to" (73 percent), "supplement my family income or make a little extra money for myself" (64 percent), and "liked the idea that the harder I worked the more money I would get" (54 percent). "I enjoy selling" (49 percent) and "give me a chance to make a significant amount of money" (45 percent) are considered by slightly less than the majority of salespeople to be very important reasons for entering direct selling. A total of 29 percent consider as very important both "give me a way of meeting and socializing with new people" and "thinking of making it as a possible full-time career." Each of the last three reasons are believed by 28 percent or less of the salespeople to be very important: "wanted recognition and support of coworkers and peers" (28 percent), "a good way to occupy my spare time" (25 percent), and "give me a chance to get more involved in the community" (24 percent).

Level of Effort and Importance of Reason

For salespeople, there is a relationship between the expressed importance of their reasons for getting into direct selling and the level of effort they actually put into their selling. Generally, the greater the number of hours per week a salesperson works in direct selling, the more likely he or she will believe a reason for getting into direct selling is very important.

Among the top reasons salespeople give as very important for entering direct selling, the best example of this relation is the reason "the idea of having my own business and working when I wanted to." Among salespeople working less than five hours per week in direct selling, 53 percent believe this reason is very important. This percentage increases to 89 percent among salespeople working full-time in direct selling (over thirty hours per week). Other reasons where the percentage increases as the hours per week increase are "thinking of making it as a full-time career," "idea that the harder I worked the more money I would make," and "I enjoy selling."

For the reason "chance to make a significant amount of money," the percentage believing this is a very important reason increases from 30 percent among those working less than five hours per week to 62 percent among those working twenty-one to thirty hours per week. The percentage remains the same (62 percent) among those working over thirty hours per week (full-time).

For the other five of the eleven reasons, the percentage who believe that the reason is very important increases with hours per week among salespeople working part-time (thirty hours or less per week) but begins to decline for those working over thirty hours (full-time). For several of these five reasons, this makes sense, in that they are relevant reasons for part-timers to enter direct selling, such as "meeting and socializing with new people," "supplement my family income or make a little extra money for myself," and "way to occupy my spare time."

A notable exception to this relationship is the reason the highest percentage of salespeople think of as a very important reason for entering direct selling—"like and believe in the product." The percentage of salespeople believing this is a very important reason remains essentially the same as the number of hours per week in direct selling goes up.

1992 vs. 1976 Results

Among the eleven reasons listed in the 1992 survey for entering direct selling, nine reasons were also in the 1976 survey. Changes in the importance of these nine reasons can be seen from 1976 to 1992.

The financial reasons for getting into direct selling appear to have become somewhat more important to salespeople. The percentage of salespeople believing "supplement my family income" or "make a little extra money for myself" is very important increased from 58 percent in 1976 to 64 percent in 1992. "Idea that the harder I work the more money I could make" and "chance to make some significant money" increased from 52 percent to 54 percent and from 37 percent to 45 percent, respectively.

Career reasons for entering direct selling have also become more important to direct salespeople. The percentage for the reason "possible full-time career" nearly doubled, increasing from 16 percent to 29 percent. The percentage for "idea of having my own business and working when I want to" increased from 70 percent to 73 percent.[3]

The importance to salespeople of nonfinancial, noncareer reasons for entering into direct selling seems to have declined somewhat. The percentage of salespeople saying that "meeting and socializing with new people" was a very important reason for entering direct selling decreased from 35 percent in 1976 to 29 percent in 1992. The percentage for "good way to occupy my spare time" decreased from 37 percent to 25 percent. The percentage saying "I enjoy selling" is a very important reason declined from 53 percent to 49 percent. The percentage of salespeople saying that the "chance to get more involved with the community" is a very important reason, however, remained the same, at 24 percent.

Among the nine reasons that were in both the 1976 and 1992 surveys, the ranking of the four reasons most often expressed as very important for entering direct selling has not changed substantially. Among the top four reasons, "idea of having my own business and working when I want to" was the reason more salespeople expressed as very important than any other in both the 1976 and 1992 surveys. "Supplement my family income" remained the second most commonly evaluated as very important. The reason "idea that the harder I work the more money I could make" went from fourth to third, while "I enjoy selling" went from third to fourth.

"Most Important" Reason

In addition to eliciting the relative importance of various reasons for entering direct selling, the 1992 survey asked respondents to select one reason as their most important. Only three reasons were rated by more than 5 percent of the salespeople as most important: "supplement my family income," "liking and believing in product," and "having my own business." These three reasons are the same three reasons that are most often expressed as very important.

When the three reasons are ranked by the percentage of salespeople who believe it is a very important reason, "liked and believed in product" is first, "having my own business" is second, and "supplement my family income" is third. When the three reasons are ranked, however, by the percentage of salespeople who believe it is most important, "supplement my family income" jumps from third to first place; "liked and believed in the product" and "having my own business" are pushed down to second and third places, respectively.

Notes

1. The percentages in this section are based on two questions in the survey interview. One question asked respondents whether they had ever exited and re-entered direct selling. If they answered yes, they were asked how many times they had exited and re-entered.

2. Two of the choices to the question on what respondents were doing before first entering direct selling were worded somewhat differently in the 1976 and 1992 surveys. The choice "working at other job" in the 1976 survey was changed to "working at other paid employment" in the 1992 survey. The choice "housewife" in the 1976 survey was revised to "unpaid family worker/housewife" in the 1992 survey.

3. The wording of this reason was somewhat different in the 1976 and 1992 surveys. In the 1976 survey, it was "I liked the idea of being independent and working when I wanted to." In the 1992 survey, it was "I liked the idea of having my own business and working when I wanted to."

Suggested Reading

Direct Selling Publications

Studies on Direct Selling Published in Academic Journals and Management Reference Books

Alexander, Roy. *Direct Salesman's Handbook.* Englewood Cliffs, N.J.: Prentice-Hall, 1958.

General "how-to" handbook for the direct salesperson. Company and market information is out of date.

Ash, Mary Kay. *Mary Kay.* New York: Harper & Row, 1981.

With the success of her company, Mary Kay Ash, founder of Mary Kay Cosmetics, Inc., decided it was time to tell her own story. This book covers her life: her childhood, her roles as mother and wife, her early career as a door-to-door salesperson and her role as chairperson of a multimillion-dollar company.

Ash, Mary Kay. *Mary Kay on People Management.* New York: Warner Books, 1984.

Discussion of how people management inspires both people and profits and how the golden rule can apply to all aspects of management.

Aspley, John Cameron. *The Dartnell Sales Manager's Handbook* (11th edition), edited by Riso Ovid. Chicago: Dartnell, 1968, esp. pp. 266–74, 774, 798–800.

General essay on direct selling, describing direct selling in the United States, advantages and disadvantages, organization, training, agents, route selling, campaigns, and combining with other channels. Definition (p. 774). Court decisions on direct selling (pp. 798–800).

Beltramini, Richard F., and Kenneth R. Evans. "Salesperson Motivation to Perform and Job Satisfaction: A Sales Contest Participant Perspective," *Journal of Personal Selling & Sales Management* 8(2) (1988): 35–42.

Salespeople's perceptions of a program of sales contests offered by several organizations over time are related to both sales performance and job satisfaction.

Bernstein, Ronald A. *Successful Direct Selling*. Englewood Cliffs, N.J.: Prentice-Hall, 1984.

Starting with a broad definition of direct selling and the industry, this text covers marketing techniques, products, and home office management among other specifics for individuals who might be considering direct selling for supplemental income or a full-time career. It also discusses how to plan, launch, promote, and maintain a profitable direct-selling company.

Biggart, Nicole Woolsey. *Charismatic Capitalism*. Chicago: University of Chicago Press, 1988.

Provides the first full-scale study of social and cultural factors that have given rise to direct selling and explores the dynamics of its organizational life.

Boone, Louise E., and David L. Kurtz. "DSA Code of Ethics," *Contemporary Marketing*. Chicago: Dryden Press, 1986.

Brief discussion on the Direct Selling Association members' Code of Ethics (p. 552).

Buzzell, Robert D., et al. *Marketing: A Contemporary Analysis* (2nd edition). New York: McGraw-Hill, 1972, pp. 237–39.

Brief description of direct selling, its advantages and problems, with examples from the United States.

Cohen, Sherry Suib. *Tender Power*. Reading, Mass.: Addison-Wesley Publishing Company, 1989.

Defines the role of the new woman—one who is both powerful and nurturing and is the stronger and happier for having achieved this balance. Discusses the new opportunities that have arisen for women from this new combination of strengths.

Court, Alice MacDonald, and John A. Quelch. "Mary Kay Cosmetics, Inc.," *Harvard Business School Case Services*. Boston: 1983.

Focuses on possible strategies Mary Kay Cosmetics could implement to maintain its impressive growth rate. Discusses product line, sales force compensation, and organization of company.

Crawford, John C., and Barbara C. Garland. "A Profile of a Party Plan Sales Force," *Akron Business and Economic Review* 19(4) (1988): 28–37.

This article addresses the particular issue of the kinds of people who are attracted to party plan selling and

investigates whether there are significant life-style differences between those who see their position as a career
and those who see it simply as a way to make extra money.

Engel, James F., and W. Wayne Talarzyk. "Mary Kay Cosmetics, Inc.,"
Parts A & B. *Cases in Promotional Strategy* (revised edition).
Homewood, Ill.: Richard D. Irwin, Inc., 1984, pp. 3–10, 226–30.
Part A discusses: (1) history, philosophy, and direct-sales strategy of
the Mary Kay organization; (2) comparison of skin care products
sold direct with those products sold through department stores or
specialty shops; and (3) consumer advertising.
Part B focuses on sales training, compensation packages, and
sales incentives for Mary Kay Consultants.

Frenzen, Jonathan K., and Harry L. Davis. "Purchasing Behavior in Embedded Markets," *Journal of Consumer Research* 17(1) 1 (1990): 1–12.
This article explores the concept of market embeddedness and its
impact on purchasing behavior in a consumer market.

Futrell, Charles. *Fundamentals of Selling* (2nd edition).
Homewood, Ill.: Richard D. Irwin, Inc., 1988, pp. 19, 469, 577.
Textbook covers the basic foundations for understanding the concepts and practices of selling in a practical, straight-forward, and
readable manner. Encyclopaedia Britannica and Avon Products are
briefly mentioned along with profiles of successful salespeople from
Tupperware and Mary Kay Cosmetics.

Futrell, Charles. *Sales Management* (2nd edition). New York: Dryden
Press, 1988, pp. 15, 355–58, 507–508, 570.
This textbook provides a basic foundation for understanding all major elements of sales management and presents sales management
concepts and practices. Motivational techniques for Mary Kay's sales
force are discussed, and a case study on a disguised direct-selling
company, House Wares, Inc.
(Case 9.1), is presented.

Hinkle, Charles L., and Esther F. Stineman. Case 26, "Mary Kay
Cosmetics, Inc.," *Cases in Marketing Management.* Englewood
Cliffs, N.J.: Prentice Hall, 1984, pp. 384–415.
Focuses on the history and philosophy of Mary Kay Cosmetics and
looks at current and future marketing strategies with emphasis on
exclusively promoting skin care products. Also discusses scientific
research undertaken at Mary Kay facilities.

Hutton, Shirley, and Constance deSwaan. *Pay Yourself What You're
Worth.* New York: Bantam Books, 1988.

Shirley Hutton, the #1 National Sales Director for Mary Kay Cosmetics, shares secrets and strategies for succeeding in direct sales in all its aspects. Experiences of others who have also struggled and triumphed are detailed and a step-by-step road map to success in direct sales is included.

Jolson, Marvin A. *Consumer Attitudes towards Direct-to-Home Marketing Systems.* New York: Dunnellin Publishing Co., 1970.

Based on the author's doctoral dissertation at the University of Maryland, this book explores several hypotheses about consumer attitudes toward direct selling in light of his research and states implications for marketing management.

Kotter, John P. "Mary Kay Ash" and "Mary Kay Cosmetics, Inc." *A Force for Change: How Leadership Differs from Management.* New York: Free Press, 1990, pp. viii, ix, 55–56, 65, 66, 67, 83, 84, 106, 112, 116.

Focuses on what leadership really means today, how it is different from management, and why both good leadership and management are essential for business success, especially for complex organizations operating in changing environments. Kotter presents detailed accounts of how senior and middle managers in eleven major corporations were able to create a leadership process that put into action hundreds of commonsense ideas and procedures that, in combination with competent management, produced extraordinary results.

Levering, Robert, Milton Moskowitz, and Michael Katz. "Mary Kay Cosmetics, Inc.," *The 100 Best Companies to Work for in America.* Reading, Mass.: Addison-Wesley Publishing Company, 1984, pp. 199–202.

Levering, Robert, and Milton Moskowitz. "Mary Kay Cosmetics, Inc.," *The 100 Best Companies to Work for in America.* New York: Currency Book, Doubleday, 1993, pp. 269–73.

Informative profiles of Mary Kay Cosmetics which discuss the company's management style, philosophy, and outstanding characteristics. Quotes from employees and anecdotes about Mary Kay Ash are also included.

Longwell, R. L. "Direct-to-Consumer Selling," *Handbook of Modern Marketing,* edited by Victor P. Buell. New York: McGraw-*Hill, 1970, sec. 19, pp. 28–38.*

General, short encyclopedia article on direct selling. Discusses reasons for selling direct, factors for success, types of companies, sales approaches, building and maintaining an organization.

Lumpkin, James R., Marajorie J. Caballero, and Lawrence B. Chonko. *Direct Marketing, Direct Selling and The Mature Consumer.*West-port, Conn.: Greenwood Press, 1989.

A research study into the behavior of mature consumers as they purchase goods through catalogs, direct-mail, direct selling, party plan selling, and in-home demonstrations. Also compares shopping behavior and attitudes of older consumers with younger groups and analyzes differences on the basis of demographic and psychological variables.

Mary Kay's Guide to Beauty. Reading, Mass.: Addison-Wesley, 1983.

Illustrated guide for discovering your skin inside and out; the skin care and make-up guide for all types of skin.

Mason, J. Barry, and Morris L. Mayer. *Modern Retailing* (4th edition). Plano, Texas: Business Publications, 1987, pp. 5–6, 67–68, 85, 116–17, 148–49, 233.

Amway, Avon Products, Mary Kay Cosmetics, and Tupperware Home Parties are mentioned throughout this marketing text, which provides new insights into the dynamics and challenges of today's retail marketplace.

Ovid, Riso. *The Dartnell Sales Promotion Handbook* (6th edition). Chicago: Dartnell, 1973, pp. 648, 738, 989.

Short notes on: door-to-door demonstrations, giveaways to open doors, backing up door-to-door salesmen.

Peters, Tom, and Nancy Austin. *A Passion for Excellence.* New York: Random House, 1985, pp. 50, 93, 180, 262, 361, 363, 366–67.

Discusses the leadership accomplishments of Mary Kay Cosmetics and profiles examples from *Mary Kay on People Management,* which organizations can implement to achieve managerial success.

Peterson, Robert A. *The Future of U.S. Retailing.* New York: Quorum Books, 1992.

Focuses on likely trends in traditional retailing, direct marketing, direct selling, and multi-channel distribution networks for the 1990s. Defines direct selling and its significance in the U.S. economy. Offers insight into the future of direct selling and strategies direct-selling organizations can utilize to ensure success.

Peterson, Robert A., Gerald Albaum, and Nancy M. Ridgway. "Research Note: Consumers Who Buy from Direct Sales Companies," *Journal of Retailing* 65(2) (1989): 273–85.

Study indicates the degree to which consumers purchase goods from direct-selling companies; documents the characteristics of purchasers and perceptions of advantages, disadvantages, and perceived risks of buying from direct-sales companies.

Pride, William M., and D. C. Ferrell. *Marketing: Concepts and Strategies (6th edition)*. *Boston: Houghton Mifflin Company, 1989, pp. 369, 544–45.*

Textbook focuses on strategic marketing methods used both inside and outside of the business world. Avon, Electrolux, Mary Kay Cosmetics, Stanley Home Products, and Tupperware are mentioned.

Quelch, John A., and Paul W. Farris. Case 1-4, "Mary Kay Cosmetics, Inc.," *Cases in Advertising and Promotion Management*. Plano, Tex.: Business Publications, 1983, pp. 54–74.

Focuses on Mary Kay's consumer advertising and its marketing communication programs designed to enhance sales growth.

Stengrevics, John, and John P. Kotter. "Mary Kay Cosmetics, Inc.," *Harvard Business School Case Services*. Boston, 1981.

Focuses on Mary Kay Cosmetics' rapid growth, product philosophy, selling policies, and organization. Also discusses the company's dynamic founder, Mary Kay Ash.

Walters, Dottie. *The Selling Powers of a Woman*. Englewood Cliffs, N.J., Prentice-Hall, 1962. Basic "how-to" manual on selling and salesmanship for women.

Though not written solely about direct selling, this book contains hints, suggestions, and advice for women in direct selling.

Wotruba, Thomas R. "The Effect of Goal-Setting on the Performance of Independent Sales Agents in Direct Selling." *Journal of Personal Selling & Sales Management* 9(1) (1980): 22–29.

Study looks at how goal-setting relates to the behavior and performance of salespeople and the extent to which salespeople set goals.

Wotruba, Thomas R. "The Relationship of Job Image, Performance, and Job Satisfaction to Inactivity-Proneness of Direct Salespeople," *Journal of the Academy of Marketing Science* 18(2) (1990): 113–21.

Examines whether the public image of the selling job as perceived by direct salespeople has an impact on their tendency to remain active or become inactive in that selling job. Relationships among job image, job satisfaction, and job performance are also investigated.

Wotruba, Thomas R. "Met Expectations and Turnover in Direct Selling," *Journal of Marketing* 55(3) (July, 1991): 24–35.

Shows that stayers and leavers differ significantly on met expectations in both cross-sectional and longitudinal analyses.

Direct Selling Education Foundation Materials

Direct Selling Association. *Member Company Responsibilities under
the DSA Code of Ethics.* Washington, D.C., 1982.
Detailed guide to the DSA Code of Ethics. Contains two sections:
(1) what the Code requires of company procedures, sales, and
documents, and (2) the simple steps companies are
required to follow in the event of a Code Administrator
contact prompted by a Code complaint.

Direct Selling Association. *We Deliver Extra Protection.*
Washington, D.C., 1979.
An easy-to-read version of DSA's long-established Code of
Ethics. The pamphlet tells what steps dissatisfied customers should
take to rectify a problem with a DSA member company and sets
forth standards that ethical independent salespeople should follow.

Direct Selling Education Foundation. *Customers Mean Business.*
Washington, D.C., 1982.
Based on studies conducted by Technical Assistance Research
Programs (TARP), directed toward business to explain how much
dissatisfied customers can harm business and how to handle com-
plaints successfully.

Direct Selling Education Foundation. *Is That Traveling Sales Job
For You?* Washington, D.C., 1989.
Brochure directed at young adults who are considering jobs with
traveling sales crews. Pamphlet offers advice on questions to ask
during an interview, warning signs of a disreputable company, and
what a contract should cover. Also outlines guidelines for ethical
salespeople and warns readers about unethical business practices.

Direct Selling Education Foundation. *Promises: Check 'em Out!*
Washington, D.C., 1980.
Brochure to help consumers avoid falling victim to business opportunity fraud. It describes the elements of a business opportunity, lists
the kind of information consumers should have, and tells where to
go for help when investing. Also available in Spanish.

Direct Selling Education Foundation. *Pyramid Schemes: Not What They
Seem!* Washington, D.C., 1989.
Brochure that explains what a pyramid scheme is and how to tell
the difference between a legitimate business and a disguised bogus
operation.

Direct Selling Education Foundation. *Questions Every Buyer Should*

Ask. Washington, D.C., 1980.

Seven questions buyers should ask direct sellers before purchasing products and what to do if dissatisfied after the purchase.

"The Personal Touch." A 16-minute videotape exploring direct selling, including an overview of this unique method of distribution with insights of direct-selling executives, perspectives of independent salespeople, and how direct selling meets the needs of consumers. (Note: can be ordered through the Direct Selling Education Foundation.)

Peterson, Robert A., and Richard C. Bartlett. "How to Achieve Retailing Leadership by the Year 2000," 1991. Report of an academic symposium cosponsored by the Direct Selling Education Foundation and the IC^2 Institute at the University of Texas, in conjunction with the Academy of Marketing Science and the American Marketing Association.

The brochure is an agenda of informed speculations regarding the nature and structure of retailing by the year 2000 and contains issues and options.